Organizational America

Organizational America

William G. Scott
  and
David K. Hart

Houghton Mifflin Company Boston 1979

Library of Congress Cataloging in Publication Data

Scott, William G
    Organizational America.

    Includes bibliographical references and index.
    1. Organization. 2. Organizational change — United States. 3. Social structure. 4. Social values. 5. Elite (Social sciences) — United States. I. Hart, David K., date   joint author. II. Title.
HM131.S39   301.18'32'0973   79-13815
ISBN 0-395-27599-7

Printed in the United States of America

S 10 9 8 7 6 5 4 3 2 1

Portions of this book were adapted from certain of our articles that appeared in the following journals: *Academy of Management Journal, Academy of Management Review, Administration and Society,* and *Public Administration Review.* We appreciate the permission of the editors of these journals for the use of this material.

Democracy has long been not only the form of government for the people of America, but a faith and an ideal, a romantic vision. This has been peculiarly our form of patriotism, our form of spiritual imperialism. The "mission of America," whether stated in religious terms or not, has been conceived as witnessing Democracy before mankind, bearing democracy's ideals of freedom and equality, and its material blessings, to the nations of the world. Belief in this mission perhaps has become less widely and intensively held during the past fifty years. Nevertheless, the romantic vision of democracy has been dimmed remarkably little by our continued experience with "realistic democracy" and *realpolitik*. Of the general influence of the democratic ideal there can be no doubt.

— Dwight Waldo, *The Administrative State*

TO OUR FATHERS
GEORGE E. SCOTT
AND
DAVID F. HART

Preface

We began this book, unofficially, nearly a decade ago with a continuing series of conversations about the kind of nation that would be appropriate for Americans in the last part of the twentieth century. There was a real urgency to those discussions, conducted as they were against the backdrop of Vietnam, campus riots, and urban violence. It seemed to many that the national fabric was unraveling and that drastic, even Draconian, measures might have to be employed to reverse the process. However, since we are professors in a school of business administration, it should not be surprising that our attention was not riveted upon the politicians, generals, and students who occupied center stage. Rather, in those tumultuous times, our attention kept returning to the managers of the large organizations, public and private. Even more, we were concerned with the essential role they would play in ushering us all into the twenty-first century.

By now the turmoils of those times are rapidly becoming ancient history. Vietnam is so far behind us that it has even become respectable to write novels and make movies about it. The passionate young radical superstars of the era have faded into middle age: some into highly chic society; a few into intense religion; while the rest have simply disappeared. They have been replaced by a new generation of conservative, job-oriented young people, who seek the rewards and salvations of the system. A cursory glance might suggest that we have returned to the placid fifties.

Yet America has undergone a profound change in the last two decades, in ways that very few anticipated and for reasons that had little to do with the pressing issues of the late sixties and early seventies. During those dramatic years of extraordinary events and dazzling surface changes, one institution remained stable, provided continuity, and in so doing grew even more powerful: the modern organization. The major transformation of America has been the consolidation of power into modern organizations, led by a managerial elite, and maintained by a cadre of professional managers.

This unprecedented growth of the modern organization in America became the subject of most of our public presentations, our seminars and classes, and our published work during the 1970s. Many of the notions in this book — among them the insensitivity of management to value questions and the pivotal concept of "the organizational imperative" — were developed, debated, and refined in those arenas. But we soon realized, as our collaboration progressed, that we could not just write articles about subjects tangential to the central theme: *the replacement of the traditional American system of values with the values of the modern organization.* We had to come to grips with it directly. Thus, this book was born.

Since that central theme concerns everything in contemporary America, it required no small amount of arrogance even to embark upon such an ambitious project. It was disconcerting, at the outset, to consider a project so vast and complicated. But as we wrote preliminary drafts, the central theme began to crystallize and we concentrated upon the values that inform the modern organizations that dominate organizational America.

In Part I, "The Values of Organizational America," we summarize our most important value generalizations, some of our thoughts about how America arrived at its present condition, and some ideas about what that shift in values has meant to the individual. In Part II, "The Roles in Organizational America," we examine the structure of roles, derived from the values of modern organization, that are necessary for "success" in organizational America. Some of the specific implications of those organizational roles are discussed therein, including the status hierarchy that the organizational imperative imposes.

We intended to end the book with Part III, "The Fate of Organizational America." We argue that the social and organizational dynamics of the modern organization are impelling us into an altered, but dimly perceived, future. We discuss some of the grim prospects for the future in the final chapter. But by then so many subjects have been covered that a summation is needed. It appears as the Epilogue, a nocturnal conversation between the shades of Chester I. Barnard and Fyodor Dostoevsky.

Writing this book has done many things for us. It is a collaboration based upon friendship, a shared sense of humor, and a willingness to disagree with each other. The most important thing, however, has been the satisfaction of putting into words what we believe: that there is nothing worthwhile for individuals in this world beyond freedom and dignity. Anything less than a free and open society is unacceptable. Granted, this is not an original position; nonetheless we had to state our own values, reckon the implications of that position, and search for the quarters from which the strongest attacks would come. We believe that the most significant source of the subversion of the individual right to "life, liberty and the pursuit of happiness" is the modern organization, with its supporting technologies and behavioral sciences. We cannot expect all of our readers to agree with us. Our modest hope, however, is that our book will help more people become aware of the potentially lethal dangers that arise from muddling along with the status quo.

We wish to acknowledge the assistance given to us during our research and writing. During one summer, William Scott traveled around the country interviewing persons who were studying various aspects of the physical control of the brain, to gather information for Chapter 8. The Department of Management and the School of Business Administration of the University of Washington made funds available for that and subsequent trips. Among those interviewed were: Colonel Wayne O. Evans, Director, Military Stress Labs, Natick, Massachusetts; Dr. Herbert Vaughan, Albert Einstein College of Medicine, Bronx, New York; Dr. José M. R. Delgado, School of Medicine, Yale University, New Haven, Connecticut; Professor Perry London, Department of Psychology, University of Southern California, Los Angeles, California; Robert Neville, Institute of Society, Ethics and the Life Sciences, Hastings Center, Hastings-on-Hudson, New York; Dr. John G. Varni, Department of Experimental Psychophysiology, Walter Reed Army Medical Center, Washington, D.C.; David Kefauver and Dr. Louis A. Wienckowski, National Institute of Mental Health, Rockville, Maryland; Dr. Vernon Mark, Harvard Medical School and Massachusetts General Hospital, Boston, Massachusetts; Dr. Arthur Ward, Department of Neurosurgery, School of Medicine, University of Washington, Seattle, Washington; Dr. J. P. Buckley, School of Pharmacy, University of Pittsburgh, Pittsburgh, Pennsylvania; Dr. J. Horowitz, staff assistant to Senator Edward Kennedy, Washington, D.C.; and Dr. Larry Halpren, Department of Pharmacology, University of Washington, Seattle, Washington. Their graciousness and courtesy are greatly appreciated.

Of course, questions of analysis and interpretation of research directions are solely ours.

With respect to the book as a whole, numerous friends and colleagues were generous with both their time and their advice. We cannot list them all, but they know who they are and how much we appreciate them. Special mention must be made, however, of a few. The final drafts of our book benefited immeasurably from the editorial guidance of Jonathan Galassi of Houghton Mifflin. We greatly appreciate the constant support of Professor Dwight Waldo, of the Maxwell School of Citizenship and Public Affairs, Syracuse University. Long before us, he wrote about the significance of organizational and administrative values as they pertain to the essential questions of "who should rule" and what constitutes the "good life" in America. Dr. H. George Frederickson, President, Eastern Washington State University, Cheney, Washington, has provided us with constant insights. James D. Hart, Executive Director, Northwest Hospital, Seattle, Washington, read and commented upon the entire manuscript.

Our colleagues in the Department of Management and in the Department of Business, Government, and Society have been most willing to argue with us or to provide us with help when needed. Valuable library assistance, together with critical readings of various portions of the manuscript, was provided by Marna Tallman, Carol Weibel, and Linda Dethman, all from the University of Washington. An ad hoc group, the "busy bee" typing service, consisting of Jacqueline Swofford and Mary Anderson, performed heroic service in the preparation of the final draft.

Finally, the rigorous, but sensitive, editing provided by the staff of Houghton Mifflin Company was instrumental in shaping this book. Without their demands for clarity and consistency, our book would not have taken its present form.

Last of all, thank you, Mary Poppins, wherever you are.

Seattle, Washington   *W.G.S.*
1979   *D.K.H.*

Contents

Preface   vii
Introduction   1

PART I   THE VALUES OF ORGANIZATIONAL AMERICA

Chapter 1   Organizational America   13
             The Shattering of Traditional Confidences   13
             The Reconstruction of Confidence   23
             The Decent Intentions of Managers   28
Chapter 2   The Organizational Imperative   32
             The Transformation of American Values   32
             The Paradox of Technological Progress   33
             Managerial Amorality   36
             *The Propositions and Rules of the
             Organizational Imperative*   43
             We All Win . . .   48
Chapter 3   The Organizational Imperative Realized   50
             We All Win . . . Or Do We?   50
             *The Collapse of the Values of the Individual
             Imperative*   55
             New Values — New Puzzles   78

PART II THE ROLES IN ORGANIZATIONAL AMERICA

Chapter 4 Organizational Roles 83
Values, Roles, and Organizational America 83
On-the-Job Roles 87
Off-the-Job Roles 90
Chapter 5 The Insignificant People 95
The "Weenie" Syndrome 95
*Insignificance: Some Strategic Role
Considerations* 99
*Insignificance: Some Tactical Role
Considerations* 117
Chapter 6 The Professional People 130
The Inhabitants of the Technical Core 130
Solving the Paradox in Professional Roles 135
Credo in Unam Ordinationem 139
Chapter 7 The Significant People 161
The Significant Job 161
Crisis and Management 164
Who Are the Significant People? 170
Chapter 8 Enhancing the Significant People 178
Improvement at the Apex 178
*The Physical Modification of Managerial
Behavior* 183
The Techniques of Behavior Modification 190
The Psycho-Economy of Enhancement 198
*The Dilemma over Enhancing the
Significant People* 202

PART III THE FATE OF ORGANIZATIONAL AMERICA

Chapter 9 The Probable Future 207
The Drift into Totalitarian America 207

*Who Will Challenge the Organizational
Imperative?*   214
The Option of Transcendent America   223
Epilogue   "The Requisite Conditions for Human
Happiness": A Dialogue   230

References   249
Index   269

Introduction

The twentieth century may rightfully be termed the American century. It has been marked by the roaring successes of the United States. Loud, boisterous, and even arrogant at times, Americans have swept over the globe like a triumphant army and the world has changed accordingly. In response, all nations, even those that hate us, have struggled to emulate our material achievements. This is understandable, for those successes are the bases of real national power.

Our claims of triumph must be tempered, however, for our present station has not been attained unsullied. By too often forgetting the guiding ideals of our Republic, we have sometimes committed terrible mistakes, inexcusable oversights, and even gross injustices. Those whose vision is so narrow that they can only see our failures believe they have cause to use the phrase "the American century" as an epithet. They are wrong, for arguably more good than bad has been achieved by the American endeavor: unmatched political freedoms, unimagined opportunities for public education, and a global generosity unparalleled in human history. For all its fault, the United States has set a worthy example for the peoples of the world.

The primary instrument of our successes in this century has been neither our military prowess nor our wealth, but our most successful social invention: the modern organization. Americans have moved into this last quarter of the twentieth century with only the slightest awareness that the modern organization, with its accouterments of power and control, has become the dominant force in our lives, shaping and changing American values and the American people to suit its requirements. Modern organizations have influenced us profoundly, but so quietly that we are scarcely aware that they are our major agencies of social control. We take them for granted in much the same way we accept television commercials, the "two-minute warning," and Muzak.

Thus it should not be surprising that the serious philosophical issues resulting from the dominance of modern organizations are not matters of major concern to most Americans. Certainly, all of us have had occasional twinges of doubt about the organizations in our lives, but they have seemed only minor irritations compared to the wretchedness of so many nations on this earth. Besides, it seems almost sacrilegious to tamper with a system that has proven itself capable of delivering so much to so many. However, there is enough evidence of present discontent and future peril to force us to look critically at the society we have created and to ask why it is not working so well. Our purpose here is to pursue and to interpret the meaning of the modern organization for the individual.

The modern organization, as noted, has produced a vast transformation of the traditional American value system. We term this new value system, and the new society it has produced, respectively "the organizational imperative" and organizational America. Further, since all value systems require forms of control unique to themselves, organizational America has produced its own form of leadership and control. The real power in America belongs to the managerial elite who administer our great organizations.

The primary concept in this book is *the organizational imperative,* and it is concerned with values. Therefore, we will use terms that belong to moral philosophy. Because it is among the most ancient disciplines, debates about the meaning of key words and phrases are historic, numerous, complex, and intense. Just a few words illustrate this: "right" and "wrong," "truth" and "falsehood," "love" and "hate," "freedom" and "slavery." Words like these refer to our most important thoughts, actions, and emotions. Human society depends upon them.

In particular, they are necessary for any reasonable discussion of the modern organization. Therefore, we must state what we mean by the word "value," since it is central to the book. It is an unusually elusive word and has caused generations of scholars difficulty. Definitions abound. However, we have found that Clyde Kluckhohn's definition is especially useful for our purposes: "A value is a conception, explicit or implicit . . . of the desirable which influences the selection from available modes, means, and ends of action." [1]

Sound and succinct as this definition is, it must be amplified. Therefore, we will use a three-part classification scheme: [2] morals, ethics, and values. When we say "morals" we mean attitudes related to specific behaviors and actions; when we say "ethics" we mean articulated, theoretical codes; and when we say "values" we mean the transcendent belief system that determines our conception of right and wrong.

At the base are moral principles, the standards of good and bad that influence our everyday choices. They are derived from the next higher level, ethical principles. These are cast in theoretical frameworks from which laws are derived and formal codes are constructed. These, in turn, are derived from the highest value principles, the commitments to right and wrong that transcend both concrete levels of moral behavior and more abstract ethical systems. Thus everything important in a society ultimately rests upon the values that the society holds.

Managers like all individuals act on moral principles. In

fact, managers often engage in moral debate as they try to decide the correct courses of action to take. Some managers are aware of the derivative nature of their moral principles and engage in discussions about ethics. But since such discussion requires valuable time, it is usually left to the organizations' attorneys to draft ethical codes and to see that practices conform to them. All this is familiar. Our concern is that managers seldom speculate about the *value* principles upon which their moral and ethical systems are predicated.

Managers are not insensitive people, so if values are of such importance, why have they not become philosophers? For one thing, such speculation requires an education that, unfortunately, most managers have not had. Moreover, delving into value problems is unsettling, for it raises painful questions about the fundamental assumptions upon which one's life is founded, and organizations certainly do not encourage the raising of value questions. In fact, they discourage it, for it also brings up the same kinds of thorny questions about the worth of modern organization. Thinking about values demands an intellectual and spiritual boldness that is not integral to the training of good managers.

Since we discuss those values in this book, it is essential to define three major terms. The first term is *modern organization.* By it we mean a great deal more than simply large institutions in the modern age. *Modern organizations are managerial systems using universal behavioral techniques to integrate individuals and groups into mutually reinforcing relationships with advancing technology in order to achieve system goals efficiently.* Most of the definition should be clear, but at the center of it is a phrase, *universal behavioral techniques,* which requires a second definition. *Universal behavioral techniques are the methods, drawn from the behavioral sciences and instructed by humanistic psychology, used to obtain obedience to managerial instructions.* One point must be emphasized. Modern organizations are unique because they are based upon *both* modern technology and modern psychology. This means they are not comparable with any organizations of the past. They are, indeed, new.

The third term is *the national managerial system*. Modern organizations are run by managers who are all schooled in the same organizational values, based upon the universal behavioral techniques. It is largely through the personae of the managers that the values of the modern organization have pervaded society. *The national managerial system is a vast complex of interlocking management systems, sharing a common set of values, which control modern organizations and which provide order and stability in our national life.* It does not matter whether the systems are public or private; by now they are so interdependent that these traditional boundaries are irrelevant.

Rule by a national managerial system, through modern organizations, represents a major departure from the way American society was supposed to be governed. We agree with Peter Drucker's evaluation, written in 1954:

The emergence of management as an essential, a distinct and a leading institution is a pivotal event in social history. Rarely, if ever, has a new basic institution, a new leading group, emerged as fast as has management since the turn of the century. Rarely in human history has a new institution proven so indispensable so quickly; and even less often has a new institution arrived with so little opposition, so little disturbance, so little controversy . . .

Management, which is the organ of society specifically charged with making resources productive, that is, with the responsibility for organized economic advance, therefore reflects the basic spirit of the modern age. It is in fact indispensable — and this explains why once begotten, it grew so fast, and with so little opposition.[3]

Drucker is correct: Management is *the* essential activity of the modern organization, which has become the primary agency of material human betterment. But the implication elsewhere in Drucker's work is that managers actively and benevolently shape organizations to satisfy public and private needs, communicated to them through a representative government and a free market. Here we part company with him. Managers have become largely powerless to affect the organizations they inhabit.

No contemporary issue is more important than the problems of the values that have emerged with the growing dominance of modern organizations: the substitution of the values of the organization for the values of the individual, and the concomitant emergence of a new and indispensable power elite of managers. None of this should surprise us, for we have had ample warning. The impact of modern organizations on American values began to receive considerable attention in the 1950s, a decade much condemned for complacency and Babbittry. Yet during that decade, a number of impressive books were written about the extraordinary effect the modern organization was having upon personal and social values. Among the leading organizational critics of that period were William H. Whyte, Jr., Jacques Ellul, Hannah Arendt, Robert Nisbet, David Riesman, Sheldon S. Wolin, and Dwight Waldo.

Their anxiety about the modern organization was publicly acknowledged by the supposed personification of complacency, Dwight D. Eisenhower. The President, in his farewell address, warned the nation of the dangers of a "military-industrial complex." That phrase received widespread publicity, but what is less well remembered is that he went on to warn against allowing public policy to become "the captive of a scientific-technological elite."[4] Unfortunately, his warning was misinterpreted by uncomprehending analysts, who took it as an admonition to be on the lookout for high-level shenanigans between business and government executives for the sake of personal gain. But Eisenhower understood that the real danger lay in the unprecedented fusion of the public and private sectors.

However, the warnings of the 1950s were largely ignored and the extremely important discussion about the pervasive use of modern organizations did not mature. Why? For one reason, 1960 ushered in a decade of distractions — wars and riots, assassinations, and dramatic attempts to radicalize public and private institutions. While these "alarums and excursions" certainly captured public attention, they also exhausted public emotion. As we debated the highly visible attacks on the status quo, we had the impression that we were facing the important issues of the moment, and to a limited extent we were. But what we failed to understand was that behind all the publicized turmoil, modern organizations continued to grow and consolidate to encompass all aspects of American life. It does not minimize the importance of the struggles of the sixties to say that eventually they worked to strengthen modern organizations. Remedies for injustice and anguish were sought in improved organizations that embodied and advanced the liberal and humane ideals expressed during this decade, and thus the "solutions" served to reinforce the basic problem.

In the early 1970s it again began to dawn upon some that an apparently implacable force had been set in motion: the modern organization, a reality more powerful than religion, politics, and economics, in which managers perform a uniquely modern role. They are the human intermediaries between the modern organization and the mass of producing-consuming citizens. Managers must reconcile the needs of the people with the needs of the organization through the efficient use of resources to increase material goods and services. The successful performance of this function has been the primary basis for the legitimacy of modern organizations, public and private. Through it, managers have assumed a new role as the mediators of legitimacy.

By now, however, modern organizations move with an inertial dialectic all their own, and the individuals trapped by such mammoth governments — or corporations or universities — are apparently powerless either to affect them or to escape from them. To survive in this new order of things, all must conform to the requirements of the modern organization, and therein lies the problem.

It is almost too late to ask whether the value requirements of organizational life are satisfactory to individuals as such. Even asking the question seems pointless. Some argue that since there is no dissenting consensus about what the individual really is, then discussions about the transcendent integrity of the individual are irrelevant.[5] Modern organizations are just too powerful. A practical person would say that if Americans have, in fact, become so agnostic about what the individual really is, then all that can be done is to leave speculation about related value issues in the hands of the managerial elite and not trouble our heads over them. Even those who would reform things are beginning to despair about their ability to affect modern organizations through appeals to idealism and improved organizational practices.

This was poignantly demonstrated at a small conference of influential scholars in public administration held late in 1977 at Charlottesville, Virginia. Some of the participants had also been at another such conference ten years before. The hallmark of the 1968 conference had been optimism that a revolutionized public administration could shatter the established organizational patterns that seemed to be at the roots of many problems identified during the previous decade, and that government could become less impersonal and more sensitive to human needs.[6]

At the 1977 conference the mood was one of abiding pessimism arising from a sense of powerlessness. The optimism as well as the outrage of the 1960s had evaporated. Instead there was a feeling that no one in government, business, education, or politics could reduce the dominance of modern organizations. The mood seemed to be, "if you can't lick them, join them." This was translated into a pervasive support for management conducted safely within its normal theoretical and practical boundaries.

However, to accuse public administrators of sidestepping the essential value questions misses the crux of the organizational problem. Trained as they are in the traditions of political science, public administrators are more attuned to value questions than their counterparts in business, and they are not as reluctant to examine them. This does not mean that business managers avoid value questions. But the values that shape modern organizations are accepted by them as *given,* beyond reflection and discussion.

It is difficult to decide which condition is worse: the sense of helplessness among some about their inability to change organizations, or the insensitive belief among others that all is well within the organizational firmament. While we would not do away with modern organizations (even if we could), we believe that the unanticipated effects of the overorganization of contemporary society are seriously harmful, and that its long-range implications for the individual are negative. Organizational America is not a permanent destination. The very dialectical forces that brought it into being are impelling it into another form. America is in the process of becoming something else, and there is real reason to believe that the something else may be quite unpleasant.

Given the current opinion about the use of discussing values, it is decidedly out of step to offer anything other than practical solutions, based upon empirical evidence, that reinforce the central values of organizational America. Nevertheless, we will reopen the case made by the organizational scholars in the 1950s. The reason for doing so is straightforward. The modern organization has been more successful and more effective than any of these critics thought possible. Therefore, there is an urgent need to re-examine the fundamental values of organizational America in the light of those successes.

This book will argue for the value of the individual over the organization. We will pick up the strands of the arguments about the individual trapped within the organization that began so well in the 1950s. The odds are astronomical against stimulating a passion for philosophic discussion among management specialists; but if we ignore or reject this chore, we are certain to wind up in circumstances that none of us either desire or understand.

Part I

The Values of
Organizational America

Chapter 1

Organizational America

Some of the owner men were kind because they hated
what they had to do, and some of them were angry
because they hated to be cruel, and some of them were
cold because they had long ago found that one could
not be an owner unless one were cold. And all of them
were caught in something larger than themselves. Some
of them hated the mathematics that drove them, and
some were afraid, and some worshipped the mathematics because it provided a refuge from thought and
from feeling.

— John Steinbeck, *The Grapes of Wrath*

The Shattering of Traditional Confidences

In modern times, the dreams of the American century were
given their most eloquent expression on the twentieth day
of January, 1960. It was bright and cold and all things could
be seen with a crystal clarity. John F. Kennedy, having taken
the oath of office as the thirty-fifth President of the United
States, stepped to the podium to give his inaugural address.
The young, articulate President seemed the perfect embodiment of all that we had tried to achieve through the many
years of our history.

The speech was impressive. More, it was the apotheosis

of the traditional ideals of America, and in one passage, past and future were fused:

We dare not forget today that we are the heirs of that first revolution. Let the word go forth from this time and place, to friend and foe alike, that the torch has been passed to a new generation of Americans, born in this century, tempered by war, disciplined by a hard and bitter peace, proud of our ancient heritage, and unwilling to witness or permit the slow undoing of those human rights to which this nation has always been committed, and to which we are committed today at home and around the world.[1]

And so the dream was secured in the hands of a new generation of our best and brightest. President Kennedy went on to express what Americans believed: We could do it all. There was nothing we could not accomplish, and the world would yield to our good intentions.

But only ten years later, the days of "Camelot" seemed as far removed from us as the Jazz Age. We had believed our leaders would be able to control events and that our collective future would be an improvement of our present. But it did not work out that way. We entered the 1970s in a condition of national discontent, with raw feelings exacerbated by assassinations, the war in Vietnam, festering domestic inequalities, government venality, crime and decay in our cities, shortages of basic commodities, and economic inflation that seemed to have no end. What was worse, our optimism had corroded and the future became threateningly unclear.

As the 1970s spin themselves out, the American people have settled into a mind-numbing routine of trying only to preserve the status quo. Our dreams are no more, our glories are of the past, and nihilism prevails. If that was not sufficiently serious, we are beginning to understand that we are in the process of becoming something else. We are not too clear as to what we are becoming, but in such epic times people can either cling tenaciously to the security of the present or they can seize the opportunities to create for themselves a better future.

Tragically, it seems that we have chosen the conservative response, and that will take us to places we do not want to go. That is why this chapter's epigraph is from *The Grapes of Wrath*. The message is that meanness comes when people are frightened, knocked loose from their security by social changes they cannot understand or control. In the face of the Great Depression, the employed majority recoiled, confined themselves to the routine of their jobs, and tried to ignore the obvious pain within and around them. And so the "owner men" forced the farmers off their land into that tragic and memorable exodus.

Contemporary America is greatly distant in time and sentiment from the Great Depression, but the tidal wave of social change has risen again. We are being dislocated by another social revolution, and while it is altering all our lives in fundamental ways, we neither understand it, although we could, nor control it, although we should. Ironically, our response parallels what Steinbeck described: We have fallen back upon the security of familiar tasks and try vainly to ignore the pain. But we cannot avoid the questions: Why, with all of our notable successes, are we not a more peaceful, a happier people? Why, with all of our marvelous inventions, does the future look so perilous? The American century was to open out into a utopian twenty-first century, but the future seems anything but ideal now. Organizational America is not working out that well and our confidence in the future is being sorely tried.

If one examines the many interpretations of our national confidence, four themes emerge as traditionally constant in the American character: a confidence in the generosity of the environment; a confidence in the benevolence of time; a confidence in American know-how to solve all problems; and a confidence that the individual will receive material rewards for diligent personal effort. No small part of the obvious national trauma in organizational America results from our increasing doubts about the validity of these confidences.

A Dun from the Environment

Our unquestioning confidence in the endless abundance of the environment produced a historically unprecedented optimism that the future would allow for all American ambitions. Granted, the record contains numerous horrifying accounts of the travails endured by our forebears — from droughts, floods, and starvation to Indian attacks, plagues, depressions, and wars. But such problems were seen as temporary and correctable situations. The continuous presumption has been that in the long run the intransigencies of the environment would be subdued, and there would be sufficient land, resources, and products to realize our individual and national aspirations. This optimism was historically warranted, as Robert Heilbroner has noted:

At bottom, *a philosophy of optimism is an historic attitude toward the future* — an attitude based on the tacit premise that the future will accommodate the striving which we bring to it. Optimism is grounded in the faith that the historic environment, as it comes into being, will prove to be benign and congenial — or at least neutral to our private efforts.[2]

Our history bore constant witness to the fact that the environment was generous, once its puzzles were solved. There was little reason to expect it to dun us for an overdue bill we could not pay. Environmental Jeremiahs have been around for a long time, but their dour forecasts were always deferred by technological breakthroughs or fortuitous wars. Now, however, we seem unable to pay our overdue bill because the environmental dun has become global: There are too many people, not enough resources, not enough space, and not enough time for all nations to realize their material ambitions.

In the face of this global situation, some influential Americans argue we should go it alone. This is a modern restatement of our traditional confidence that Americans could, and should, avoid foreign entanglements and live independently in "Fortress America." Such an attitude is now pathetically and dangerously passé. For better or worse, we are inextricably entangled in a global society that is so interdependent that there is no foreseeable way for nations to get free from one another.

The main reason the problems of global interdependency include the United States is that we are dependent upon other nations for critical, nonrenewable mineral resources. As Nicholas Wade wrote: "In 1970 the United States possessed five percent of the world's population but consumed 27 percent of its raw materials, a share that will be difficult to maintain in an increasingly competitive world." [3] Further, we use most of these products for domestic consumption and, even more significantly, we are being forced to import more and more of what we need. Unless we are willing to reduce our standard of living drastically, we are highly dependent upon the supplying nations.

Nowhere is this more evident than with oil, the most critical nonrenewable resource. Because we are an energy-intensive nation and are now dependent on others to supply us with over half of our crude oil requirements, we have come to live with it as our particular Sword of Damocles. John Blair made the following assessment:

Behind every energy policy, program, legislative proposal put forth by the practical men of affairs lie assumptions (usually implicit) concerning the adequacy of petroleum reserves. These assumptions range from the alarmist position which envisions an imminent exhaustion to the euphoric view that the reserves are adequate to last indefinitely. For the United States, the pessimistic position under any reasonable forecast of demand is very definitely in order.[4]

While the world position is somewhat better, all nations are under sentence of a diminishing oil supply. However, for the next twenty-five years the significant fact is that the oil crisis will be the result of the politicization of oil. OPEC's discovery of the enormous political leverage involved in its oil reserves has altered world politics and economics dramatically. By itself, the global politics of oil is sufficient to produce major changes in the living standards and politics of the United States. With oil added to the multitude of other environmental problems, the American confidence in the generosity of the environment has been badly shaken.

Traitorous Time

American history demonstrates our unquestioning confidence that time would never be wicked to us. It was understood that we might sometimes be caught unprepared by change, but we could always count upon a stalwart few to stand fast and purchase whatever extra time was needed. Time has been our kindly friend and staunch ally.

But lately we have arrived at the shocking realization that time has turned traitor and works against us. We are faced with a host of time-related difficulties, the anguish of which was eloquently stated by David Easton:

Mankind today is working under the pressure of time. Time is no longer on our side. This in itself is a frightening new event in world affairs. An apocalyptic weapon, an equally devastating population explosion, dangerous pollution of the environment, and, in the United States, severe internal dissension of racial and economic origin, all move in the same direction. They move toward increasing social conflict and deepening fears and anxieties about the future, not of a generation or of a nation, but of the human race itself. Confronting this cataclysmic possibility is a knowledge of the enormous wealth and technical resources currently available in a few favored regions of the world, the spectacular rate of increase in man's material inventiveness and technology, and the rich potential just on the horizon for understanding social and political processes. The agony of the present social crisis is this contrast between our desperate condition and our visible promise, if we but had the time.[5]

Easton has effectively summarized the paradox of the time crunch. The brutal but inescapable fact is that we now must work within narrowing time spans that we do not fully understand, and this is having a decisive effect upon the means we select to satisfy various economic, social, and political demands.

The guiding principle of statecraft behind national survival under the conditions outlined by Easton will be in the form of a new mercantilism. We will dust off this doctrine because it seems suited to future economic realities. Given the constraints of time, centralized management of the political economy seems more effective than our pluralist tradition. It quickly reconciles the relationships between commercial, financial, and industrial strength on the one hand and political and military power on the other.[6] Obviously, under these circumstances individual welfare must be subordinated to the single purpose of national security. This view is clearly at variance with the economic and political models of competiton, free trade, and pluralism in which we had such confidence in the past.

The Frustration of Practicality

The real significance of practicality to Americans was that it relieved an individual of dependence upon others for the necessities of life. Our language is filled with approving expressions for those who are able to solve practical problems ingeniously: from "Yankee know-how" to nicknaming a military division "Can Do." It has been axiomatic that there are no practical problems, particularly technological ones, that we cannot eventually solve. Thus, Americans could laugh at the amateur-loving British, or the emotional Italians, or the contemplative Chinese, and then proceed to solve practical problems with confidence in technical skills and organizational expertise.

But this confidence in our practicality, and hence in our independence, has changed for two reasons. First, we are learning that we do not have a monopoly on solutions to practical problems. Our industrial and technological know-how is not quite the prime export commodity it once was, and we have been astonished and even chagrined at the ability of other industrialized nations to match us product for product and process for process in areas of technology where we once excelled. Second, our lives are arranged by organizations too complex for an individual to comprehend, and these organizations are in turn served by machines that often perform beyond human capabilities. The confidence Americans had that they could be useful in the world, and could effect that world to their advantage through personal efforts, is being sorely tried. As individuals, we stand increasingly helpless before machines and organizations. We are proficient at doing things that really do not matter much at all and that have meaning only in terms of their relationship to organizations.

The incongruity between our professed belief in individual practicality and our undeniable dependence, both as individuals and as a nation, has led to public frustration. Other countries can now ignore our demands because they realize we need them as much as they need us. On the plane of personal feelings, the effects of dependency are even more acute, since they reflect the utter reliance of the individual American upon impersonal, and too often ineffective, delivery systems for goods and services. Our frustration stems from this pervasive personal sense of our own powerlessness.

The Erosion of Expectations

Finally, no small part of American confidence was the expectation that the future would be better than the past — if not for the present generation, then for the next one. This confidence was, in many respects, a summation of the others: Given an abundant environment and adequate time, the individual, with proper diligence and ingenuity, would be able to achieve economic security and a reasonably comfortable life. Further, there was the confidence that such personal efforts would put one's children at a better starting point for their own lives.

By most standards, these expectations have been met for the majority of Americans, and therefore it seems unreasonable to talk about austerity, especially when our stores are piled high with a prodigious variety of goods. However, it is not enough that present living standards are high. What is important is that people believe that their future will be more affluent so long as they apply themselves assiduously to socially approved tasks.

Even though public moods fluctuate quickly, polls taken over the last fifteen years indicate a growing pessimism about the future.[7] We are becoming less certain that the future will be better than the present no matter how hard we try to make it so. Such pessimism comes not so much from our concern for the problems of paying back the environment, or the fickleness of time, or that most industrial nations can solve problems as well as we can. Rather, we are experiencing the frustration of expectations more directly.

The inflationary trends in housing costs in the late 1970s struck directly at the heart of the American dream of home ownership. According to an authoritative study, housing costs between 1970 and 1976 nearly doubled, and the percent of families able to afford a medium-priced new home dropped from 46 to 27 percent.[8] Similar statistics could be presented for other vital commodities, such as food, clothing, and medical care. Taxation is placing increasingly heavy burdens upon the middle-income majority. The political implications are enormous, as the taxpayer revolts of the late 1970s have demonstrated. Of course, compared to the Japanese, English, and Canadians, we are better off on most counts. But this is beside the point, since the problem is American expectations, not the rest of the world's.

If some Americans are optimistic about the next twenty-five years, they have little reason to be. The cards are heavily stacked against the possibility that the future will be better than the past. Some observers contend that we are becoming more interested in nonmaterial higher values that do not require the massive consumption of scarce natural resources. Such asceticism may appeal to some younger people or to some of the already affluent, but this austerity does not have much attraction for the majority, who are constantly and intensively coerced by business and government to consume more and more. Certainly tightening the belt has no appeal whatsoever to those whose jobs depend on increasing mass consumption of goods and services. The question becomes whether the majority will voluntarily accept a diminished material standard of living, replacing it with a more austere style?

The leaders of modern organizations, whose careers depend upon growth, show no inclination to change the status quo; in fact, the tendency is to persuade the public that their lives are getting better all the time. But this is not the case. Already, the quality of our goods and services is declining without most of us realizing it. We are suspicious, of course, but the advertising media, which carries both corporate and government copy, smother our suspicions with superlatives about the superiority of their goods and services. We can see these trends, for example, in the downgrading of meat standards, the growth of fast-food franchises, and in the supposed superiority of government-sponsored medical programs.

What does it all mean? It means that decline will have to be managed. At the simplest level, Americans are lowering their expectations because the bases for realizing a higher material standard of living are simply evaporating. The interesting point, however, is that the decline in the standard of living is not accompanied by a decline in the size, power, and ubiquity of the modern organization. Rather, the opposite is the case. Decline can be managed; the larger problem is maintaining morale in the face of decline.

The Reconstruction of Confidence

As traditional beliefs are being shattered, the leadership of contemporary society is confronted with the staggering problems of creating new confidences, for confidence is the essential component of legitimacy. Where the old legitimacy was fashioned out of confidence in the efficacy of individual endeavor and the effectiveness of our pluralistic institutions, the new legitimacy is being forged from assumptions that support the modern organization. Recognition of this change is seen in the considerable literature concerning the growing "crisis of legitimacy" in America.[9] Many commentators have noted that confidence in all American institutions is declining and that the public mood is decidedly gloomy. It is axiomatic that such a condition cannot be tolerated by any political system, for unless there is public support for prevailing social, economic, and political arrangements, those arrangements will not last long.

For this reason alone, legitimacy is fundamental to the political, economic, and social order. Therefore, a crisis of legitimacy utlimately raises the question, who governs? The basic issue is: Why should the governed obey the governors?

The question of who governs is being settled, albeit in ways the public does not really comprehend and might not be very happy about if it did.

When people are fearful and uncertain about the forces affecting them, they tend to fall back upon what they do best, regardless of its relevance to the problems at hand. In the face of doubts about who governs, there has not been a re-examination of values, where real answers lie. Instead, increasing reliance has been placed upon the most successful American social invention, the modern organization. The resolution of the modern crisis of legitimacy has been achieved through the modern organization and the kind of leadership it requires. As a result, the principles and practices of the modern organization have pervaded every nook and cranny of American life — to such an extent that whoever controls modern organizations controls the nation. This solution to the government question has been clearly understood for years and by more writers than we can conveniently mention here. However, it is instructive to note the progression through time of the ideas about organization government through the work of Robert Michels, James Burnham, and Jacques Ellul.[10]

The political sociologist Robert Michels is not very fashionable these days. Theoretically, he was not highly rigorous and his historical examples are obscure. Further, his major contentions are much too unsettling. Nevertheless, his ideas apply to our situation. The essence of his argument is that in spite of the most honorable intentions, the democratic waves in history were forever breaking over the same shoals: the immutable needs of organization that create the "tyranny of expertise" and its corollary "iron law of oligarchy."[11] Depending upon one's ideological preferences, the cycle Michels described can be judged favorably or unfavorably; either way, his analysis was essentially correct.

Two points must be emphasized. First, given the inevitable rise of organizational oligarchs, Michels believed that the "ideal government would doubtless be that of an aristocracy of persons at once morally good and technically efficient." [12] This is now the ideal of modern organizational theorists and practitioners, although they often camouflage it with democratic euphemisms. Second, the people had little to say about all of this: They would be governed by an elite, like it or not, whether in political parties, labor unions, government agencies, or private businesses, because this was an inescapable law of nature. In other words, Michels considered the idea of the legitimacy of rule by a managerial elite to be beyond question; one does not discuss the legitimacy of a natural force.

The triumph of managerialism was spelled out by the reformed American Trotskyist James Burnham. While his book, too, has drifted into relative obscurity, most of what he predicted has come true. *The Managerial Revolution* has a distinctly old-fashioned air today, for Burnham was busy settling accounts with various Marxist factions and speculating whether capitalism could survive. But his contention that the managerial elite was winning everywhere was correct, even though their organizational techniques were then most primitive.

Burnham understood that the principal element of control inherent in modern organizations was the expertise of management, which involved a new kind of knowledge. Because it took managerial knowledge to keep an organization alive, this led inevitably to an elitist oligarchy. Because of its indispensability, the managerial function had to be made legitimate. Certainly this is most evident today: In modern organizations, power accrues to those who have expert knowledge in management. Those who occupy the key managerial posts constitute a governing elite. Regardless of our democratic and humanistic intentions, the inescapable admission is forced upon us: "THAT which IS oppresses THAT WHICH OUGHT TO BE." [13] People still use their learning to obtain influence and power, but those prizes now lie within managerial positions. Once such positions are obtained, the power of the incumbents is used to preserve and nourish administrative oligarchies.

No one has analyzed the developing organizational culture better than Jacques Ellul. It is impossible to summarize him — he strides through all subject matter, disdainful of small thoughts and precise expression. However, he repeatedly stresses one point of enormous importance to our argument: the adoption of "technique" by the state. In 1954, he wrote:

From the political, social, and human points of view, this conjuction of state and technique is by far the most important phenomenon of history. It is astonishing to note that no one, to the best of my knowledge, has emphasized this fact. It is likewise astonishing that we still apply ourselves to the study of political theories or parties which no longer possess anything but episodic importance, yet we bypass the technical fact which explains the totality of modern political events.[14]

This situation has resulted partly from a fusing of the traditional legitimacy of the state with the modern organization. It is further compounded because we cannot readily observe the managerial elite who are commanding us. The old-time dictators were obvious and there was little doubt about their intentions.

If anything, managerial elites in the national managerial system are even less accessible today than when Michels, Burnham, and Ellul wrote. They are shielded from public appraisal by the cloak of organizational invisibility and further insulated by the arcane languages and practices of managerial specialties. Indeed, the symbolic jargon of management reinforces the uncanny feeling that when one deals with someone who does MIS, PPBS, CPM, and OD, one is not dealing with an ordinary person. Managers alone understand the sacred language of the new secular priesthood, and their sense of legitimacy and elitism is intensified the higher they move up through the organizational hierarchy.

But, on the one hand, a tough-minded person will argue, so what? Michels, Burnham, and Ellul have spelled out the facts of life, so why fight the inevitable? The national managerial system probably is a blessing, for it creates order and, through some mystical form of organizational Darwinism, the fittest managers rise to the top. Since we want to be managed by the best and the strongest, Thrasymachus has been reincarnated in a gray flannel suit. This is one of the most lethal mistakes made by the supposed tough-minded apologists. Certainly, order is imposed by the national managerial system, but neither Michels nor Burnham nor Ellul believed that the rise of managerial power also brought with it some form of winnowing by which virtue triumphed. To the contrary, they believed that managerialism encouraged organizational stagnation, the spoiling of idealism, official insensitivity, despotic repression, and the blighting of human aspirations.

A humanist will argue on the other hand that one reason for these early, unfortunate results was that the managers were forced to use very crude techniques of leadership. Not much sensitivity can be expected from managerial leaders if the primary instruments in their behavioral repertoire are autocratic command and coercive power, coupled with a raw kind of expertise in the use of influence within organizations. In reaction to such obvious organizational barbarisms, most managerial scholars and practitioners have turned to other, more "humane" modes of behavior control. For instance, considerable attention has been given to alternatives to the crudities of past management theory and practice. These alternatives are found in processes like participatory management and organizational development, which stem from the humanistic psychology of Abraham Maslow, Douglas McGregor, and others of their persuasion.

Ellul foresaw this development of humanism and discussed it in a chapter entitled "Human Techniques." [15] He observed that much of the new behavioral research would eventually be adapted to serve as rational tools for managers. This did, indeed, happen, and management practices were sanitized along humanistic lines. The significance of this cannot be overemphasized. The behavioral sciences added to management's legitimacy a previously missing dimension: a demonstrable intention of benevolence toward the people being managed. Since everyone is either a manager or is managed, humanistic practices have become extremely important in establishing the right of the new managerial elite to rule. Legitimacy is augmented by niceness.

This new order of things, an organizational America governed by a managerial elite, has been announced and accepted as routine by such skillful writers as George C. Lodge and Harlan Cleveland.[16] They, among many others, believe the triumph of the modern organization has created new possibilities for America and that further social changes in this country can be effected without a falter in stride. Whatever our problems, they can be solved by making our organizations better, especially as we enter the Age of Decline.[17] Their optimism is not warranted.

The Decent Intentions of Managers

There has been a very important shift in emphasis in our perceptions of leadership in organizational America. In the past, the public has always placed its confidence in the individuals who run the organizations, whether public or private, rather than in the organizations themselves. When something goes wrong, the cry goes up to "kick the rascals out!" With respect to the top leadership, much of the civil ruckus in our society has been over the conduct of those at the helm of the ship of state — or the corporate galley ship, for that matter. Put in simple terms, most of us want to equate good and evil with identifiable people: Evil people do evil deeds and vice versa. Obviously, once the "good guys" are in control, all will be well. This is now a child's game. Does anyone honestly believe there will be no more Vietnams now that Lyndon Johnson has passed away or no more Watergates now that Richard Nixon is on his own Elba? Obviously not. So we are again confronted with the eternal question of democracy: How can a free people guarantee that only worthy persons move into the positions of leadership in both the public and the private sectors? The answer is, they cannot. There are no guarantees. But that is the essence of democracy, that a free people must constantly search for virtue, in themselves and in their leadership.

But modern organizations cannot tolerate such uncertainty; they have too much invested to allow for the ambiguities of searching for virtue. Therefore, within management theory and practice has developed the belief that by designing "perfect" organizations, the individuals who occupy positions in them, especially high positions, become morally cauterized. Consequently, it does not matter what individuals were like before they entered these positions; they become virtuous by their incumbency. If organizational rule structures are informed by humane psychology, then incumbents will automatically do good. This rather stands Lord Acton on his head!

Karl Popper has written that "Who should rule?" is no longer the question but rather "How can we so organize . . . institutions that bad or incompetent rulers can be prevented from doing too much damage?" [18] He contends that the strength and vitality of organizations must never be predicated on the assumption that the best people will rule, since if it turns out that such is not the case, as often happens, the survival of political and private institutions is compromised, along with our freedom, welfare, and national security. Therefore, our energies should not be consumed with the issue of quality in professional management. Popper was not writing an apology for the modern organization; rather, he was reaffirming an almost Jeffersonian position. The difference is that the Founding Fathers wanted strong organizations in order to enhance and preserve the values of the individual. Modern organizations seek strength to preserve themselves.

Management scholars and practitioners have tried to do what Popper said, even though they misperceive the ends. They have worked from the premise that good organizational structures not only function well, they also produce good people. Virtue, then, lies *first* in the organizational structure and *second* in the individual. Laying aside this issue for the moment, we believe that most managers are honorable. Therefore, we have assumed throughout this book that *the intentions of managers are decent and that they want the best, not only for themselves and their organizations, but for all people as well.* But if this is the case, then why is there such growing discontent in America?

The problems that beset the nation now lie not so much in the managers but in the very nature of modern organizations. The basic trouble is in the self-justifying ideology upon which organizations are founded. But we know very little about the value foundations of the society we have brought into being. We have substituted our extensive and useful knowledge about behavior in organizations for the essential discussion about the values of organizations.

The power of the modern organization is such that it has reformed the qualitative expectations we have for our lives and reordered the priorities we assign to our values. Invariably, organizational values will take precedent over individual values. The individual is now being made for the organization rather than the organization for the individual.

But even granting this point, is it necessarily bad? Humanist managers argue that there is no cause for alarm, for all personnel problems can be countered by techniques of humane management: job enrichment, participatory democracy, the decentralization of decision-making. In other words, mold individuals nicely to fit the needs of organizations. The difficulty with this argument, of course, is that it proposes to solve the problems of organizations by techniques that owe their existence to them.

This is where a major Catch-22 arises. The decent intent of managers has its origin *within* the justificatory value system of modern organizations, to which they owe their loyalty. Thus, their very definitions of "good" and "bad" are predicated upon their prior acceptance of the values of the organizational imperative. The measure of their decent intentions is determined by the organizational imperative. If, then, they dismiss philosophical considerations as irrelevant, it is simply because they have been trained that way, and within their value framework, philosophy is foolish. Therefore, why should they examine the a priori values upon which their organizational faith is based? It is the *unexamined* determinism that grows out of the blind acceptance of the values of the organizational imperative that is at the root of our contemporary malaise.

Chapter 2

The Organizational Imperative

What has in fact happened during the past half century is that the bulk of power in our society, as it affects our intellectual, economic, social, and culture existences, has become largely *invisible,* a function of the vast infragovernment composed of bureaucracy's commissions, agencies, and departments in a myriad of areas. And the reason this power is so commonly invisible to the eye is that it lies concealed under the humane purposes which have brought it into existence.

— Robert Nisbet, *Twilight of Authority*

The Transformation of American Values

The American value system has undergone major transformations. The pluralistic forces that shaped our national character have disappeared,[1] and the collective strivings of our society have been consolidated into the modern organization. In contemporary America, its needs overwhelm all other considerations, whether of family, religion, art, science, law, or the individual. We have become a different people than we imagined we would be, than we think we are.

Central to our tradition has been the assumption that individuals could determine their interests better than any collectivity. We were confident that such knowledge gave individuals the possibility of control over their destiny. The lodestar of the American dream was the individual. Embodying the spirit of the times, Walt Whitman wrote:

I swear I begin to see the meaning of these things,
It is not the earth, it is not America who is so great,
It is I who am great or to be great, it is You up there, or any one,
It is to walk rapidly through civilizations, governments, theories,
Through poems, pageants, shows, to form individuals.

Underneath all, individuals,
I swear nothing is good to me now that ignores individuals,
The American compact is altogether with individuals,
The only government is that which makes minute of individuals,
The whole theory of the universe is directed unerringly to one
    single individual — namely to You. [2]

But as time passed, the contribution of individuals became more and more minor as new collectivities emerged. They were vast, complex, technologically based modern organizations or their precursors, which synthesized clusters of resources into rationally functioning wholes. We have accepted what we have received from modern organizations neither gratefully nor ungratefully, but as an earned and just inevitability. Recently, however, we have begun to comprehend that a technologically based affluence has not led to a commensurate personal happiness. Indeed, as Heilbroner has written, affluence seems to have unmasked an agonizing "existential hunger." [3] How did we drift into this situation?

The Paradox of Technological Progress

The paradox of technological progress rests upon two contradictory beliefs: that technology is an ungovernable force, and that technology can be controlled by people because it is created by them.

Our deep belief in unremitting technological progress involves more than the superficial confidence that the problems caused by technology can be solved by technology. It reflects a deterministic view about the inevitability of technological change in engineering and the natural sciences and in the social and behavioral sciences as well. While most people think these changes are signs of progress, there is also no shortage of critical comment about the potentials for global catastrophe born from technology.

The nondeterministic belief affirms that because people made technology, they can know it. And since they can know it, they can control it. But who has this responsibility? There is the completely naive assertion that since scientists made technology, they are responsible for controlling it. This position is totally impossible to support. Scientists cannot control technology because the machinery for control is not in their hands. Instead, the managers, and to a lesser extent the politicians, who make scientific and technological policy decisions, control its development and use. This fact, however, does not refute the nondeterministic belief. It merely identifies, more realistically, the locus of responsibility for control.

If the control of technology is a management policy problem, then the obvious question is, how does management go about solving it? Not very well, according to some writers. John Platt, for instance, listed "administrative management" third among the top American crises, surpassed only by total nuclear annihilation and great destruction short of annihilation. He argued that unless we become better at management, our nation faces unbearable tensions. But he believes that such tensions will yield to enlightened management practices. In his opinion, management failures result from insufficient research and development of better managerial techniques: "The cure for bad management designs is better management designs"[4] Platt's stand will gain nods of assent from within the managerial fraternity. But, like too many others within this brotherhood, Platt has fallen for the deception that good methods guarantee good results.

Regardless of how well managers perform their administrative functions, it is absolutely unwarranted to suppose that socially progressive control of technology will follow. Management may serve organizational America in many ways, but the one thing it does not necessarily provide is leadership. Richard A. Gabriel and Paul L. Savage made this point unequivocally in their study of the management (mismanagement) of the army in Vietnam. The deterioration of the field army, they claimed, was a direct result of the false premise that equated good management practice with good leadership. Discussing Robert S. McNamara's role as secretary of defense in promulgating this idea, they wrote:

He was the ideal corporate man, and during his tenure as Secretary of Defense the Army moved ever closer to the modern business corporation in concept, tone, language, and style. Further, the individual military officer became identified with the corporate executive to the point where the functions of command were perceived as identical to the functions of departmental management. More and more of its officers were sent to graduate schools to take advanced degrees, almost all receiving degrees in business management or administration.[5]

Management is not leadership. This dictum applies equally to the army, corporations, universities, labor unions, and government agencies. Given the option, management will pursue those conservative alternatives that are derived from the organizational status quo. Leadership has the foresight to extract itself from the status quo and seek options that will allow for the possibility of social improvement.

Thus, the question is not whether technology is a governable force. It is. The pertinent question is whether the organizational imperative is governable. Organizational America is run by managers who will control technology in ways that will serve modern organizations. Certainly, some of our present difficulties arise from managerial incompetency. But much more basic, however, are those difficulties that stem from the values that all managers must hold and that must be imposed upon all connected with modern organizations. C. P. Snow wrote: "We are immensely competent; we know our own pattern of operations like the palm of our hands. It is not enough . . . It would be bitter if, when this storm of history is over, the best epitaph that anyone could write of us was only that: 'The wisest men who had not the gift of foresight.'"[6]

Managerial Amorality

Organizations are so familiar that their presence among us is either accepted uncritically, ignored, or mindlessly despised. Nonetheless, because modern organizations have created and have largely defined the American value system, they must be considered the most important socializing agencies in America. The managers who control the great system of organizations will continue to have an increasingly dominant role in defining values by the decisions they make. But managerial decisions are always those required by the organization. All the organizational standards used to assess managerial effectiveness in decision-making measure contributions to the health of the organization. The key word here is "health."

The Criterion of Organizational Health

At one time, organizational health meant adjusting organizational inputs so that they were minimized relative to outputs. Success in this endeavor was called *efficiency,* and the object of management was to increase it. Efficiency meant lower costs, lower prices, higher profits, and better competitive status in the marketplace. The continuous growth of efficiency meant that everyone — managers, employees, customers, and ultimately, all of society — would be better off.

At the time when efficiency measures were about the only formal standards for judging managerial performance, the word "health" was seldom used in connection with organizations. It has appeared more frequently, in the last fifteen or twenty years, as the analogy of the organization to an organic system has gained widespread acceptance.[7] It assumes that an organization, similar to all living things, must manifest two characteristics to be judged healthy. First, it must either be growing or be mature and stable. Of these characteristics, growth is preferable, since the economic system depends on it.[8] Maturity and stability are acceptable, too, of course, but not for long; managers get fired for failing to return to growth patterns. (How quickly the organic analogy can be forgotten!) Above all, the organization must never be allowed to decline, contract, or shrink, as these conditions are unhealthy in the "organic" organization. Second, the organization must be adaptable, since healthy, complex organisms adjust to environmental contingencies in order to survive.

Thus growth and adaptability have been added to the older notion of efficiency as criteria for organizational health. The sum of these factors is now expressed by a new term, *organizational effectiveness,* a new ideal for managerial success. Unfortunately, few people are sure what the term means, let alone how to measure it.[9]

The criterion of organizational health has two very interesting managerial consequences. The first is that managers must be expedient — in fact, amoral — in order to obtain the most benefits for their organizations. Second, managers need not worry about their actions if they *are* expedient, for organizations shield them from public accountability. We term these conditions "the methods of expediency" and the "shield of elitist invisibility."

The Methods of Expediency

When management theory emerged as a discipline, in the early twentieth century, the theories and methods of natural science were well advanced. One of the basic features of the natural sciences is the separation of "fact" and "value." This separation allowed scientists to avoid troublesome value questions and to concentrate on the comparatively simpler world of nature. Scientists confined their inquiries to the puzzles presented by the natural order and developed, concomitant with these puzzles, techniques that enable them to predict, and often to control, the events of the empirical universe. By limiting itself to a world capable of being known, science thus identified research goals that could be objectively verified and replicated. And there are an endless number of puzzles for scientists to solve.[10]

The enormous success of natural science was not lost on management. Scholars and practitioners optimistically presumed that their field could enjoy similar explosive progress by using the methods of science in managing organizational affairs. Accordingly, management began to transpose those methods into guidelines of its own, and scientific management, the earliest movement in that direction, was created by Frederick W. Taylor around 1900.[11]

To an extent, management's borrowing of the scientific method has been justified. Over the years major problems have been solved and management has learned a great deal. Unfortunately, the methodological single-mindedness with which management embraced scientific methods has resulted in a dangerous unwillingness to question values or discuss anything that cannot be treated empirically.

This failure to consider values is risky for any applied behavioral science, and it is lethal in the case of management. Clearly, management's value poverty is not the fault of science. It is the result of a combination of circumstances that elevated a false model of scientific method into a model suitable for management theory and practice. The need for empirical methods, joined with the need for solving the immediate problems of modern organizations, provided the foundation for managerial amorality. The methods of expediency are rooted here.

These methods are largely a practical exercise in puzzle-solving. The rational requirements of technology, the coordination requirements of job specialization, and the productivity expectations of society require that managers direct their energies and talents to finding solutions for the immediate, practical, and material problems that confront them. So the pressures for solving these concrete problems have overriden any propensities for thinking about values.

Management has not, however, reluctantly turned away from such thinking. The motivation for it was never there to begin with; organizational puzzle-solving is so engaging that serious concern about values is condemned within. the management profession as a wasteful excursion into mysticism. Consequently, managers are rewarded only for the expedient solution of organizational problems; those who think about anything else are derided. To illustrate, Daniel Katz and Robert L. Kahn, two experienced management scholars, wrote:

A technologically oriented organization has its rationalized purposes geared to the world of empirical fact rather than to transcendental value. Absolutistic beliefs, unquestioning loyalty, and the excommunication of heretics just do not fit into a value system of pragmatic operationalism . . . The technological system creates experts who are heavily task oriented, who fly no flags, and who are completely bored by ideological considerations.[12]

So the policies, practices, and thoughts of management are heavily weighted toward the expedient by people who have been trained to consider value questions as impractical, even foolish. Managers, trained in the scientific management of organizations, enter into an orderly, purposeful, and balanced empirical world of puzzles "that only their own lack of ingenuity would keep them from solving." [13] That world offers managers security and status so long as the methods of expediency remain intact. Since questioning values is a threat to this security, there should be little wonder that it is neglected.

But there is a hitch. In the name of organizational health, managers must make decisions affecting the lives of many others, and while these decisions may be organizationally justified, they may also be morally indefensible. Are individual managers accountable to higher public tribunals of opinion for the morality, distinct from the legality, of their decisions? The answer is no, for personal responsibility is inconsistent with expediency. Therefore, managers must be shielded by the organization from accountability.

The Shield of Elitist Invisibility

Some might claim that the exposure, prosecution, and jailing of managerial miscreants disprove our last statement, and that there is some ultimate accountability for managers whether they serve in public or private enterprises. Theoretically, this is true, and from time to time dramatic examples of mismanagement or executive misdeeds are exposed. Certainly an epic disaster like the collapse of the Penn Central Railroad was well covered by the media. Other indiscretions have also been reported, like the Lockheed scandal. But these exceptions prove the point, if for no other reason than that the cost and the effort required precludes the exposure of many or even most gross misdeeds.

However, it is not only misdeeds that are hidden; almost all managerial actions are shielded by the impenetrability of modern organizations, whether they be offensive, innocuous, or even gratifying to public opinion. We can recall seeing, years ago, a picture of a corporate president saying goodbye to one of his subordinates at the gate of a federal prison. He was about to start serving time for a price-fixing conviction. Of course, it was the subordinate who was going in, not the president. The situation was the electrical industry price-fixing case in the late 1950s and early 1960s. The question then was, as it still is, why was the president of the company shielded from conviction and not the subordinate?

Other incidents come to mind. The Senate, investigating oil company practices during the OPEC embargo, simply could not get enough information from testifying executives to determine whether anything shady had been done to restrict oil supplies. But Senate investigators are not the only ones deprived of information for investigatory purposes. The shield of elitist invisibility even protects managers from inopportune inquiries from their own boards of directors. For example, the board of Gulf Oil, looking into the machinations of the company's chief lobbyist, was led astray by the top management through the 1970s. The clash between the board and management came to a head in 1975. It was asked why the board had not done more:

Why did the directors behave as they did? In part, because they were led astray by the management. Gulf's general counsel and lawyers retained by the company withheld from the board some devastating details that they had turned up while looking into the company's transgressions. And Dorsey [the CEO] kept secret from the board, for more than a year and a half after the scandal broke, the fact that he had personally authorized the largest political payments — $4 million to the party backing President Park Chung Hee of Korea.[14]

It is often said by public administration observers that government agencies are open with respect to their policies but very secretive about their procedures. The General Services Administration scandals of the late 1970s support this claim. The public was treated to an ever-lengthening list of contracts awarded on comradeship, vacationing civil servants sunning themselves in luxury, and extremely strange accounting procedures. The point is that in organizational America it is extraordinarily difficult to get at managers, at very high levels, to make them accountable for the legality, much less the morality, of their administrative decisions.[15]

One of the most effective shields protecting managerial performance is the personification of the organization in familiar phrases, like "the company feels," organizations "do" this or "decide" that, organizations "behave" "responsibly" or "irresponsibly." This is consummate nonsense and we all know it. Yet we continue to write and speak about organizations as if they were persons. This personification obscures the fact that it is individuals who make decisions within organizations. To suggest that organizations "do" anything masks these individuals from view and depersonalizes both the value and moral issues implicit in their conduct, thus relieving them of individual responsibility and public accountability.

A second way in which the invisibility of the managerial elite is preserved is that their performance is measured by purely operational criteria. Because Americans are so dependent upon the efficient performance of organizational systems, they tend to hold managers operationally accountable for their actions and excuse all else. In other words, a manager's morality is equated with the utility of his actions, as they contribute to the health of the organization. As we have seen earlier, the measures of that utility are efficiency, growth, and adaptability. A manager may behave like Attila the Hun, but if he contributes substantially to organizational effectiveness all is forgiven. This is not because the public is

morally insensitive, but because it lacks the technical expertise needed to manage the modern organization. Thus, they
can only turn to the criterion of effectiveness to judge performance.

There is a third result of this shielding, and it is extremely
important. The value system of modern organizations has
developed behind closed doors, so to speak. Managers continue to do what they must do and the organizational values
that guide their decisions are clear to them. But ordinary
people still cling to the now-outmoded values of the American tradition. This has led to a widening gap between the
popular assumption of the nature of the American values and
the actual practices of managers in modern organizations. In
the remainder of this chapter, we outline the primary values
of modern organization; in the next chapter, we shall discuss
how those primary values have altered some particular
American values.

The Propositions and Rules of the Organizational Imperative

The major force that has produced the transformation of
American values is the organizational imperative. It consists
of two a priori value propositions and three ethical rules for
behavior. The imperative is based upon a primary proposition, which is absolute: *Whatever is good for the individual can
only come from the modern organization.* The question of what
is good for the individual is left open for the moment. What
must be beyond doubt is the belief that the only way to
achieve anything of significance is through the modern organization. The secondary proposition derives from the first:
*Therefore, all behavior must enhance the health of such organiza-
tions.*

Out of these propositions come three rules for organizationally healthy behavior, which define, guide, and measure

all managerial performance. They apply to every manager in every organization in modern society. These behavioral rules require that the manager be technically rational, a good steward of other people's property, and pragmatic. Since the concepts of rationality, stewardship, and pragmatism carry a heavy burden of numerous interpretations, we must specify their exact meaning with respect to the organizational imperative.

Rationality

The rule of technical rationality is the common denominator for all scientifically conditioned, technologically oriented organizations in advanced industrial nations. We do not refer to the philosophic tradition of rationalism, but to that form of rationality central to scientific method, which requires the economizing of means to achieve ends.

Drawing upon its heritage of science, engineering, and economics, management has made rationality indistinguishable from efficiency — the equation of $E = O/I$. The task of administration, guided by this formula, is to increase the value of E by adjusting the relative values of outputs and inputs. While we often argue over definitional refinements and are sometimes confused by our own rhetoric, this statement must be accepted, along with its behavioral implications, because ultimately there is no other satisfactory way to account for what managers do in modern organizations.

Stewardship

The organizational imperative requires competent stewards whose primary loyalty must be to the organizational imperative's a priori propositions. They must be defenders of the faith, and beyond that, must proselytize on its behalf.[16] Their secondary loyalty must be to the "others" in whose interests the organization is managed. It does not make a particle of difference who the "others" are: the public at large, the stockholders of a corporation, the members of a consumer cooperative, or the members of labor unions. The rule of stewardship applies with equal force in all cases. For one thing, it legitimizes the hierarchical structure of organizations: If stewards are to fulfill these obligations, those who work for them must obey their commands. Therefore, managers are stewards for the combined destinies of their subordinates. Additionally, stewardship requires the husbanding of organizational resources. If the stewardship rule is successfully executed, the health and wealth of the organization are protected and increased, the welfare of those dependent on the organization is improved, and the fortunes of its managers are advanced. As with rationality, divergent ideas about the nature of stewardship are unthinkable within the framework of management theory and practice as it has developed during the last seventy-five years.

Pragmatism

Pragmatic behavior enables the organization to survive in good health in changing environments, as circumstances continually impose different necessities upon managers. The rule of pragmatism requires no more than devotion to the methods of expediency, guided by the primary and secondary propositions. Beyond this, the rule for pragmatic behavior has no other content.

The organizational world of management is one where complex problems of short-term duration must be dealt with expediently in order to advance the a priori propositions. Pragmatism demands that managers direct their energies and talents to finding solutions for practical, existing problems within an immediate time frame. The language, reward systems, and activities of management demonstrate this concern for the present. Its attention to putting out fires, meeting competition, adjusting to "inputs" from the public, insuring the smooth day-to-day running of departments, and short-range planning horizons indicate its devotion to securing an orderly, purposeful world composed of interesting, narrow puzzles to be solved. This pragmatic puzzle-world encourages managers not to reflect on larger, less immediate issues of long-range effects or needs.

Each of the behavioral rules involves the others. To be pragmatic is to be rational, in the sense that efficiency and expediency often amount to the same thing in practice. To be a competent steward means finding expedient solutions to pressing problems within boundaries defined by rationality. Therefore, the three behavioral rules exist in an interrelated web within the imperative, the primary purpose of which is to strengthen the a priori propositions of the imperative. What does all of this mean to American society?

The Significance of the Organizational Imperative

The organizational imperative is the sine qua non of management theory and practice. It cuts across organizational boundaries. It changes slowly, if at all. If it is affected tangibly by political and social turmoil, or even war, the imperative is *strengthened* by them. The organizational imperative is the metaphysic of management: absolute and immutable. It is persuasive (it alters values in order to alter behavior), it is universal (it governs through the a priori propositions all collective efforts for achieving major social and individual objectives), and it is durable (it is the one source of stability and continuity in a turbulent world).

Before explaining these contentions, we must remember that the management of organizations is a practical and mundane effort. Implicit within the pragmatic rule is a warning against philosophizing. Management does the vital job of linking organizations, which are the most elaborate of abstractions, with the people. Organizations are run by managers who must make decisions about goals, policies, and strategies of action that influence human values and behavior, both within and outside the organization. They respond with varying sensitivity and accuracy to the needs and interests of the different groups affected by their decisions. But their loyalties seldom belong to those they affect most profoundly, and certainly they are neither trained nor encouraged to speculate about the value implications of their decisions. The vice president for personnel of a large company that must lay off five hundred employees is certainly not encouraged to consider the impact of this action on their lives. Instead, consideration is given to the health of the company.

Conventional wisdom has it that the primary loyalty of managers should be to those who own their organizations: the stockholders, if it is a private company, or the citizens, if a public organization. While that wisdom may have been correct once, it is certainly not so now. *The overriding concern of managers is to keep their organizations healthy*; if their clients are served as a consequence, it is a happy secondary result of the primary managerial concern.

Organizational health is best achieved through management's total allegiance to the organizational imperative. To advance this cause, the values of *all* persons who influence the organization, whether from within or without, must be modified so that they complement the organizational imperative. This "imperialism" is a distinctive characteristic of the organizational imperative. Managers, therefore, must discipline themselves, their subordinates, and even their clients to arrange their values, expectations, and practical affairs so that the organizational imperative is served. This may necessitate the modification of traditional beliefs. The rugged individualism of our pioneer past is certain to get one fired in any large organization today, particularly one with a dress code. The results of such modifications are the conversion of almost all actions into organizationally supportive behavior and are alterable to suit the needs of changing times, tastes, and circumstances. Changes in public behavior, however, do not produce changes in the organizational imperative, which holds absolute sway. But such behavioral and value alterations are not that painful, for we have created a society in which those who are loyal to the organizational imperative, managers and civilians alike, are amply rewarded.

We All Win . . .

As early as 1910, Frederick W. Taylor argued that scientific management had to be used to expand the productivity pie. He taught that individual advantage was best served when human energy was directed rationally toward increasing productivity rather than spent squabbling over the relative size of the shares of the pie. According to Taylor, workers, managers, owners, and consumers had a mutual interest in the continuous growth of productivity. Growth created surpluses in the forms of economic abundance, which could be applied to finance still another cycle of growth.[17]

Out of this dream came the belief that material growth was absolutely essential to the vitality of national life and that the material abundance obtained from such growth was limitless. These were the necessary preconditions for the "good" that modern organizations created for the individual. Whatever else Americans sought as individuals, they could find in the consumption of products and services. Material well-being was, to an appreciable extent, the basis for the *consensus* that cemented the social order, especially after the American Industrial Revolution of the late nineteenth century.

There has not been much difference between how Americans define their individual aims and what managers try to accomplish within organizations. Management practices generally are consistent with the expectations of Americans at large, since successful practices are thought to contribute to individual welfare. However, as technology has been carried by modern organizations into nearly every corner of society, a new and extremely important factor has been added to the equation for a good life. This factor has not eradicated customary materialistic conceptions of individual good. Rather, it has converted them to organizational terms. The organizational imperative was this factor, and the single most important change in public attitude it wrought was the creation of the idea that individual welfare can only be realized through the modern organization and its managerial systems.

Thus growth is a good, but the most important growth is organizational. Abundance is a good, but it is an organizationally produced abundance. Consensus is a good, but the crucial consensus is among potentially conflicting interest groups within organizations. For the most part these organizationally derived goods have benefited individuals. By managing organizational resources efficiently, growth results in financial surpluses that, when distributed in a reasonably equitable way, promote positive attitudes about the validity of the organization, the legitimacy of management, and the general community of interest in the work of expanding productivity. The goods of growth, abundance, and consensus have become guidelines for management practice that reconciled the organizational imperative with the people's expectations. Everyone can be satisfied when the productivity pie grows. But, as we enter an age of economic decline, there is growing doubt that "everyone" can win, that growth can continue.

Chapter 3

The Organizational Imperative Realized

People grow restive with a mythology that is too distant from the way things actually are, and as more and more lives have been encompassed by the organization way of life, the pressures for an accompanying ideological shift have been mounting. The pressures of the group, the frustrations of individual creativity, the anonymity of achievement: are these defects to struggle against or are they virtues in disguise? The organization man seeks a redefinition of his place on earth — a faith that will satisfy him that what he must endure has a deeper meaning than appears on the surface. He needs, in short, something that will do for him what the Protestant Ethic did once. And slowly, almost imperceptibly, a body of thought has been coalescing that does that.

— William H. Whyte, Jr., *The Organization Man*

We All Win . . . Or Do We?

The benefits of the organizational imperative do not come for free; everyone must pay. And paying the debt has required us all to surrender our allegiance to the traditional American values. As technology, organization, and management have penetrated the social order, collisions of increasing severity have been unavoidable between the values that originated in our agrarian and early industrial past and the new values of the organizational imperative.

This revolution in values was largely unanticipated as recently as two decades ago, although warnings were sounded by such perceptive observers as William H. Whyte, Jr., whose book *The Organization Man*[1] enjoyed great success in the 1950s because it was a sensitive, accurate, and timely appraisal of some extraordinarily important events. Whyte argued that America was shifting from an individualistic ethic to a social ethic, which was not yet articulated. His contention was that organizations, through their management systems, had imposed their values upon all they contacted, in nearly every human situation imaginable. This had produced a value lag, which he described well in the quotation above.

Unfortunately, most people misunderstood that message as a statement about conformity and read the book simply as a nonfiction version of the popular novel *The Man in the Grey Flannel Suit,* which had appeared a year earlier, in 1955. The theme of conformity was emphasized out of proportion, and the essential meaning of Whyte's book, his identification of an organizational imperative behind the change in values, was almost completely overlooked.

Somehow, in the turmoil of the 1960s, Whyte's warnings were forgotten. But in spite of campus riots, civil rights demonstrations, militant peace movements, and all of the other distractions of that era, the organizational imperative continued to work, and to work very well. As America drifted even further into an organization-dominated society, the contemptible organization man of the 1950s turned into a laudable model of managerial dedication. In order to bring coherence and security into his life, he constantly exerted pressure to bring social values into a harmonious and reinforcing relationship with the organizational imperative, to which he had pledged total allegiance.

The Organizational Imperative Realized   51

So, contrary to the shortsightedness of the media, the "ideal" individuals of the 1960s were not the "with-it" hippies, the peace activists, the committed and articulate university students, or the humanist psychologists. Rather, they were the superbly trained, functionally devoted, amoral managers — the "best and the brightest" among us. They were us, and most of us became them, if not in actuality, then at least in spirit. The irony was that we presumed we were following another model: John F. Kennedy set a style and proclaimed a doctrine of accelerated national performance in 1960. But we did not become like him; we became like those he hired.[2] Whyte's prophecy was fulfilled with only the slightest public recognition of what was happening.

Securing the dominance of the modern organization has been the major triumph of management in contemporary America. Because of their vital posts in all organizations, managers are uniquely able to influence the substance of public values. Through the mediating role of management, social values, either actually or potentially, have become reinforcing to the organizational imperative. Outrageous as it may seem, the fact is that a new value system dominates America. The organizational imperative, while originally a subset within the context of the overarching social value system, has now become the dominant force in the homogenization of organizational America, displacing the more individualistic values of the past.

The new order of organizational dominion requires specific responses from individuals if our society is to survive. The basic response, above all others, is the transformation of all social values so that they are consistent with the organizational imperative, and managers are both the facilitators and the arbitrators of this radical metamorphosis.

We shall discuss six values central to the American tradition that have changed due to the irresistible pressures of the organizational imperative. The values have been paired: the first indicating a dominant value of our tradition and the second, the value now dominant. The six pairings are: from innate human nature to malleability; from individuality to obedience; from indispensability to dispensability; from community to specialization; from spontaneity to planning; from voluntarism to paternalism. These pairs are not exhaustive, but they delineate what we see as the major value changes that have produced organizational America.

We must digress for a moment. It is not our purpose to analyze the traditional American value system. But since we argue that those values have been displaced by the values of the organizational imperative, we need to say something about our former values. In general, the idea at the inception of the Republic was to create a society that would allow for the full development of a set of individual values believed to be innate to all individuals. We have termed them the values of the "individual imperative." The primary proposition of the individual imperative is: All individuals have the natural right to realize the potentials of their unique selves throughout the stages of their lives. It thus follows that the primary purpose of any organization, public or private, is to allow for the realization of individual potentials.

We will have more to say about the values of the individual imperative in the last chapter. Suffice it to say that the nation produced by the values of the individual imperative was individual America. The nation produced by the values of the organizational imperative is organizational America. In Figure 1, the values in column A are some of the values of individual America. The values in column B are the values of organizational America.

Let us use a hypothetical situation to illustrate our contention that the values of the organizational imperative have displaced the values of the individual imperative. Suppose the personnel manager of a large, modern organization is designing a battery of tests to pick new candidates for a

FIGURE I

The Changing American Value System: From Individual
America to Organizational America

A		B
The values of the individual imperative		The values of the organizational imperative
From		*To*
Innate human nature	——	Malleability
Individuality	——	Obedience
Indispensability	——	Dispensability
Community	——	Specialization
Spontaneity	——	Planning
Voluntarism	——	Paternalism

management training program.* Among the tests is the inevitable personality test. Instead of measuring only the usual anal and oral fixations, this test also has questions that measure the intensity of the candidate's commitment to organizationally expedient values. Such questions would concern attitudes about flexibility, obedience, dispensability, and teamwork, among others. "Correct" attitudes would be those that indicated a tendency toward obedience, for example; "incorrect" attitudes would be those that indicated a strong propensity toward individualism.

Figure 1 depicts the array of values our personnel manager is measuring. The reader is asked, Which candidate would get the management trainee job, the candidate who scores heavily in the A column or the candidate who scores heavily in the B column? The answer is obvious: Column B values are overwhelmingly preferable.

We have used this example in numerous executive devel-

---

* We are in debt to William H. Whyte, Jr., for this illustration. In the Appendix to *The Organization Man,* Whyte discusses the use of personality tests to select persons for employment who demonstrate "organizationally correct attitudes."

opment courses, and practicing managers are unhesitating in stating their preferences for employees schooled in the values in column B — the values of the organizational imperative. Further, while they may personally admire the values in column A — the values of the individual imperative — they sheepishly agree that they themselves must possess B values or forget about advancement in their organizations.

The Collapse of the Values of the Individual Imperative

From Innate Human Nature to Malleability

The study of organizations must begin with an answer to a fundamental question: What vision of innate human nature instructs and legitimizes a system of authority? In other words, one must comprehend the prior vision of innate human nature upon which that system rests. This has been central to political philosophy throughout its history. If the assumption is that people are innately evil from birth, then it is nearly inevitable that government will be authoritarian, rigid, and cruel. It can be reasonably argued that Western civilization has been profoundly shaped by the notion of original sin; there is no doubt that the doctrine has been central to Western political systems for nearly two thousand years. But there are other visions that call forth their own forms of government. If one assumes that people are innately compassionate, a different kind of governmental system will emerge.

The same is true for organizational America. Behind the organizational imperative is a vision of innate human nature that is absolutely necessary for modern organizations. From the outset, management has been necessarily concerned with questions of organizational government. Usually these questions have been subsumed under studies of structures or systems or economic processes. But management had to create rational ways to bring people, resources, and specialized tasks together into efficiently functioning arrangements. So, consistent with the methods of expediency, management has created powerful organizational methods of control. But it is rare to find equally forceful attempts in managerial thought to understand what is the innate nature of the individual who is to be controlled. We do *not* imply that managerial thought does not have a vision of innate human nature. On the contrary, management has been dominated by a succession of images of human nature. These implicit value assumptions are seldom recognized as the foundations of managerial thought, but they are deeply imbedded in both theory and practice.

In an essay entitled "The Moral Nature of Man in Organizations," we examined some of these images, comparing the ideas of three management theorists (Frederick W. Taylor, Elton Mayo, and Douglas McGregor) with three political philosophers (Hobbes, Locke, and Rousseau). Noting some basic similarities and differences, we wrote that

Taylor and Hobbes believed in the need for maximum control to beat back *predatory* man. McGregor and Rousseau, in opposition, agreed to a minimization of the institutions of control to allow man's *innate compassion* to be released . . . Mayo and Locke occupied somewhat the center ground where man, being *basically indeterminate,* had to be formed through education to develop his own rational controls.[3]

The conclusion we drew there was that the view of human nature held by management theorists necessarily influences all their prescriptions for the management and design of organizations. A Frederick W. Taylor would prescribe differently from a Douglas McGregor. This particular point is so obvious in management thought that the models of the individual proposed by Taylor and McGregor are often used as examples of the extremes in organizational government: autocracy and democracy, respectively.

But theoretical fashions change, and the good–evil, democracy–autocracy polarities in the old management thought are fading fast. A new vision of innate human nature has become predominant. It can be seen lurking in the shadows of the currently fashionable ideas that hold that there are no "right" or "wrong" ways for management to organize and control. The new idea of what managers should do depends upon the practical demands of organizational size, environment, and technology.* Thus, management thought not based upon moral and ethical relativism is condemned as reductionist and determinist.

The point is that this pragmatic approach ascribes to managers a marvelous plasticity in adapting themselves and the people in their organizations to technological change and environmental tempests, whatever happens and as often as they occur. This conviction about human malleability is, in fact, the necessary view of innate human nature required by the organizational imperative; thus it is imbedded solidly within every modern organization. This image is based on the belief that the individual is, by nature, nothing and has the potential to be made into anything. Therefore, organizations must be designed to mold individuals, since there is nothing in their nature to prevent their adapting to whatever

---

* Of course, the primary propositions of the organizational imperative are absolute and unchanging. The fads of managerial thought stem from the rules for behavior connected to the primary propositions. "Contingency theory," for example, comes directly out of *pragmatism* (see pages 45–46). This position has become a most influential, albeit implicit, ethical foundation of contemporary management thought. Unfortunately, this assumption about human nature has profound consequences that are barely understood. Let us expand upon its implications by restating a point.

We believe that the predominant value criterion that influences management thought and practice is based on the second proposition of the organizational imperative. What is desirable in our society is measured by the degree to which it contributes to organizational health. It is axiomatic that an advancing technology is essential for "progress." Consequently, we have created a society completely dependent upon technology. By now, most people simply cannot conceive of a society that is not dominated by technology — it is unthinkable.

value premises and organizational contingencies are required. There can be little doubt that in the eyes of management the contemporary image of the individual's nature is one of malleability.

The psychologist Elton Mayo postulated, in the 1930s, the notion of human malleability in a way that management found extraordinarily useful. In his influential book *The Human Problems of an Industrial Civilization,*[4] he argued that the individual has an indeterminate nature. This vision of innate malleability has created unprecedented problems. Contemporary technological culture is historically unique, since it is neither a simple evolutionary change in the use of tools nor a linear extension of the Industrial Revolution. To put it in our terms, organizational America is a mutation with certain historical roots but which is in itself quite new. Since the technology upon which our society is built is so complex and expensive, people must be changed so they will be in a harmonious relationship with their machines. The instrument used to accomplish this goal is the modern organization. Since it is assumed that ultimate ends will take care of themselves, we have not questioned whether malleability is harmful to the individual as an individual. We have simply accepted our pliant role.

This is a dangerous situation, but it has been fully embodied in management thought, which does not allow for the serious consideration of such abstract topics as whether it is *right* to presume that individuals are, by nature, completely malleable. Management lives in the present. It gravitates toward the tangible realities of immediate organizational problems. It seeks solutions that "work" without disturbing the organizational cosmos. But with no consideration of the past and little consideration of the future, except in organizational planning, is it any wonder that the present seems capricious and contingent? Therefore, management has accepted completely the concept of total human malleability, since modern organizations could not otherwise survive in the status quo we have created.

And so we have adopted a malleable view of innate human nature. Simply, the individual need not get in the way of managerial responses to technological and organizational requirements, since nothing innate in individuals will force them to resist if the rewards for adaptation are sufficient. In other words, individuals can be shaped into anything the organization wants them to be. Given this base of innate malleability, an unspoken proposition of management can now be stated: With the discovery of appropriate scientific techniques, the individual can be shaped or, given a shift of contingencies, reshaped for maximal organizational utility. This proposition is of unprecedented importance, for now the individual, in principle, need never impede the management process. The problems of the individual are reduced to technological puzzles that can be solved without disrupting modern organizations. With more advances in mind technology, the proposition will become the third a priori of the organizational imperative: The individual can be shaped or, given a shift in events, reshaped for maximum organizational utility.

There is no value content in the malleable individual thesis of human nature unless, in some perverse way, nihilism can be considered a value. Acceptance of the individual as malleable is a managerial escape route, since it absolves managers from any need to consider individual rights or from any personal responsibility for the lives of the people they manage.

A bastardized variation of Mayo's image of the individual is now dominant in contemporary management thinking. It is a vision of individuals who are innately malleable and, thus, completely susceptible to techniques of education, development, and control through the modification of the environment and mind. This extreme vision of malleable human nature is a value position that is far beyond anything

Mayo wanted or anticipated. This new vision is a mutation, much as the technological society is itself a mutation and its guru is B. F. Skinner. Examples of the growing influence of the Skinnerian philosophy abound; one has only to look in on schools of psychology, education, penology, and social work. The neo-Skinnerians are carrying the day. And, bit by bit, their philosophy is infusing schools of administration.[5] Business organizations have not been exempted from the Skinnerian influence. For instance, Emery Air Freight has incorporated Skinnerian reinforcement techniques into its employee motivation programs.

The only element still needed for the fulfillment of the new vision is for individuals to accept their own malleability. Not only must all people believe they are, by nature, malleable, they must also accept this condition as a positive value.[6] When that happens, the behavioral conversion of society will be complete and the circle of managerial proselytizing will be closed.

This is a major movement toward the complete cultural renovation of America, and is why we argue that ours is the first organizational culture in history. But the change began long ago, in the 1930s, when influential writers like Elton Mayo, A. A. Berle, G. C. Means, and Chester I. Barnard were struggling to understand the then-emerging national managerial system. It was clear to them that management was in *the* strategic position for planning and bringing into being changes in values. Barnard, in particular, foresaw that management had to be the final arbiter of social values. He wrote: "The distinguishing mark of the executive responsibility is that it requires not merely conformance to a complex code of morals but also the creation of moral codes for others."[7] Mayo and Barnard never dreamed how right, or how naively optimistic, they were about the evolving managerial society.[8]*

* Elton Mayo, together with Thomas Henderson, Fritz Roethlisberger, and William Dickson, formed an intellectual hub at Harvard University in the early 1930s

Managers, as the elite of advanced industrial society, have set the tone of that society and established its cultural pace by their influence on values. Since managers control all modern organizations, they can write programs of social control for people who cannot hope to accede to managerial power but whose support is absolutely necessary for maintaining the managerial regime. These are the "insignificant people," whom we write about in Chapter 5, who must be convinced of their malleability and insignificance. Whether or not this persuading should be a part of managerial responsibility, in the sense that Barnard writes of, is a supreme question in any discussion of values, ethics, or morals. But the inescapable fact remains that management scholars and practitioners accepted the premise of innate human malleability without a trace of philosophical reflection. That demonstrates an appalling philosophic bankruptcy.

From Individuality to Obedience

De Tocqueville, among others, correctly observed that Americans have ranged, with marvelous inconsistency, from individuality to conformity. Nevertheless, individualism has

---

around which revolved the humanistically enlightened approach to management. It was an outgrowth of the famous Hawthorne Studies at Western Electric Company. The general sense of this group was that the new managerial leadership was bound to direct the course of values in a benevolent manner; that human potentials in industrial employment could be realized; that a renaissance in the social, economic, and governmental institutions would result from the rise of the new managerial elite. While none of this was foreseen by these thinkers as inevitable — they had some twinges of doubt — they nevertheless leaned toward optimism. The late 1930s, of course, were times of concerted social experimentation, and their optimism is therefore understandable. What none of them anticipated was that the organizational imperative would engulf managers and nonmanagers alike in its a priori assumptions and its behavioral rules.

While Chester I. Barnard was not a participant in the Harvard group, since he was located in New Jersey as president of New Jersey Bell Telephone Company, he influenced the thinking of its members, and vice versa, by his friendship with Thomas Henderson. See William B. Wolf, ed., *Conversations with Chester I. Barnard,* ILR Paperback #12 (Cornell University: New York State School of Industrial and Labor Relations, 1973).

held a unique and dominant place in our tradition, no matter how badly we have abused it. It has been interpreted in many ways, but central to them all was the confidence that individuals knew, or could know, what was best for themselves. As John Stuart Mill wrote: "With respect to his own feelings and circumstances, the ordinary man or woman has means of knowledge immeasurably surpassing those that can be possessed by anyone else."[9] Legitimacy was conferred upon American social, economic, and political institutions when they conformed to the individual's perception of right and wrong. Granted, this was an ideal, but it was nonetheless an ideal we tried to put into practice. David Riesman provides an excellent definition of that individuality in his description of the "inner-directed man."[10] The most significant justifications for action came from the individual, and the satisfactions derived from such personal actions were infinitely superior to those that came from obedience to collectivities. The ideal of rational individuals was the essential foundation for our notions about representative government and the free market.

In our time, the source of legitimacy for institutions is the organizational imperative, which requires individual obedience to it. What is more, such obedience is now a value in and of itself, supplanting the presumed ascendency of individuality. Poignantly, influential Americans still proclaim the importance of individuality on public occasions, knowing all the while that very little of importance is accomplished outside modern organizations. Given that reality, our allegiance has shifted quietly from individuality to obedience to the organizational imperative. The claim is now made that obedience to organizational rules results in far superior personal satisfaction. In short, it is good for individuals to be obedient.

Obedience is the cornerstone of the organizational edifice because it is essential to the chains of command. Superiors in a hierarchy of authority depend upon obedient subordinates. We will limit our discussion here to some observations about two particularly important aspects of obedience: homogenization and organizational amorality.[11]

Stanley Milgram distinguished between conformity and obedience as follows: "Conformity [is] the action of a subject when he goes along with his peers, people of his own status, who have no special right to direct his behavior. Obedience [is] the action of the subject who complies with authority."[12] Americans have become an *obedient* people; we have accepted the reality of the organizational imperative. In this process we are becoming all the same, not so much because we are "other-directed," looking to significant others in search of security in conformity, but because we have individually committed ourselves to a single ultimate value. By accepting, most often implicitly, the organizational imperative, and by agreeing to abide by the managerial rules derived therefrom, we are becoming extraordinarily homogeneous. Our problem is not conformity, as so many critics have argued. Our problem is homogeneity, which is more like the unanimity among members of an intense religious sect. They become the same from observing the same standards, *not* from observing each other. In a similar way, the traditional value of individuality was *not* abolished, but converted into an individual commitment to obedience to the demands of the organizational imperative. This conversion is important because it implies that people are not coerced into accepting the organizational imperative; they do so freely out of a sense of belief.

The second aspect of obedience we need to discuss is organizational amorality. It is a management truism that individual values must be congruent with organizational values. Individual idiosyncrasies cannot be allowed to impede the effective operation of the organization. Hence, the desired stance for individuals within the organization is organizational amorality: the willingness to substitute organizational values for personal values. In order to be of the greatest usefulness to the modern organization, individuals must be personally amoral and organizationally moral. That is, they must willingly internalize the goals of the organization as their own goals, without a qualm. We do not say that individuals must be immoral, only that they must be malleable.

But what if an organization requires individuals to do wrong things, such as lie or cheat? Unfortunately, the comparative goodness or badness of specified individual actions is not the issue. The key issue is the acceptance of the superiority of the organizational imperative over individual moral commitments. Obedience of this kind is so deeply ingrained that it takes a formidable personality to be disobedient to the demands of managers responsible for the health of their organization.

This is not altogether new. Human history is full of accounts of "true believers," individuals who gained meaning for their lives by committing themselves totally to a cause or a movement.[13] What is new is that the organizational imperative does not require the fanaticism so common to mass movements; in the popular parlance, one should be a cool "gamesman." Indeed, the organizational way of life is far from a calling. But one central feature of mass movements is present: the substitution of the collective absolute for personal values.

The values of the organizational imperative are clear and easily understood. Further, their application has produced observable and beneficial results; this is the stuff of conversion. On the other hand, individual values are not easily determined and held in the best of times. They are usually not clearly understood and, hence, are weakly defined. When confronted with the clarity and force of the organizational imperative, conflicting individual values are easily swept aside or, more likely, converted into organizationally useful values. By adopting the organizational imperative as the foundation of personal values, the agonies of introspection and the articulation of personal value commitments are removed and purpose is given to individual lives.

This situation is strongly reinforced by the fact that such a conversion is usually painless, materially rewarding, and brings with it the approbation of one's employers. The rule that emerges, which is nearly universal throughout our institutions, is that efficient performance in the service of organizational values is considered moral behavior. Thus, our standards of personal morality are defined by their usefulness to organizational goals.

So something like the following sequence has occurred. First, because of the successes of the modern organization, conventional wisdom has elevated its imperative over individual values. Second, since organizational values are given precedence over individual values, individuals are invariably rewarded for believing in their personal malleability. Third, once individual malleability is accepted, individual morality becomes synonymous with organizationally useful attitudes and behaviors. Individuals are rewarded for "adjusting" their personal attitudes and behaviors to bring them into congruence with the organizational imperative. The result is the substitution of obedience for individualism so the organizational imperative will be better served.

From Indispensability to Dispensability

An important value in the American tradition has been the belief that individuals were justified in feeling indispensable to the groups, organizations, and communities of which they were a part. Honorable people had the right to expect that their absence would have a profound effect upon those who worked and lived with them. For example, when the great historian Frederick Jackson Turner was a young assistant professor at the University of Wisconsin, in 1889, a senior professor of history died, and his death was felt by all: "His passing plunged the university into mourning; classes were canceled, the massive pillars at the entrance to the campus were draped in black, and all social events were put off until after the funeral, three days later."[14] The community was sorrowfully diminished by the passage of one individual. One might ask what would be the response of a major university today upon the death of a single professor? At best, the deceased would earn a mention in the mimeographed notes of the next faculty senate meeting, and perhaps a minute of silence at the beginning of the meeting, during which time those attending would surreptitiously look at their watches so that they could be first to be recognized by the chair after the inconvenience was over.

Throughout history, including parts of our own, people have dispensed with one another in callous and brutal ways, and most people have probably never really felt indispensable. Nevertheless, the ideal of personal indispensability has been central to our tradition and its attainment has been held out as one of the most important rewards of an honorable life. Simply, indispensability meant that individuals could have a sense of being necessary to their communities. This theme was seldom depicted as well as in the 1946 Frank Capra film, *It's a Wonderful Life*.

But the organizational imperative requires that nothing and no one be indispensable and that, indeed, dispensability be a prized attribute. Modern American society is built upon the dispensability of things, and our economy is founded upon the necessity of the dispensability of products through the consumption cycle. The major purpose of obsolescence is to enrich organizations. Our lives are spent in surroundings of constant material replacement because our technology and our economy have made it more efficient to dispose of things rather than reuse them.

All of this is well known. What is less well understood is how individuals in a society that exalts dispensability might eventually come to view themselves. Further, how does a society that demands that nothing, save modern organizations, be indispensable come to regard individuals? The answer is obvious: The organizational imperative requires that all people believe they are dispensable and, further, that this is a good thing.

Modern organizations cannot tolerate necessary individuals. If they did, organizations would become dependent upon these individuals, and such a situation is anathema to managerial thought and practice. Let us illustrate this point by using the familiar metaphor of the organization as a machine. In a machine, each part is linked as efficiently as possible with all the other parts. Each performs its specific tasks in a productive rhythm with all the others. If there is an ample supply of spares, any part of the machine is dispensable, even though some parts are more expensive to replace than others. The engineer must not only keep the machine running, but also insure an adequate supply of spare parts.

In the modern organization, the manager, analogous to the engineer, must keep the organization running as efficiently as possible. Like the engineers, managers must insure that an adequate supply of spare parts, including their own, is immediately available through the personnel department. The motto of the modern manager demonstrates the principle: "I've trained my own replacement." At all levels and in all capacities, personnel must be immediately replaceable by others of similar abilities with a minimal loss of efficiency during the transition. If there are enough human spares, there need never be any major upheavals because of turnover. The difficulty here is that while no machine part needs to be convinced of its dispensability, a human being does.

The organizational imperative demands that people accept the principle of dispensability, and one of the main tasks of the American educational system is to reinforce that idea. From the earliest grades on, books, articles, teachers, and professors hammer away at the theme that individuals have no right to expect that they might become necessary, nor should they attempt to do so. It is stressed, as a fact of life in the "real" world, that the dream of personal indispensability is selfish, and even worse, organizationally intolerable. A graduate student, asked to comment on what an MBA program should do for him, observed that he was like a sausage being prepared for consumption by a large organization. He argued that nothing should be stuffed into him that would give his employer indigestion. Some variant of this sentiment is drilled into students as an essential part of the mangerial attitude they should take with them to the job. Certainly it is quickly learned the moment students are employed.

But the process of organizational socialization does not stop at the boundaries of the employing organizations. As the organizational imperative has affected more and more social values, the attitude of dispensability has extended into all areas of our lives, and there is now a widespread belief that indispensability is an illusion, nowhere to be found.

If individuals do indeed have an innate need to be necessary in their world (and we believe they do), this particular value transition is quite destructive. A society of people convinced of their personal dispensability has many baleful characteristics, from alienation to nihilism. And the condition worsens with age, for the aging and the elderly are the most dispensable of all.[15] And so the terrible paradox: As people flee more deeply into the organization, searching for security, they find only that there they are the most dispensable commodity of all.

From Community to Specialization

Part of America's magnificent inconsistency has been a stubborn commitment to the seemingly contradictory values of individuality and conformity to community norms, be they of family, farm, small town, ethnic group, church, occupation, or whatever. But the values of community and indispensability went hand in hand, for individuals prized for their personal qualities contributed something unique to the continuity, warmth, and support found in community.[16] When they were gone, the quality of those multiple community virtues was lessened and the people left behind realized that the "bell tolled" not only for those gone but for themselves as well. The life of the community could never be experienced again in quite the same manner.

The organizational imperative has diminished and transformed the value of community, as it has the other values discussed here. In this instance, the organizational imperative requires that the individual's dedication be primarily to a specialty that is harmonious with and contributes to the total needs of an organization. Clearly, specialization does not exist for its own sake. For specialization to have any meaning, it must have utility for the organization. So, regardless of the functions managers perform, the stewardship of their responsibilities is measured by their utility to the organization. Loyalty must not, therefore, be given to the work group, to the place, or to some abstract ideal of honor, hospitality, or obligation; rather, loyalty must be to the specialized function, the successful performance of which adds to the whole organizational effort. The emphasis on transient, temporary systems and "ad hocracies"[17] simply increases the importance of specialization; while personnel, projects, departments, and jobs may come and go, specialization goes on forever.

The criteria by which an individual's worth is evaluated in a community are quite different from those by which an individual's utility is assessed in an organization. The organizational imperative requires a denial of community. An individual's worth, in organizational terms, is not measured by the quality of his relationship with others. When has friendship ever been considered a standard in wage and salary administration? Instead, worth is measured quantitatively, wherever possible, by the level of one's specialized performance relative to the achievement of organizational goals.

Finally, specialization and dispensability are comfortable, even necessary, partners. Specialization has always been considered impersonally in management. The efficient way to manage people in modern organizations is to objectify, as far as possible, their jobs and to assign quantitative standards in order to judge their performances. These standards allow little room for affective considerations other than those with organizational utility, such as interpersonal competence, which helps people work together temporarily in more effective teams.[18]

There is no room for community, in the traditional sense of the word, within modern organizations, since it requires individuals to become indispensable to one another. No modern organization could tolerate such *real* interpersonal relationships. The loss of meaning in one's life because of the absence of community cannot be replaced by the dispassionate rewards that come from specialization. Yet specialization predominates because it is required by the organizational imperative.

From Spontaneity to Planning

Another value central to the American tradition has been spontaneity. As usual, it has been interpreted in a number of ways. Its most dramatic example was the entrepreneur who was willing to stake everything on high-risk ventures for the sake of personal gain. There was a spontaneity, also, among the pioneers who opened the West. But the most significant form of spontaneity was found in problem-solving. Americans believed that the really serious problems would most often be solved by individuals through spontaneous, creative action. While such individual spontaneity, by definition, could not be anticipated in detail, it was assumed that it would somehow occur, in mysterious ways and at appropriate times, to the benefit of society in general or specific organizations in particular. The spontaneous, creative, enterprising individual would work wonders in all areas, from farming to industry — even in the political system — and the results would be better ways of doing things, creating on the way more jobs, goods, and services, and ending with improvement in the welfare of society.

Thus, spontaneity became an integral part of the American business character, popularized as ingenious "Yankee know-how." The moral lesson in the Horatio Alger and Frank Merriwell stories was simply that anyone with "pluck and luck" would succeed. Pluck meant the motivation to act creatively in unforeseen circumstances to solve problems. Luck referred to the risk that a plucky person had to assume if he was to make his way successfully. The interesting implication in these stories was that if individuals took action from an instinctual knowledge of what was right, Lady Luck would bend in their favor. Individual, spontaneous action was prized because it brought favorable outcomes for all concerned, especially when guided by a sense of moral rectitude. In this sense, the uncertainties of life were seen not as fearsome but as sources of opportunity.

Management needs in modern organizations have changed this. The world of management is composed of short-term, complex, immediate problems. But the future must also be taken into account in setting goals, mapping strategies, making budgets, establishing policies, allocating resources, and so on. In short, managers must plan. However, they cannot plan spontaneity. There is not only a low premium placed upon spontaneity in management theory and practice, it is also beginning to be seen as harmful. The future cannot be left either to chance or to spontaneous individual reactions. Organizations need systematic and informed projections about the future.

As more investment capital is committed to plant and

equipment, as the time span between the beginning and the end of tasks or projects lengthens, as more specialized personnel are hired, and as the flexibility of an organization diminishes in relation to its increased fixed resources, planning activities expand dramatically. First, managers must eliminate as much guesswork as possible. This requires the development and application of an advanced technology of forecasting. Second, managers must control as many external variables as possible, because they influence the direction of the organization in uncertain ways. By controlling these variables, today's forecasts become tomorrow's self-fulfilling prophecies. Third, managers must reduce the possibilities that aberrant, including *spontaneous,* individual behavior will unpredictably alter the course of planned future events. Finally, managers must control behavior in the planning process itself. This means that planning ideally should be a collective activity, because group performance is more measurable and predictable than individual performance.

That control and planning are conceptual counterparts is a frequently cited management adage. However, it is certain that as managerial planning grows, controlling also grows, if for no other reason than to prevent random or deviant occurrences from confounding plans. This explains why spontaneity is by now a doubtful and even dangerous behavioral commodity. It is unpredictable, hence, uncontrollable. And while the organization may lose some advantage from spontaneously creative acts, this loss is offset by the more easily controlled behavior that arises from collective planning activities.

From Voluntarism to Paternalism

In the past, when individuals required concerted action to achieve common aims, it was assumed that they would combine voluntarily into interest groups and that their communal efforts would be effective. Associations of freely participating individuals were so much a part of the American way of doing things that the traditional political theory of pluralism and the economic theory of countervailing power[19] rested to a substantial degree upon the principle of voluntarism. This principle underlay the familiar American ideals of industrial democracy, collective self-determination, federalism, decentralization, and government by consent.

The labor movement is an example of how voluntarism worked successfully and dramatically. Samuel Gompers was aware that American public opinion, around the turn of the century, was not receptive to radical, politically oriented labor movements, so he rooted the organizational philosophy of the American Federation of Labor in two tenets — voluntarism and economic unionism. In its early days, the success of the A.F. of L. vindicated his judgment. No small reason for its survival, when other attempts at labor federation were failing, was due to the fact that the ideas of free association and economic self-interest corresponded to widely held American values. So, while the unionization of workers was a bitter prospect for many in business and government, they began to realize after a long struggle that it was better to have a labor movement congruent with prevailing values than one that subscribed to alien, revolutionary philosophies.

Voluntarism, of course, had many adherents outside the labor movement. Farmers, accountants, consumers, doctors, professors, engineers, businessmen, lawyers, and many others have formed voluntary associations at different times, with varying degrees of success. Our point is that voluntarism reflected a compromise between individualism and collectivism, presenting us with an ingenious amalgamation of these extremes.

We have traditionally believed that social structures were the result of deliberate decisions traceable to individual acts. This belief implied autonomy, free will, individual responsibility and accountability, and generally accepted values that guided the conduct of individuals in making choices. It is also true that we believed in the usefulness of collective action, especially when additional leverage was required to advance one's own interests in the face of opposing collective interests. So voluntarism allowed the people to retain the rights and privileges of individualism, but also permitted them to take advantage of the power of concerted action within a self-governing organizational framework.

Voluntarism was an effective but fragile compromise. It was always under assault from both individualist and collectivist fronts. On the one hand, even the most conservative craft unions still are condemned in some quarters because they allegedly curtail individual autonomy. The argument used against the unionization of university professors is that individual freedom, for many the essence of scholarly excellence, will be destroyed. But, the most devastating attack upon voluntarism presently is not coming from those who advocate individualism but from those who advocate and practice organizational paternalism.

Paternalism is nothing new to organizations. The benevolent concern of management for the welfare of their employee "children" has been prevalent, especially in Great Britain and the United States, for a long time. Paternalistic feeling initially grew out of the social doctrines of Calvinism, which imposed upon the "elect" the responsibility for the collective spiritual welfare of their charges. Following the Industrial Revolution in England, such responsibilities were reflected in the rules of work and worship that were widely circulated and applied in factory towns. Regardless of how primitive, convoluted, and cynical this early paternalistic thinking may seem to us now, it was defended by its practitioners as a manifestation of religious responsibility.

Paternalism changed as social innovations swept through the industrial Western nations. The religious justification for paternalism correspondingly diminished with the secularization of America and Great Britain, and organizational and economic benefits became the dominant reason for management's interest in employee welfare. As Andrew Carnegie put it: "The employer who helps his workmen through education, recreation and social uplift, helps himself."[20] Responding to the challenge of unionism in the 1920s, management adopted the paternalistic "American plan" as a counterstrategy. In the "American plan" employees would be given benefits directly by the employer that they would otherwise have to bargain for indirectly through their union.

Thus, by the first part of this century, paternalism was used by management for practical purposes: fighting unions or raising worker productivity. But while the focus of paternalism shifted from the spiritual to the temporal, it remained basically a collective undertaking, ideologically justified as the means of promoting general employee welfare. Regardless, there was nothing in business paternalism that encouraged the voluntaristic principles of self-determination.

Another shift in the doctrine of paternalism occurred in the 1930s, against the backdrop, interestingly, of changes in criminal justice philosophy. These changes were partially attributable to the growing dominance of organizations in America and to the increasing influence of the behavioral sciences, particularly psychology, on social policy–making. Nicholas N. Kittrie, discussing the changes from a legal perspective, stressed that criminal justice systems progressively de-emphasized the punishment of deviant behavior and substituted psychiatric treatment for it. The impetus behind this change stemmed from a rising humanist sentiment, a broadened conception of the welfare function of the state, and the spreading importance of the behavioral sciences in the welfare sphere. The net effect was that the state applied therapeutic means even more in the treatment of antisocial behavior. Kittrie wrote:

Historically, the therapeutic ideal is traceable to the common law concept of the benevolent role of the sovereign as the guardian of

his people. "The king, as *parens patriae,* has the general superin-
tendence of all charities," said Blackstone . . . At the inception of
the therapeutic revolution, it was thought that the individual required no protection against the state acting in his behalf as *parens
patriae.* [21]

Concomitantly, a shift in the doctrine of paternalism occurred as the rise to power of professional management accelerated during the 1930s. This shift was directly traceable
to the rule of stewardship, because it did not take long for
the grasp of professional management to reach from the
material and financial resources of the organization to the
human resources. Although there was not a one-to-one relationship between Kittrie's model of the state as *parens patriae*
and the new doctrine of managerial paternalism, there were
some instructive similarities. For example, employees do not
need to be protected from the decent intentions of their
managers. But far more important is the notion that deviant
behavior in organizations is a sign of illness, which should
be treated medically (psychiatrically). It is not a very long
step from this point of view to the next: the prescription of
measures to prevent mental illness. As E. Fuller Torrey
wrote: "Prevention is powerful, efficient and American." [22]
To illustrate, an acquaintance interviewed for a job with
a large management consulting firm. The interviewer carefully described all the employee benefits, including the offer
to pay for his attendance at twice-yearly sensitivity-training
programs. Our friend replied that he really didn't want to
attend such programs, to which the interviewer replied: "But
don't you want to be happy?"
What does this anecdote reveal about therapeutic paternalism? At one level it says that management knows best
what contributes to good employee mental health. But at
another level it demonstrates the proposition that, given
appropriate standards of mental health, there should be no
incompatibility between the goals of organizational perform-

ance and individual satisfaction. In other words, there is an optimal cluster of behaviors and attitudes that contribute to both these goals. This cluster defines "normal" behavior. It does not take much to move from here to the next stage, wherein the norms for employee mental hygiene are specified. A deviation from these norms defines mental illness, organizationally speaking. Therefore management, following the model of therapeutic paternalism, ought to use all the means at its disposal to prevent employees from getting "sick."

The preventive methods of mental hygiene were quickly learned and put into practice with the assistance of psychologist-consultants. These methods are based on the following premises. First, people are organizationally maladjusted if they do not accept organizational rules because the rules define "normality." Second, management has sovereign power and responsibility to inculcate organizational rules for the employees' own attitudinal welfare. Third, organizationally "deviant" employees should be cured by using applied behavioral science techniques rather than punished by disciplinary action.

Organizational paternalism has come a long way, beginning with a concern for spiritual welfare, moving through the economic considerations, and ending with the mental welfare of employees. Of them all, the last is the most insidious, because in our age the best way to insure obedience is to create a state of psychological dependency. This is exactly what the new form of paternalism does. It defines anything but the most innocuous expressions of self-determination, autonomy, and other conditions of individualism as illness. Consequently, the authority of management is complete, for there is no more despotic authority than that of "father" — the manager who righteously legislates the terms of mental health for his "children," the employees.

New Values — New Puzzles

The organizational imperative that has displaced the values of individual America is now the central part of a new, well-entrenched system of American values. Obedience is essential to organizational discipline; dispensability is necessary for organizational adaptation to change; specialization is required for organizational efficiency; planning is needed to reduce organizational uncertainty; and paternalism is the psychological justification for management's dominion over the work force. But, most of all, the denial of an innate human nature has thrown open the door to the complete domination of most Americans by the organizational imperative.

Of course, not all Americans are committed to these values. There are still clusters of people who live in ignored corners of our society who have little to do with them, including large numbers of the poor and the elderly. We will have more to say about them in Chapter 4, but regardless, most of us in the production and consumption mainstream of American life are inextricably involved in and/or committed to these values. They are contemporary articles of faith that we must embrace if we expect to gain any rewards from the system we have made for ourselves. They are the definition of organizational America.

It is important to re-emphasize this point: The organizational imperative is dominant because we made it so. We did this because we believed that the modern organization would provide us with material affluence, physical safety, and peace of mind. We were not aware, in the beginning, that we would have to buy a whole sack full of new values in the process. But something does not come for nothing; once the organizational imperative was set in motion, it became so powerful that we lost our sense of how to control it, let alone how to turn it off.

Yet, in spite of negative feelings, we seemingly cannot escape organizational America. Its basic values are at the root of our national malaise. But there is no way we can ever return to a simpler life. Would we, or could we, voluntarily go the "small is beautiful" route if we had a choice? Probably not. We are too enchanted with material abundance to turn our backs on it. We have no Cato the Censor calling for a reassertion of the old values. Instead we have legions of politicians calling for an increased GNP, and we will probably continue to cling to the status quo until it is unhinged by some global disaster.

But if we are willing to adapt ourselves to the value system of organizational America, why should anyone fret? We see at least two reasons. The first is because ordinary people are trying to run a nation of almost hopeless complexity. In plain language, management cannot cope with this complexity by any technical or governmental means yet devised. But management is urgently seeking new technologies and forms of control in an almost desperate attempt to regain control of the system and the faith of the people. This desperation does not bode well for us, for if history teaches us anything, it is that control achieved in the face of panic is almost always authoritarian.

This leads us to the second reason. It may well be that this new set of organizationally fostered values offends our deepest sense of humanity, and we know that the combination of management and technology holds both promise and danger. In our view the danger of this combination is out of proportion to its promise because of the unwillingness of those who should know better (e.g., management scholars) to reflect upon the values that underlie modern organizations and their implications. The fact that the discussion of values in management has not developed along with the development of our core technology creates pressing human problems that cannot be ignored, unless one believes that our present condition is acceptable.

It may seem unfair to blame managers for not being concerned with value questions. After all, their responsibility is to the organizational imperative and to the people who depend on it. Why do we insist that managers be philosophers any more than are scientists, teachers, physicians, or engineers? The answer is simple: because managers have *power*. [23]

Those who manage, and those who theorize about management, are the human intermediaries of technologically based modern organizations. They provide a link between the abstract idea of the organizational imperative and the mass of Americans. They control the material resources and reservoirs of technical knowledge necessary for continued development. They occupy the central positions in the communications and decision networks in private industry and government. They have and use a unique set of managerial skills that are quite different from the conventional skills of science and engineering associated with technology. Without the managerial component, large-scale technological advances would be impossible. The managerial function is indispensable, and therefore those who manage have enormous influence over public attitudes — more than any other group in society.

Management, as we have described it, is a recent phenomenon, not more than seventy-five years old. But the presence of management in organizational America, although obvious, has not been given attention commensurate with its importance. Therefore, our contention that managers have the greatest privilege of power in American society is hardly unreasonable. They hold these privileges because they *alone* have the skills to keep modern organizations, as presently constituted, alive. With this awesome power, it is appropriate to expect managers to have greater sensitivity to the implications of their premises. Because all things are possible in a technical, and thus in a managerial, sense, managers should be concerned with and reflect upon values. The question is, why are they not so concerned? Why are they not so reflective?

Part II

The Roles in
Organizational America

Chapter 4

Organizational Roles

It should be stated, first of all, that the role concept
is not an invention of anthropologists or sociologists
but is employed by the very people they study. No
society exists which does not in this sense classify its
population — into fathers, priests, servants, doctors,
rich men, wise men, great men, and so forth, that is,
in accordance with the jobs, offices, or functions which
individuals assume and the entitlements or responsibilities which fall to them; in short, every society gives
such linguistic notice of the differential parts individuals
are expected (or "briefed") to play. What anthropologists and sociologists have done over and above recog-
nizing the existence of these categorizations has been to
turn it into a special analytical tool.

— S. F. Nadel, *The Theory of Social Structure*

Values, Roles, and Organizational America

Very few persons go searching for values in order to learn
how to act. Rather, the values of a society are embedded in
the tangible realities of daily roles, as Nadel observed above.
Individuals are socialized from birth to be alert to role behavior cues, and they have only to look around for them.
Social roles mediate between cultural values and individual
behavior. They convert the abstractions of values into con-

crete role expectations from which people learn what attitudes they should have and what actions they should take in everyday life. Therefore, following Neal Gross, and his colleagues, for our purposes, a *"role* is a set of expectations applied to an incumbent of a particular position." [1]

Beyond this, roles exist in a multitude of configurations, and as Georg Simmel noted, the nature of the configuration makes each individual, and thereby each society of individuals in the aggregate, different from each other.[2] However, these webs of human affiliations are very complex, and the roles within them are often conflicting. Take, for instance, the realities of American society that were beautifully depicted by Sinclair Lewis. In 1922, people were urged to "stand on their own two feet" and "to speak their own mind." Yet Babbitt was the personification of other roles, the malleable, consuming citizen that an emerging organizational America required:

Just as he was an Elk, a Booster, and a member of the Chamber of Commerce, just as the priests of the Presbyterian Church determined his every religious belief and the senators who controlled the Republican Party decided in little smoky rooms in Washington what he should think about disarmament, tariff, and Germany, so did the large national advertisers fix the surface of his life, fix what he believed to be his individuality. These standard advertised wares — toothpastes, socks, tires, cameras, instantaneous hot-water heaters — were his symbols and proofs of excellence; at first the signs, then the substitutes, for joy and passion and wisdom.[3]

Babbitt can be visualized as a composite of roles assigned to him as a consumer, a Republican, and a Presbyterian. Today, one may be a hyperconsumer, an est graduate, and a Democrat. It does not really matter. The multiple roles people must play in organizational America are defined for them externally by schools, television, corporations, government agencies, and many other socializing institutions. Whatever conflicts might occur in these roles can be resolved by reference to the overarching framework of values from which they are derived. For example, the role of corporation manager might conflict, in its demands on time, with the role of father. However, the conflict is settled by the father's belief that his organizational commitment will provide economic benefits for his family. This belief is reinforced by organizational rewards as long as he performs his corporate role satisfactorily.

Role is often described in contemporary terminology as wearing different hats. During the day people perform various roles symbolized by the hats they wear. An individual must constantly switch from a boss hat to a subordinate hat to a peer hat. In the evening, some men put on husband hats for their wives, who are in turn wearing wife hats for them. Later, some may don their parent hats to cavort with or discipline their children, while others put on their joggers' hats and get down to the real pleasures of the day. The list could be expanded, but the message is clear. The symbol of the different hats is a recognition that roles, while they differ, are always present, whether one is on or off the job.

In organizational America a new emphasis has been given to role, in which organizations have become more instrumental in making and imposing role definitions. Job and leisure roles are organizationally specified and conformity to them is required if an individual desires the rewards that come from participating in organizational America. Granted that some slack is allowed in the performance of these roles; nevertheless, it is obvious that our days are ordered in roles that are defined in organizationally useful ways.

The reason for this is clear. Organizations need people, but they need people who are reliable. This means that individuals must be schooled in behaviors appropriate to their organizational roles. For instance, we have seen that modern organizations cannot allow any individual to become indispensable. An indispensable individual is the axis around which the wheel of an organization must turn, and this is heresy. Consequently, all organizational roles must be carefully depersonalized so that no individual will become indispensable. But what is more, people must also interpret their roles in a way that the required dispensability seems positive. Such role specification provides for consistency and uniformity of personnel and also permits efficient job force planning.

It might be thought that while the above applies to people of lesser rank, it does not hold true for those higher up, but such is not the case. The higher one rises organizationally, the more one is dominated by the demands of managerial roles. Promotions seldom bring more freedom, even though they bring more money and perquisites. Instead, advancement entails greater personal commitment to the values of the organization. Most top managers have so internalized their organizational roles that they find it difficult to separate the values that are derived from them and the values they hold as individuals. As a practical matter, there is in fact no difference between personal and organizational values for top managers.

In some respects the clarification of roles is good, since people are able to talk objectively about what they must do in their jobs and who has authority over what in the organization. Such role specification reduces uncertainty. Nevertheless, these benefits often mask harmful consequences, of which three should be mentioned.

First, the various roles individuals must play cannot be compartmentalized, and the values and attitudes of dominant roles will spill over into the other areas of a person's life. Those who manage, especially at the higher levels, carry the values of the organizational imperative. These values are bound to influence their attitudes in other roles. Even those who do not manage must be managed by people who have committed themselves to the organizational imperative. These values, therefore, will have to influence how others perceive themselves and those things that are important to them.

Second, excessive commitment to organizationally authorized roles leads people to define themselves in terms of these roles. Note how often people respond with the titles of their jobs when they are asked who they are. This may be organizationally useful, but it dashes any hope for the realization of one's individuality.

Third, the excessive reliance upon organizationally defined roles creates greater potential for human control. Totalitarian regimes control their people through interlocking systems of roles. The control possibilities in these systems were pinpointed by the political philosophers Harold D. Lasswell and Abraham Kaplan: "A system of maximal regimentation is called totalitarian; the scope of the power is all inclusive . . . All practices are coercively controlled; in the familiar phrase, everything that isn't forbidden is obligatory."[4]

The key lies in that final sentence. Total control is obtained by placing rules upon everything, positive and negative, and enforcing obedience to those rules. All roles are defined and authorized, and behavior outside the official role structure is illegitimate. Thus, in Lewis H. Coser's terms, modern organizations are "greedy institutions," demanding total obedience at all times,[5] in roles off the job as well as on it.

On-the-Job Roles

Like Gaul, the organizational world is divided into three parts, as Figure 2 illustrates. The "significant people" are at the top of the hierarchy because they occupy the most important positions. The incumbents of those positions must make cardinal choices about strategies that ultimately affect the lives of everyone in organizational America. They will be discussed in Chapter 7. Below this set of roles is the technical core of the organization,[6] composed of scientists, engineers, and technicians, as well as a vast cadre of lesser managers ranked according to function and position. We

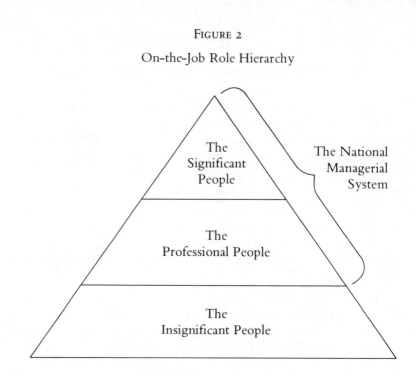

FIGURE 2

On-the-Job Role Hierarchy

have termed them the "professional people." They make the technologies run, make the policies work, do research, perform routine housekeeping tasks, and, in general, maintain the health of the organization by keeping its internal affairs tidy. In short, the professional people staff the bureaucratic apparatus of the modern organization and operate the technological system. However, if these technological specialists want to move up the ladder into leadership positions, they must abandon their specialized fields and pick up managerial skills and attitudes. The rule is unavoidable: Access to power in the modern organization comes almost exclusively through higher managerial positions. The professional people will be discussed in detail in Chapter 6.

Taken together, the significant people and the professional people make up the national managerial system. Status in this system is identified by one's role in the hierarchy. The leadership hierarchy in the national managerial system is based upon the strategic importance of the job to the modern organization. It is only secondarily based upon personal qualities, such as sensibility, compassion, or intellect. Finally, it must be noted that the national managerial system exists without a consciousness of solidarity among the incumbents of the organizational roles.

The lowest on-the-job roles are occupied by the majority of the people, those who perform the ordinary tasks of the organization, from assembling automobiles to frying hamburgers to sheet welding to typing. We have termed them the "insignificant people" and they will be discussed in Chapter 5. Suffice it to say here that the insignificant people are treated as units rather than as individuals. It is a vile term, but it fits reality. A unit is a functional, completely interchangeable, low-priority component of the organizational machine. This is the role the majority of people have been assigned in the modern organization. Units have no sense of "unitness," of their relationship to other units. Like the other members of the modern organization, they only take on meaning through the roles they perform. They may feel isolated or alienated, but such feelings only become important to modern organizations when they interfere with productivity. Thus, units must understand that their primary role is to serve as elements in the total organizational environment. They must understand that they are powerless to affect it, and that their best course is to adapt as often and as well as possible.

The on-the-job relationships of all individuals to the modern organization, which we have briefly summarized, are ordered hierarchically according to the utility of an individual's contribution to its production of goods or services. Our analysis of this role system differs from conventional analyses, especially in terms of the content of the roles performed. This aspect of our argument is so important that we devote a separate chapter to the interpretation of each group.

Off-the-Job Roles

One of the most pervasive myths in contemporary society is that, regardless of what people must do on the job, when they leave work, their time is their own. Further, it is assumed that in leisure time, satisfactions not found on the job can be fulfilled. The sacrifices and responsibilities that organizational obedience entails are amply rewarded by salaries that enable people to exploit their leisure time to the fullest. This is a cruel deception.

There is really no such thing as leisure time in organizational America, in the sense that people can be free of the binding rule of service to the organization. The reality is that what one does away from the job is also determined by the needs of the organization, even though the range of options is great. Because of vast possibilities for choice, the illusion exists of the free use of leisure time. This illusion masks the fact that most options, and therefore most choices, are organizationally predetermined.

The predetermination of leisure activities is a logical extension of the second proposition of the organizational imperative — that all behavior must enhance the health of modern organizations. Service to the organization must be constant, even off the job. Then the rule is: The primary obligation of the individual off the job is to consume. John Kenneth Galbraith emphasized this point in his discussion of the importance of the production-consumption cycle in a technological society:

The small volume of saving by the average man, and its absence among the lower-income masses, reflect faithfully the role of the individual in the industrial system, and the accepted view of his function. The individual serves the industrial system not by sup-plying it with savings and the resulting capital; he serves it by consuming its products. On no other matter, religious, political, or moral, is he so elaborately and skillfully and expensively in-structed.[7]

One of the most fascinating aspects of leisure time is that it is the time when people in organizational America are most equal. The "blithe and jocund peasantry mingle with their superiors"[8] with scarcely any recognition on either's part that there are any on-the-job role differences between them. When hunting, one is just as likely to encounter a production manager as a production worker, a corporation lawyer as a court clerk, an aerospace engineer as an aircraft mechanic, a hospital administrator as a janitor. It is virtually impossible to tell them apart since they have similar vehicles, similar clothes, and similar access to the hunting terrain, which is frequently federal land. The same can be said for other leisure pursuits, such as skiing, fishing, mountain climbing, and jogging. Those are all participant activities, of course, and most people prefer to attend spectator sports, concerts, mov-ies, and other entertainments where they can relax. But in those halls and arenas, too, almost all differences disappear.

Organizational America has democratized leisure time, but this has *not* relieved its citizens of the obligation to support modern organizations continuously through consumption. Some will argue that where consumption is concerned, peo-ple are very unequal because of the differences in their dis-posable incomes. But this misses the point: We are equal in our responsibility to consume up to the limits of our dis-posable incomes and, through credit, beyond that. Is this overstating the case? No. Actually, we are understating it. Since the early 1950s, personal debt has risen astronomically and is now at an all-time high. If all people do not consume as much as possible, then most modern organizations will fail, and that is an unthinkable proposition.

The personal pleasure derived from consumption in off-the-job pursuits takes a distant second place from the standpoint of the modern organization. The primary purpose of consumption is to enhance organizational stability. But personal pleasure does have a lesser use for the modern organization. For the vast majority of people, their off-the-job activities are organizationally so determined that they will create no debilitating incongruities with what they must do on the job. "R and R" (rest and recreation) are necessary for continuous organizational efficiency. Individuals should come back to their jobs refreshed and better able to perform their organizational roles.

Everyone needs a break with routine; but beyond that, there is a training purpose to leisure-time consumption. Our supposed recreation teaches us, subtly, to appreciate technology in countless ways. We cannot play tennis or golf, ski, jog, or climb mountains without using and appreciating the irresistible new technological products that abound. For instance, the jogging craze that swept through organizational America in the late 1970s produced an innovative explosion in the technology of running shoes, and the shoes purchased in May were obsolete in September. The same thing happened (and is happening) in nearly every participant sport. In the spectator sports, like football, basketball, and hockey, other lessons are taught that are useful to modern organizations. In fact, they are more important lessons because they demonstrate to all the futility of individual effort.[9] The on-the-job usefulness of teamwork and organizational dependence is constantly reinforced. Even television viewing is but an endless round of obedience-training in consumption, and there is growing evidence that television may be the most powerful training tool in the arsenal of modern organizations.[10]

However, there are some living in organizational America who cannot, and a few who will not, participate in authorized leisure activities. Such people are the casualties of contemporary society. They do not match the rest in their responsibility to consume because it is physically, financially, or philosophically impossible for them to do so. Whatever the reasons, these individuals compose a distinct subgroup of the insignificant people, defined by their relationship to consumption.

In identifying the casualties, one thinks immediately of those who are no longer necessary because they are neither organizationally useful nor able to consume much. The most obvious example is the elderly, the vast majority of whom live on inadequate, fixed incomes. Their consumption is extremely limited, and they are taking huge sums of money from the federal and state treasuries in Social Security and other promised benefits. This group is growing in number, and it will increasingly become more of a national problem, perhaps our most difficult internal problem.[11] The elderly are useless in organizational America.

Social "dropouts" are casualties. Some just disappear into transient rooms somewhere, but most eventually re-enter the job force. However, one batch of casualties is most intriguing: the artists, poets, and musicians who do nothing but add grace and beauty to our society. A few, of course, write enormously popular novels or turn into rock stars with vast followings. They are very useful to modern organizations — but they are also the minority. Most work away, impoverished and ignored. Who is more organizationally useless than a talented but impoverished poet whose books do not sell? There is just no place in the organizational society for those who do not contribute to the production-consumption cycle.

We must emphasize that organizational America is not intentionally unkind to its casualties. The wounded and the stragglers are picked up and cared for, after a fashion, out of productive surpluses. Nevertheless, just as the primary mission of an army is not the care of its wounded, so the primary mission of the organizational culture is not to look after its casualties. There is real tragedy in the blighted lives of our wounded, but the modern organization is not to be deterred from its main goals by sentimentality.

Chapter 5

The Insignificant People

Among the constant facts and tendencies that are to be found in all political organisms, one is so obvious that it is apparent from societies that are very meagerly developed and have barely attained the dawnings of civilization, down to the most advanced and powerful societies — two classes of people appear — a class that rules and a class that is ruled. The first class, always the less numerous, performs all political functions, monopolizes power and enjoys the advantages that power brings, whereas the second, the more numerous class, is directed and controlled by the first, in a manner that is now more or less legal, now more or less arbitrary and violent, and supplies the first, in appearance at least, with material means of subsistence and with the instrumentalities that are essential to the vitality of the political organism.

— Gaetano Mosca, *The Ruling Class*

The "Weenie" Syndrome

Management cannot be confident about mass support. It must actively solicit it. Managerial rule is becoming more evident, and the public is beginning to raise questions about its sagacity. Therefore managers increasingly are confronted with the age-old political problem of how to gain public approval. And they are solving the problem of public support using the assumptions and techniques that are most familiar to them and are derived from managing their subordinates.

Two dominant assumptions in management today are that the individual, relative to the organization, is insignificant, and that innate human nature is malleable. Little could be more comforting to managers than the belief that people are innately nothing and can therefore be molded into anything. When these assumptions gain acceptance and respectability among the elite, management can actively pursue policies where molding, shaping, changing, modifying, and controlling human behavior are legitimate parts of their responsibility. Convincing people of their insignificance and malleability is all that is left to do before the complete dominance of the organizational imperative is achieved.

If there is a managerial elite, as we have argued, then there must also be a nonelite, who are less significant to the total society than its leaders. Hence, where there is an accepted theory of elitism, there must necessarily be a corollary theory of nonelitism. Gaetano Mosca, who is quoted above, did not mince words. He understood clearly the need for a theory of the insignificance of the nonelite. In a supposedly democratic society, insignificance is the seamy side of elite theory. For this reason, while insignificance is a fact of contemporary management, it is seldom, if ever, considered in management ideology. However, this conspiracy of silence does not negate the fact that within organizational America, the great majority of people are insignificant.

This situation has existed for years without much notice. But now an uncomfortable paradox is forcing managers to face the realities of insignificance. As modern organizations have grown increasingly complex, it has become necessary to educate more employees to handle the increasingly technical demands of their jobs. There is peril for the modern organization in such training, for in spite of its routine nature, training nevertheless requires people to think, and thinking may lead people to contemplate the nature of their jobs, and they may not be altogether happy with what they find.

For example, a young person may enlist in the navy and be assigned to naval aviation because of scores on various selection tests. The enlistee is trained in the care and operation of advanced radar gunnery systems. The training will be intense and the person may find the work personally rewarding. Alternatively, another young person may be employed by a large supermarket chain and be assigned to work the cash register at the check-out counter. Most supermarket chains have changed over to computer-based cash registers, which also maintain an inventory control system, so the new employee will have to be trained in their operation. Yet it is safe to argue that within a week the cash register operator will find the job dull, routine, and personally unrewarding. In organizational America more people tend cash registers than sophisticated electronic gunnery systems, and they are the ones most apt to be perturbed if they even consider the nature of their jobs.

While he stated it a bit dramatically, E. F. Schumacher was correct in his description of the modern job:

That soul-destroying, meaningless, mechanical, monotonous, moronic work is an insult to human nature which must necessarily and inevitably produce either escapism or aggression, and that no amount of "bread and circuses" can compensate for the damage done — these are facts which are neither denied nor acknowledged but are met with an unbreakable conspiracy of silence — because to deny them would be too obviously absurd and to acknowledge them would condemn the central preoccupation of modern society as a crime against humanity.[1]

If most employees were ever to comprehend the life-consuming implications of their jobs, there would be a frightful turmoil. Obviously, escapism through leisure-time consumption is the prescribed method of offsetting the problem of doing dumb things eight hours a day. But as we have seen, continuously growing consumption patterns are less likely in the future. Therefore, more overt managerial attention must be given to controlling the attitudes of the mass of people. They must be trained, from their earliest days, to understand and accept the insignificance of their own lives in relation to the more exalted collective goals of the modern organization. Put differently, they must be scared enough at the start so that they will understand their extreme personal vulnerability and will gladly accept the security of managerial paternalism.

This is in fact what has happened, and we term this phenomenon of vulnerability and dependence the "weenie" syndrome. Earlier, we described a student who demanded that we treat him as a weenie, a sausage to be stuffed with appropriate attitudes to make him digestible to his employer. Suffice it to say that now managers generally believe they are the stuffers, and the insignificant people — the weenies — the stuffees. This is not, in fact, the case, since managers get stuffed themselves.

The weenie syndrome involves the assumption by the elite that the mass of people are empty of understanding and that they need to be stuffed with relevant instructions. The world of the modern organization is far too complicated for them, and they therefore must quietly await instructions from a paternalistic elite. A classic example of the weenie syndrome was President Nixon's casual dismissal of the furor over the early Watergate revelations in 1973. He contended that since the pro football season was then just getting under way, the public would forget Watergate in about three weeks. Give the weenies a six-pack of beer and plenty of television and they will be quiet. (This proved to be one of the larger miscalculations in American history.) The weenie syndrome implies that people do in fact want to be led and that the managerial elite performs an altruistic and selfless task when it takes upon itself the burden of leadership.

The elite divides the world into those who manage (the minority) and those who are managed (the majority). Most managers would publicly deny that they conceive of themselves as an elite, but their actions betray this. They firmly believe that only managers can integrate all of the diverse efforts within an organization into a harmonious whole; and they are correct. They know that only managers can guide people through the mazes of technology and intricate organizational interdependencies. The managerial claim to elitism has a definite messianic ring. Managers are the secular priesthood of modern society, their authority symbolized by neat pinstripe suits and appropriate graduate degrees. They alone are privy to secrets of technologically sophisticated organizations, and without them the mass of people would not have the comforts and securities that organizational America wants so much to provide.[2]

It is tempting to write exclusively about these interesting and powerful people.[3] But in fact, without the masses they are nothing; leaders require followers. Mass support is a necessity for a managerial elite. While this assertion has been muted in the past, it is getting louder and louder, and management is listening. Management must obtain popular support that justifies its positions and practices, or it will lose its claim to legitimacy.[4] The attempt of the managerial elite to establish its right to rule is based upon its assumptions about human malleability and insignificance.

Insignificance: Some Strategic Role Considerations

While many persons may easily accept the notion that human nature is malleable, it may be difficult to convince them that they are individually insignificant, for this is contrary to our deepest cultural heritage. Our heritage includes the ideas of John Locke that *almost* completely malleable persons must be shaped into worthwhile citizens in ways consistent with their potential. But great care had to be exercised to preserve the *inherent* characteristics of the individual. It was like delivering a raw diamond of rare size and quality to a stonecutter in Amsterdam. The stone, altered from its primitive state, must be shaped in a way that will enhance its beauty and value; a wrong blow will shatter the gem into worthless chips. But people are not diamonds. People are conscious of themselves, and this self-consciousness, especially in the American tradition, led to our belief that personal development gave unique meaning to the individual in terms of his or her singular importance to family, community, and society.

To demonstrate this point for your own satisfaction, go up to an acquaintance and say, "Clyde [or Zelda], you are insignificant." Most of the time a clouded look will cross your friend's eyes while he or she tries to decide if you deserve to be punched. This little experiment should show even the most skeptical that considerable effort is required to change the term "insignificant" from an insult to a compliment. Most people understand fully that they have little or no significance for their organizations, but they certainly do not want to be reminded of it. We all want to hold on to our traditional and treasured notion of our importance and uniqueness. These American attitudes are still deeply ingrained, and they will not go away easily. But go they must; the traditional American vision of the individual is not consistent with the needs of the modern organization.

As a result there is a tension in modern life between how we would prefer to conceive of ourselves and how we are forced to conceive of ourselves by organizational realities.[5] The tension comes from the incongruity between traditionally based personal preferences (freedom, fraternity, etc.) and the beliefs required by the modern organization (obedience, tractability, etc.). This tension is exacerbated for most Americans because they believe they have a choice: They can select from different organizational realities the one that best fits their concept of themselves. Illusion or not, the dream of choice went a long way to affirm Everyman's conviction that one's individual life had a truly special meaning.

But the issue of choice must largely be spoken of in the past tense. For most people there are no longer real choices, regardless of what they think, because one organizational reality is basically very much like another. Changing a job, for example, changes an individual's circumstances in only trivial ways, for the roles required by the organizational imperative uniformly pervade virtually every modern organization. Furthermore, the idea of choice and, particularly, the tension between self-conception and organizational reality are highly disruptive to the managerial equation.[6] Therefore, one of the most important missions for the managerial elite is to convince people that their feeling of tension is not real, that the real issue is the achievement of a general harmony between the individual and the organization through a mutually shared set of values. The essence of this harmony is simply that *individual happiness is insignificant when compared with the overwhelming potential for the collective well-being offered by the modern organization.* The strategy for the managerial elite is to gain mass acceptance of this organizational ideal by assaulting the foundations of our traditional faith in individual worth. These foundations are innate human nature, intellect, and work.

Innate Human Nature

As we have said, organizations are necessarily built upon assumptions about innate human nature. In the past, the innateness of human nature was considered unalterable and was therefore accepted as a constant. One of the most common assumptions made by Western philosophy was that individuals were born into the world with an innate nature that motivated their moral actions (e.g., individuals were inherently evil or good). If each individual has an innate nature, obviously human action arises from forces inside the individual; whatever these forces might be called — soul, mind, ego, self, personality — they were rooted within each person, and human destiny was ultimately the result of the interaction between an individual's internal qualities and the external forces of the world. Obviously, most human behavior could be planned for and controlled, and it became the subject of political and social debate. But essential human nature was assumed to be beyond the capacity of human understanding and control.

Many of the traditional and venerable interpretations of innate human nature attribute to the individual internal, unreachable, even mystical forces that elude human powers of explanation. Clearly such ideas of innateness are anathema to the modern organization, which must ascribe causality to all things in its domain. As science came to master more and more of the empirical world, some scientists became increasingly confident that individuals could be completely understood and that their behavior could be predicted and controlled. Then the inaccessible "ghoulies and ghosties" of innate human nature would be banished forever. This approach, which we call "externalism," has gained adherents and influence. The old notions of innate human nature have given way to new externalistic explanations in which individual behavior is seen as a reaction to the pushing and pulling of external forces.[7] For management, it means that all organizational roles can be imposed.

The rise of externalism is understandable even without evoking the critical need of management for behavioral control. The enormous complexity of the physical, biological, human, and organizational events surrounding us has made the search for innate explanations of anything seem quixotic. It is best, so the argument runs, to assign complex matters like the brain, or the organization, or the relationship between the individual and the organization to the status of a "black box." Since only the inputs and outputs of the black box are scientifically knowable and controllable, these are the interesting elements.

Many complex phenomena can be easily regulated by controlling their inputs. The only necessary assumption is that the black box have a structure that causes it to respond with predictable outputs to controlled inputs. Black box thinking, which is an intimate part of externalism, rejects any philosophy that inquires after the essence of things. Instead, it exalts technology that allows for the manipulation of things. Externalism requires an engineering perspective of human behavior: Outside causal forces determine behavior. Once these forces are identified and regulated, the individual will be as controllable as any other physical process, especially through the assignment of specific roles.

But in spite of the pre-eminence of science, technology, and modern organizations, the triumph of externalism is not complete. It demands that all believe the individual can be psychologically disassembled and then reassembled with the best behavioral technology to suit organizational needs. Un-. til the last soft-headed humanist holdouts get over the idea that these are unseemly goals, externalism cannot completely sweep the field.

Unfortunately, the sad truth is that these objections are being overriden. So many things point this way: the triumph of the organizational imperative; the compulsion of managers to reduce all problems to technical puzzles; the steady diminution of the status of the individual; the triumph of external explanations of human behavior; and the public unwillingness to counter the totalitarian potential in organizational America. All that remains is to convince the individual that the innate self is a chimera that must be replaced by a technical reality. This new reality, consistent with the requirements of externalism, defines the individual as innately nothing. Each person is but a series of chemical and electrical processes that have the capacity to be shaped into just about anything necessary to suit organizational needs. Since the Industrial Revolution, that a priori image of the individual was most useful in organizational design. But early managers still clung to the lingering notion that there was some small corner of innateness to remain in human nature, some space and time within which the fruits of the human spirit could flourish.

But even that minuscule amount of innateness was too restrictive to the modern organization, for it contained too much opportunity for variability in behavior. In order for behavioral science to make real progress in its service to organization, all innateness had to be expunged. Further, the process needed an ideology justifying the conceptions of the individual as totally malleable. The cause has found its most effective spokesman to date in B. F. Skinner. He attacks the most fundamental principle of innateness — the possibility of individual autonomy — by taking aim at the institutions in which it is embedded. In *Beyond Freedom and Dignity* he wrote:

We have moved forward by dispossessing autonomous man, but he has not departed gracefully. He is conducting a sort of rearguard action in which, unfortunately, he can marshal formidable support. He is still an important figure in political science, law, religion, economics, anthropology, sociology, psychotherapy, philosophy, ethics, history, education, child care, linguistics, architecture, city planning, and family life. These fields have their specialists, and every specialist has a theory, and in almost every theory the autonomy of the individual is unquestioned . . . *The result is a tremendous weight of traditional "knowledge," which must be corrected or displaced by a scientific analysis.*[8]

Skinner rejects any possibility of innate free will and questions the appropriateness of any institution based upon it. For him, real scientific progress can take place only when all people accept the fact that they have no autonomy and that all of their behavior is totally determined by external forces in the environment: Understand external forces and you understand individuals.

Skinner's most important contribution in this respect is not scientific or psychological; it is philosophical and political. As Skinner himself admits, there is no final empirical justification for a malleable, externalistic image of human nature. Acceptance of the premise of total malleability requires an act of faith, and while he marshals much scientific evidence to justify his theory of human malleability, what he is really after is the conversion of all people to his vision of the individual. In this quest, he powerfully reinforces the managerial elite, for his image of human nature is the optimal image for the organizational imperative.

Therefore, the first and indispensable step in the strategy of insignificance is to gain mass acceptance of the idea of individual malleability, since no other single idea is more important to the modern organization. Skinner is wide-ranging in his attack on free will, blasting some of the bastions of innate human nature, such as autonomy, choice, independence, uniqueness, personality, and soul. In our time the main source of strength for those conducting the "rearguard action" referred to by Skinner is a belief in intellect. In order to demolish the idea of innateness, this belief must also be altered, for in it is a major defense against individual insignificance.

Intellect

Intellect is the most imposing barrier to mass domination[9] because it is the basis of human difference. "But," a modern manager will say, "the very complexity of modern organizations requires that we employ greater numbers of intelligent people. How can modern organizations, therefore, be opposed to intellect?" The problem lies in differentiating "intellect" from "intelligence." They are two different things, and the difference is critical.

The distinction between intelligence and intellect is both fairly commonplace and quite controversial. We follow the distinction made by the eminent scholar Jacques Barzun in *The House of Intellect.* Early in the book, he set the lines of debate:

There is an important reason for not calling this domain more simply the House of Mind. Mind is properly equated with intelligence, and by Intellect I most emphatically do not mean intelligence. Intellect is at once more and less than Mind. The House of Mind may turn out to be as large as the universe; to treat it would require dealing with the mental prowess of apes and bees and, for all I know, of fishes and flowers. Mind or intelligence is widely distributed and serves an infinity of purposes.[10]

A little further on, he wrote: "Intelligence is the native ability of the creature to achieve its ends by varying the use of its powers — living, as we say, by its wits."[11] Thus it may be said that a person is very intelligent but is not intellectual. The obverse does not hold true — intellectuals are always intelligent. They may be frivolous or lack common sense or something else, but they *are* intelligent.

Thus intelligence, while it does not preclude intellect, can be applied to solving puzzles within the conventional framework of modern organizations. Indeed, an intelligent, literate mass is essential to the organizational imperative. The job force must be intelligent enough to contribute positively to modern organizations. As the complexities of production and consumption in technological societies increase, people must be prepared to cope with them in the course of their day-to-day lives. Mass education is the method for meeting this need. For instance, it requires educated people to appreciate, purchase, and use such gadgetry as miniature electronic calculators, microwave ovens, quadraphonic sound systems, the Pill, megavitamins, and running shoes. One must have intelligence to be a good consumer nowadays. And nowhere is intelligence more prized than in organizational America.

Therefore, we must amend our statement about malleability and insignificance: The cultivation of *intelligent,* malleable citizens is of critical importance to the modern organization. Organizational America must encourage advanced education as a matter of high priority in order to insure the widespread cultivation of persons who are able to produce and consume intelligently. At the same time, educational policy must be controlled to insure that the forms of intelligence that are fostered serve organizationally useful purposes. Therefore, intelligence alone is not a redoubt of individual autonomy, especially since the prized intelligence is that which advances the cause of modern science and modern organizations. One can be intelligent and still be convinced of one's insignificance and malleability.

Conversely, there is no easy way to grasp the meaning of intellect. Let us return to Barzun's definition:

Intellect is the capitalized and communal form of live intelligence; it is intelligence stored up and made into habits of discipline, signs and symbols of meaning, chains of reasoning and spurs to emotion — a shorthand and a wireless by which the mind can skip connectives, recognize ability, and communicate truth. Intellect is at once a body of common knowledge and the channels through which the right particle of it can be brought to bear quickly, without the effort of redemonstration, on the matter in hand.[12]

Upon a quick reading, Barzun's statement may seem to complicate matters. But from a careful rereading, the missing element emerges. *Intellect is quality.*

Intellect entails the ability of people to transcend the commonplace, to perceive quality, and to appreciate variety. Intellect does not necessarily work within conventional frameworks, for it has the capacity both to rise above them and to comprehend inconsistencies within them. It is intellect that is able to distinguish between philosophic, as opposed to legal, issues of right and wrong. Intellect has the capacity to determine excellence as opposed to trivia. In other words, intellect cuts through appearances and exposes essential differences. In fact, this ability to identify, judge, and appreciate the *quality* of differences is perhaps the main factor that sets intellect apart from intelligence.[13] Intellect applies to qualitative differences in people, in material goods, in entertainment, in art; indeed, it applies in every case where it is necessary to say that something is better or worse than something else. Intellect is not democratic, nor is it necessarily action-oriented. It despises uniformity, and it is utterly opposed to mediocrity. Reason, employed in the service of intellect, is the primary means of identifying the unique and inviolable "self."[14]

So intellect is more than making discerning judgments. As noted above, Barzun described intellect as a "capitalized and communal form of live intelligence." As such, intellect exists in its own right, larger than any single intelligence, in fact, greater than the combined intelligence of all living people. It is evident in language, law, architecture, science, and all other human endeavors that represent the accumulated experience, thought, and wisdom of centuries. It is very interesting to note how the sorties against intellect proceed. They are all based on a single premise, which is repeated over and over in the media and the schools. This premise is simply that those characteristics that humanity shares are more important than those that make people different.

Barzun uses the photographic art book *The Family of Man* to demonstrate the premise of commonality.[15] *The Family of Man* is a glorification of being common, and it presents photographic "evidence" to support the idea that commonness is better than difference. Even the word "family" in the title suggests the point of view. But what is it that people have in common, according to *The Family of Man*? Mainly, it is biology, expressed in human behaviors such as sexual love and the consequences thereof, infancy and childhood innocence; toil, or "earning bread by the sweat of the brow"; misery; and death.

While there is much that is grim and desperate in *The Family of Man,* its overall message is overwhelmingly optimistic. This optimism is summed up by the last picture, which shows two innocent children walking hand in hand down a dirt road lined with trees toward a glowing horizon. The message is: Be like children, believe in the essential goodness of people, understand that true wisdom is "earth wisdom," and above all put your trust in your animal functions. If all this is done, the human condition will improve.

Why is the glorification of commonness a critical strategy for the promulgation of insignificance? First, it reduces the number of variables that managers must manipulate in order to control mass behavior effectively. Second, behavioral technology requires it because in assuming away differences, the amount of variation in behavior to account for is diminished. Third, an essential criterion of the organizational imperative is served, since organizations must treat people uniformly as producers and consumers. Therefore, the emphasis on common elements of humanity is of the highest usefulness to the organizational imperative and the managers who serve it, whereas the needs of intellect are downright dangerous. Nevertheless, intellect will not be altogether abolished, if for no other reason than that it has some assets that are valuable to the organizational imperative. Just think of the mess if every new generation of managers had to rediscover everything known about organizations. The House of Intellect preserves such knowledge.

The connection between intellect and the organizational imperative is not obvious because they are very nearly polar forces. Intellect allows the individual to say: "I am different, and this difference is important." The private decision to participate in the life of intellect is an ultimate expression of autonomy. But the organizational imperative requires an entirely opposite commitment to homogeneity, or commonality. This conflict between intellect and the organizational imperative has led to the only possible practical form of resolution: the control of intellect by making it appear undesirable to the majority. In operational terms, the value of intellect must be demeaned so that the motivation of most individuals to participate in intellect is destroyed. One does not get ahead in a modern organization by being an intellectual. The few who are left clinging tenaciously to the option of exercising intellect can be easily identified and, if necessary, discredited. In totalitarian societies, they most often become serious threats to the ruling elite, and they are declared psychopaths and sent away to lunatic asylums to unlearn dangerously deviant values. This has been illustrated by the work and experiences of Russian dissidents like Alexander Solzhenitsyn.

In America, freedom of intellect has generally been respected. Granted, the way of intellect has not been easy. Our society has always had a dark undercurrent of anti-intellectualism running through it, surfacing occasionally with disgraceful results — from the Know-Nothing party and the fundamentalist wars against a mythic "Darwin" to the vicious purges run by Senator Joseph McCarthy and his followers and the never-ending attempt to censor schoolbooks.[16] Nevertheless, in the more open environment of the American past, the intellectual could usually find space to do his or her thing: Henry Thoreau could retreat; Walt Whitman and Samuel Clemens could wander; Charles Sanders Peirce, William James, and John Dewey could even stay within organizations and exercise intellect.

But in swarming, teeming organizational America, there is little room for intellect because it threatens the effective operation of modern organizations. Freedom of intellect is now under much more subtle, much more dangerous attack: in education, in television, and in psychotherapy.[17] The denigration of things intellectual by the organizational imperative has very personal consequences. As intellect is phased out in organizational America, as the chief means for persons to discover and to differentiate themselves, organizational values will be substituted. Since they include malleability, dispensability and paternalism, they reinforce the legitmacy of the managerial elite.

Work

The distinction between work and labor is as fundamental as that between intellect and intelligence. The problem, again, is how to make it clear. Work means an activity, both mental and physical, whereby individuals can impress their personal identity upon a tangible object: a painting, book, machine, accounting problem, or food preparation. Work, therefore, is an aspect of intellect closely allied to creativity. When persons create a work of art, the implication is that the artists have achieved something distinctive: an object that differentiates them from all other artists working in the same medium. The idea of work does not apply solely to art, but to just about any activity that permits the expression of individuality.

Labor implies toil, but much more as well. The activity of labor does not permit one person to be differentiated from another. It does not allow individuals to impress their distinctive character upon an object. What room is there for individuals laboring in a mass-production automobile factory to stamp their personality upon an engine piston? A cook in a fast-food franchise labors; a chef in a fine restaurant works.

Work does not preclude labor, and in fact requires it. Much labor goes into writing a book; for example, typing rough drafts of manuscripts. Nevertheless, work is present in the writing process in the form of making a distinct, personal, and unique creation. Through work, individuals try to express excellence in their lives. Hannah Arendt wrote: "The standard by which a thing's excellence is judged is never mere usefulness . . . but its adequacy or inadequacy to what it should look like." [18] Some individuals are better able than others to perceive "what things should look like" and then to translate these perceptions of form and style into tangible artifacts.

However, labor often conspires against work, and interestingly enough, this conspiracy exists in its most pernicious form at two extremes of a technological continuum. At one end is a sort of tribal toil for the necessities of life, where people are pitted against a hostile nature with primitive technologies, trying to extract a livelihood from the earth. *The Family of Man* depicts toil of this kind in the mistaken belief that there is something noble in the struggle of backward peoples to survive. While laboring people must *never* be scorned, labor is not ennobling; it is poignant perhaps, but certainly not noble. Nevertheless, the myth persists and the undifferentiated struggle of individuals against nature for the collective welfare of family or tribe is lofty and purifying. This myth persists in modern times partly because that kind of fidelity is expected of the employees of modern organizations.

At the opposite end of the technological continuum is labor of another sort, equally undifferentiated and depersonalized, but light-years more advanced in terms of tools and processes — toil in the modern office or factory, a form of labor noticeably de-emphasized in *The Family of Man* photographs. Nevertheless, it is obvious that the personality of an employee has no place in putting compressors in refrigerators or programming computers. One reason why the machine is interposed between the employee and the task is to protect the product against deviation from specifications. The logic of mass production requires the interchangeability of parts. The product made or the service rendered must not be contaminated by individual differences.

The analogue of the machine in the factory is the rule in the office. It evokes a standard and predictable performance so that no individual imprint will disrupt the smooth and uniform flow of paper through the organization. Further, in the modern organization the rules of bureaucracy have invaded the factory just as the office has become mechanized. Rules and machines in nearly every activity of large organizations have united to remove people from the opportunity to exercise discretion in performing their tasks. The logic of the organizational imperative requires that the personal stamp of individual work be eradicated from the job; otherwise it disrupts carefully calculated, interlocked functions, impeding the efficiency of the entire organization. While interposing rules and machines between people and work has alleviated some of this concern, it has created other problems.

That the lot of most people is to labor is an ancient and dreary fact of history. But what is fascinating in our society are the efforts made by apologists to elevate this situation. Without exception, the argument is that individual sacrifice for the good of the collectivity is ennobling. Collective welfare supersedes individual welfare, and this formula applies across the board to a tribe in New Guinea, to a large insurance company, and to an appliance assembly line.

The estrangement from the collective enterprise of people who only labor has been a long-standing issue for management. Too much depersonalization of jobs brings about alienation, a dysfunctional consequence that no one wants, least of all managers of modern organizations. Considerable effort and money, therefore, has gone into creating harmonious and satisfying organizational environments wherein people will find collective comfort for their sacrifice of individuality.

Few people who seriously follow trends in management practice have not heard of human relations, organizational development, or job enrichment programs. These programs emphasize individual involvement in a group engaged in collaborative decision-making. Rolf H. Wild refers to this process as "management by soviet," [19] but it is more fashionably known as participatory management. This phenomenon is widespread in Europe and America. Participation in job design and goal-setting is seen by many as the way present and future organizational societies will achieve maximum effectiveness, with minimum alienation of the masses of producing-consuming citizens. While these programs still have little room for intellect and work, it is assumed that the individual employee can be convinced that collective participation in job decision-making is an adequate, indeed a superior, substitute.

But the key question is, why should people participate? One answer given with increasing frequency is that it's good for them. Carole Pateman argues that some form of true industrial democracy at the grass-roots level of workers' councils is an essential preliminary to the re-inculcation of democratic values into society at large. [20] The participation movement in organizations is, according to Pateman, a modern version of the classical ideal of human ennoblement through political activity.

If organizations are, as some contend, a contemporary substitute for the *polis* in ancient Greece, it follows that some process that satisfies a basic human need for political activity must also be substituted if alienation is to be averted. This argument is persuasive and it has numerous adherents, particularly in the field of public administration. However, it fails in one critical respect: Modern organizations are not the analogue of the *polis* as described by Plato and Aristotle.

Another answer to the participation question is more realistic: People should participate because it is good for the organization. Management does not use participation for human ennoblement; it uses it for organizational efficiency. Participation in this respect is a rational management practice for making better use of human resources. There is much support for this contention in behavioral science research.

It would be easy, but wrong, to say that the sole aim of

participation is to make people happy and productive in their labors. The participatory process is far more significant than this. When people are convinced that they can achieve higher satisfaction from participation, they often will become more obedient, since they feel they are making a direct contribution to the decisions affecting them. This is correct psychological theory. However, A. S. Tannenbaum observes that participation actually increases the power of managers over employees.[21] Research in several industrial countries, including the United States, supports this contention.

One of the facts of modern organizational life is that labor has changed. It is no longer the grinding toil shown in *The Family of Man,* but a process in a collective enterprise, and a rather comfortable process at that.[22] At no other time have so many people with so many roles and skills been involved in so fundamental a social transformation. It is by the mutation of labor to a physically comfortable activity that justification is made for ignoring the absence of work in the daily lives of the insignificant people. This change requires that people become effective contributors to the organizational process so that what ensues is seen by them as neither work nor toil but as something else, *the modern job,* whose comforts they are conditioned to prize above work and intellect.

Of the three concepts we are discussing — work, labor, and the modern job — it is the modern job that concerns most Americans. They make a living from it; they get agitated over it; they derive multiple levels of satisfaction and dissatisfaction from it; and they are alternately depressed and gratified by it. The physical and mental activities people perform on the job are the focus of their attention and consume a great deal of their energies. The modern job embodies the tangible, concrete factors of human existence in organizational America. Therefore, to be able to manipulate how people regard their jobs is as essential to management as how people perform them.

Modern jobs are sensitive to the influence of the organizational imperative because most of them are performed within large organizations. For example, the total employment of the *Fortune* 500 corporations in 1977 was 15.3 million. This was 79 percent of the total manufacturing employment in the private sector and 22 percent of the total nonagricultural, nongovernmental employment nationally. The 1977 *Forbes* magazine survey of the 1000 largest employers in the private sector, which included both manufacturing and nonmanufacturing firms, showed a total of 20.7 million wage-and-salary employees — or 31 percent of the total employment in the private sector. Many of the gainfully employed are with the government, at all levels. In December 1977, the number of people employed by federal, state, and local governments was 15.5 million. Roughly, then, in 1977 about 43 percent of the total work force, or 36.2 million people, was employed in large organizations in either the public or private sector.[23]

These organizations are at the forefront in applying the principles of modern management, and they spend considerable effort and money to change attitudes toward jobs. But the importance of these large organizations does not end there, for they are the managerial exemplars for all the smaller organizations that follow their lead. This vast employment network includes nearly every working adult in the United States. In the end, the loss of the opportunity to work must be made as palatable to people as the loss of opportunity to use their intellect. Technology and the modern organization have not made work available to the masses, as promised. Rather, the insignificant people have been trapped by a mutated form of labor called the modern job.

But our argument is not complete, since we have not demonstrated how the strategy of insignificance, summarized in Table 1, will move people from obsolete beliefs about human nature, intellect, and work to the organiza-

TABLE I

Strategic Beliefs in the Role of Insignificance

Positive Beliefs	Negative Beliefs
1. The malleability of human nature allows it to be shaped to suit the needs of the organizational imperative.	1. There is no such thing as innate human nature, and therefore there is no such thing as innately necessary human needs.
2. Intelligence is necessary for rational production and consumption and therefore its cultivation is important to the modern organization.	2. Intellect is a dysfunctional form of personal fulfillment for most people, since it tends to separate people from the collective enterprise of the modern organization.
3. The modern job is the chief source of personal satisfaction for people committed to the collective enterprise of the modern organization.	3. Work is an undesirable means of individual expression in the modern organization because it results in variability rather than uniformity.

tionally necessary beliefs about malleability, intelligence, and the modern job.

Insignificance: Some Tactical Role Considerations

The tactics of role insignificance are the means for achieving the strategic goals of insignificance. They are well known in political science literature. Carl J. Friedrich and Zbigniew Brzezinski, over twenty years ago, discussed various coercive tactics, including propaganda and the monopoly of mass communication, education, terrorism, the secret police, purges, confessions, and concentration camps, in their work on totalitarian government.[24] Many of the tactics they described now seem rather dated, as they are methods applied by malevolent, insecure, and primitive totalitarian systems, and they are not suitable for the domination of the insignificant people by technically oriented, decent managers.

This is not to say that the traditional tactics of malevolent totalitarianism have been forgotten. These tactics wait, as it were, in the wings, to be applied if necessary. However, the modern tactics of crisis management, pre-emptive control, and integrative propaganda are more appropriate in a managerial society functioning under the organizational imperative.

The Tactic of Crisis Management

The word "crisis" evokes visions of institutions failing, governments in upheaval, and the economy on the point of collapse. There are crises in religion, psychiatry, education, and energy. You name it, and a related crisis would be easy to find. But despite overuse and misuse, the phenomenon of crisis has a function as a tactic of mass control.

Crisis, in its original sense, suggests a decisive turning point with an element of the unexpected. Contrary to popular usage, a crisis has a limited focus; the notion loses all meaning if it is applied to a prolonged confrontation or to a long-standing policy question. In this sense, we used the word too loosely in previous chapters and must try for greater precision. We define "crisis" here as a short-term episode of conflict or confrontation on definable issues that requires decisions and reactions by persons in managerial authority.[25]

The fuel shortage in the Northeast and Midwest during the winter of 1977 is a good example of a crisis. The long-term problem of diminishing organic fuel resources is not a crisis. It is worse. However, crises in a managerial framework are often related to long-term policy questions. This relationship was illustrated in President Carter's first "fireside chat," in February 1977. He noted the regional calamities caused by fuel shortages in severely affected areas and used this situation as one of the justifications for calling upon Congress to enact a national energy policy.

Two connected principles seem to be working in this situation. The first principle is that as a period of tension grows, often rapidly, to the point of crisis, decision-making becomes more centralized and organizationally elevated. Thus big crises go all the way to the top of an organization for official action; smaller ones are relegated to subordinate levels of managers. The second principle is that short-term crises and long-term policy issues tend to shade into one another. The management of a crisis cannot be thought of as occurring either in the crisis itself or in the long-term policy formulation exclusively. Rather its management incorporates both, such that managerial responses to a crisis further the organization's goals, policies, and strategies. Therefore, one of the major organizational benefits from a crisis is the management of it so that greater support is generated for the organization. It does not make much difference if such crises are real, imagined, or contrived, although from the standpoint of management "real" crises are preferred. The important thing is to manage crises in organizationally enhancing ways.

A maneuver by the Carter administration in the 1977 energy episode is an example of crisis management. At the same time that the President was requesting a comprehensive energy policy, he also convened a committee to investigate the reality of the energy shortage; that is, to find out if the shortage had been concocted by the oil companies to raise the price of fuel. Regardless of the committee's findings this was a no-lose situation for the government. The discovery of true shortages or cynical corporate manipulation, *or both,* would point directly to the need for greater federal control through a national energy policy. Thus a crisis properly managed turns a threatening situation into an opportunity for the organization.[26] We have now a consolidated Department of Energy with its own cabinet office in the executive branch of government.

Why is crisis the source of such enormous managerial leverage? The simple answer is fear. But a crisis is much more than a frightening time. It is an episode that appears to have a destabilizing effect on organizations and on the people who depend on them. People sense that such times may alter their lives greatly, so it is little wonder that crises can distract people from personal pursuits, mold their opinions, and gain from them commitments to struggle for the survival of organizational goals and managerial ideals.

But how is the course of this struggle managed? How will the insignificant people know what is expected of them? These are critical questions in understanding the tactics of insignificance, and their answers bring to the surface an important, but curiously discounted, fact of modern life. One of the most dramatic aspects of organizational America has been its increasing reliance upon formal regulations to guide public behavior rather than the informal norms characteristic of the simpler American past.

Ours has become a rule-dominated society, and examples of this are nearly endless. But to illustrate, let us refer to the rules of safety concerning both the workplace and consumer products. In the past, it was assumed that the workplace might be dangerous: Whaling vessels were not models of safety and logging camps were nearly terminal. But the worker was thought to be aware of such risks and willing to take them. Contrast this with the overprotective sign on the typewriter being used at this moment: "Warning! Keep fingers, hair, jewelry, etc., away from this area when the machine is in operation." The rule is, put signs on machines when the remotest danger of employee injury exists.

Furthermore, in our past it was assumed that manufacturers would not make products designed to kill consumers. Perhaps this assumption was unwarranted, but the plethora of formal rules governing the safety of consumer products in our time is positively staggering and cloyingly paternalistic. Recently, for example, the Bureau of Alcohol, Tobacco, and Firearms (BATF) has recommended putting a label on wine bottles to the effect that the product might be dangerous to pregnant women.

Rules upon rules governing work and play constrict the life of the insignificant people in organizational America to a drab and humorless chore. But rules are vitally important to organizations; in an age of crises the pervasive acceptance of the necessity for rules by the insignificant people makes them extremely susceptible to control. *What is demanded of the insignificant people during a crisis is unreflective reaction according to preordained rules that align a particular crisis with an organization's long-term goals.*

Since the nature of crisis is immediate, there is little time to reflect on causes and to consider alternatives. Executive action has to be taken "now," and the obvious course to follow is one along the lines of rules already laid out by crisis managers. If the crisis is favorably resolved, which it should be when managed properly, the insignificant people will be relieved and their faith strengthened in the power of the national managerial system to see them through an unraveling period.

The Tactic of Pre-emptive Control

For crisis management to be effective, as many factors of the crisis as possible must be controlled. Otherwise, events could get out of hand. But regardless of precautions, crises do involve a certain degree of managerial risk, because uncertainty is present in every organizational environment in the form of unplanned change. Pre-emptive control is a tactic for minimizing this risk.

All advanced systems of control are planning systems as well. Control, the logical counterpart of planning, prevents random or deviant events from confounding future expectations. Pre-emptive control, going one step farther, is the conscious managerial effort to anticipate and to control *in advance* all organizationally critical variables, both internal and external, in accordance with the managerial policies. Ideally, pre-emptive control makes managerial plans self-fulfilling prophecies.[27]

The impetus to move toward greater pre-emptive control capabilities is clearly present in management. Computer technology and management information systems have given this capability its biggest boost in the last twenty-five years. However, while technology is necessary for effective pre-emptive control, it is not sufficient. There is an ancient military adage that says, a commander should give battle only when the conditions are favorable to his victory. In managerial language this means that pre-emptive control is possible only when managers have the power to influence and to manipulate the strategic variables in an organization's environment. Thus power, apart from technology, is necessary, since managers will use pre-emptive control only when they master the main variables in their organization's environment.

In 1965, the decision-makers of a public utility projected that the company's size would double over a ten-year period. This doubling was the long-range plan. Further incremental, short-term increases on a year-by-year basis were also forecast. Reviewing the plan at the end of ten years, the decision-makers found that not only had the long-term objective been met, but each intermediate yearly goal had also been met according to plan. Everyone congratulated each other on what marvelous planners they were. Actually, the decision-makers had nearly complete control over many important variables — the market area, the financial resources for expanding plant and equipment, the supply of fuel necessary for generating energy — so that their "planning" was close to predictable from the beginning.

This is instructive of the kind of pre-emptive control that occurs in managerial situations where the top managers have the power to mold such variables to the shape of the plan. The problem is not planning for an uncertain future, but controlling the strategic variables in an organization's environment to insure that the desired future emerges as forecast. The extent to which pre-emptive control can be practiced depends, of course, on the type of market in which a business or government agency operates. Different market structures have different degrees of uncertainty with varying susceptibility to control. But as management reduces these uncertainties, they increase their chances to exercise pre-emptive control. Uncertainty reduction is, therefore, the name of one very important managerial game.

However, critical unplanned organizational changes often occur outside the framework of pre-emptive control. These changes frequently are organizationally destabilizing. But, paradoxically, unplanned change is a dynamic condition that Americans have traditionally welcomed as necessary for progress. Interestingly, the positive benefit of change is central also to all major management theories because of the opportunities it allows for organizational growth.*

We might be led to believe, then, that there is a managerial dilemma between the desirability of unplanned change versus pre-emptive control. However, no such dilemma exists because the organizational imperative has resolved it in favor of pre-emptive control, where planning is less a matter of crystal-ball gazing and more a matter of manipulating strategic factors in the environment. Hence the managerial response to crisis and change is not spontaneous, creative adaptation; rather, it is the construction of predictive models

---

* Pre-emptive control is just as important in situations of decline as of growth. We have argued elsewhere that decline, in fact, will probably accelerate managerial tendencies toward more centralization of planning and controlling activities.[28]

based on the assumption that managers, through modern organizations, can cause events to flow into a predetermined path.

This is a very large order, but it is not as great as it might first appear. Simulation models, with the help of science and technology, have gone far to account for many of the confounding variables in a modern organization's environment, so crises and unplanned changes can be offset by anticipatory managerial actions. These actions are based upon three tactical requirements: (1) most organizational variables must be made amenable to control; (2) those variables not immediately susceptible to control must be converted to become so; and (3) if a variable cannot be converted it must be eliminated.

These conditions have been met in modern organizations to a surprising degree. However, people are the one crucial variable in the organizational environment that have eluded complete pre-emptive control. If all their behavior can be made predictable in organizational life, nearly all conceivable crises and changes can be planned for within a framework that is healthy for the organizational imperative. Thus, the primary target for pre-emptive control has to be the individual.

Pre-emptive control requires the fusion of managerial and organizational technology into a tactical assault on the human variable. This assault has a single aim: *to impose uniformity on all people as a requisite condition of existence in an organizational culture.* Pre-emptive control operates on the lowest common denominators in human behavior, exalting them in the minds of the insignificant people, but managing them in ways that result in predictable organizational outcomes. Human behavior is reduced to a scientific problem, an engineering puzzle to solve. Ideas of innateness, consequently, give way to malleability. Conformity of thought has priority over intellect, and work is ignored as a means of self-expression.

But, to paraphrase George Orwell, "while all people are

common, some are more common than others." What makes this difference in status possible is the modern job. Differentiations that must exist among employees are authorized by organizational roles of hierarchy and specialization and in no other way. Hierarchy is determined and legitimized according to organizational necessity. The organizational imperative provides the necessary justification for the power positions of managers and their control of the insignificant people. It makes managerial efforts to impose pre-emptive control on mass behavior right and reasonable. However, right and reason are not in themselves enough to accomplish the tactical objectives of crisis management and pre-emptive control. These tactics must be reinforced by integrative propaganda.

The Tactic of Integrative Propaganda

Like crisis management and pre-emptive control, integrative propaganda is a modern phenomenon, made possible mainly by the mass audience for electronic communications that makes modern propaganda more powerful than any other means of mass domination yet devised. This statement may seem extreme, but it is not. The popular and old-fashioned view of propaganda is largely incorrect. This view held that propaganda consisted of the big lie. Conventional wisdom had it that propaganda based as it was upon falsehood and used to inflame emotions against an enemy, would be easy to identify and, therefore, easy to avoid. Certainly, rational people could never be fooled by propaganda. It is dangerous, however, for anyone living in organizational America to hold such a naive opinion. Propaganda is based upon selective facts; it is congruent with and supportive of dominant social values. But most important, modern propaganda is designed to integrate all people into a commonality. For this reason, modern propaganda is nearly invisible and therefore nearly irresistible.

Jacques Ellul observed this change in the nature of propaganda, and it led him to distinguish between agitational and integrative propaganda.[29] Agitational propaganda is used to incite people to a frenzy of loyalty or animosity. It is always aimed at outside enemies, be they Jews, blacks, or capitalists. The enemy is made responsible for all the problems that beset the society. However, agitational propaganda is inefficient as a tactic of insignificance. Integration is now the primary objective of our propaganda.

Integrative propaganda is directed within, toward the resolution of conflict and toward the promotion of consensus among the people who inhabit modern organizations. It has a single vision, that humanity is a harmonious whole in which people share essential similarities. The purpose of integrative propaganda is to stimulate and to reinforce this vision of harmony, either in one organization or in a whole society. Modern propagandists concentrate upon integrating attitudes; they teach us to love human similarities.

The ideal of harmony started after World War II. Why it became popular is more difficult to sort out. Initially, it was partly a revulsion from the horrors of the Nazi era and the war itself, reinforced by the humanistic and egalitarian sentiment that had swept over Europe and America during the previous twenty-five years. It was further strengthened, as John Keegan points out, by the change in public attitudes toward violence.[30] Integrative propaganda, based upon nonviolence, suits the needs of the national managerial system. Agitational propaganda, which encourages antagonists to hate each other, is not organizationally useful at this moment.

The fact that integrative propaganda arises from the needs of the modern organization gives an unprecedented twist to the function of propagandists. There are two sides to their role, relative to the organizational imperative. One side, already mentioned as the cultivation of consensus, is well understood in management thought.[31] The absolute need for organizational harmony, as opposed to conflict, is a widely documented managerial belief that has persisted as a central theme in management for years.[32] The other side of the propagandist's role is less well understood since it involves the amelioration of individual alienation. Clearly employees have to be at peace with themselves before they can reach harmonious accommodation with their organizations.[33]

The subject of organizational alienation has not gone unexamined.[34] The problem is that within management, alienation is perceived as an individual's illness. Moreover, it is seen as an illness that is not responsive to conventional means of treatment, because alienation probably transcends any single management group's capacity to cope with it directly. More pay or job enrichment or greater participation in decision-making is like putting a Band-Aid over a ten-inch laceration. They are palliatives, not cures. Through them and similar techniques, the individual does not necessarily rise to a self-accommodation with the imperatives of organizational living.

Can modern propaganda reduce alienation and promote consensus? There are reasons to believe that it can to a rather large extent and more now than ever before. The modern propagandist has available advanced information about the human brain from the findings of medical and behavioral sciences. More is known about processes that alter individual attitudes. Further, the technologies of persuasion available to the modern propagandist are considerably more formidable than earlier ones. If nothing else, television provides the most expeditious access to the masses in history. When its propaganda potential is coupled with applied behavioral science practices, television becomes an awesome control device.

Of great importance to the integrative propagandist is the fact that the people are already in their seats. In other words, they are inextricably involved with, and reliant upon, modern organizations. The modern propagandist will not have to chase around looking for an audience; it is already gathered into receptive and interdependent clusters. But the real power behind integrative propaganda rests upon the value foundation of individual malleability and the absence of free will. The modern propagandist can thus act as the master molder without any silly pangs of conscience. The way is cleared for a systematic attempt to mold and maintain insignificant people in a preselected, role-reinforcing, organizationally "healthy" model.

Ellul noted this trend among modern ideologies:

There is, on the one hand, a mold of the perfect Socialist man which appears as the absolute ideal. There is, on the other hand, a method to press people again and again into this mold, to give them this shape conforming to this idea . . . For Mao, the idea of the mold implies the idea of a recognizable ideal prototype to which every man must be tailored.[35]

There is great force in the creation of an ideal, prototypical man, socialist or otherwise, and full use of it will be made by propaganda in the service of the organizational imperative.

The role of the propagandist as master molder naturally involves tactical questions about method. One very important means is through the manipulation of language. Jacques Barzun concluded:

Intellect watches particularly over language because language is so far the only device for keeping ideas clear and emotions memorable. And language is liable to abuse and decay; it can be ruined as quickly by its guardians, the linguists, or its workmen, the critics and artists, as by the indifferent — the scientists and the democrats.[36]

Turned around, Barzun's statement becomes a tactical principle for integrative propaganda. It must operate through language to assault individuality. Without doubt, the propagandist, confronting alienation on the one hand and the need for consensus on the other, ultimately has to eliminate the words through which people can think alienated thoughts and to implant words through which they can think collective, integrated, and harmonious thoughts.

The tactical principle is straightforward: People can only act collectively upon what they can think about. Conversely, they cannot act wrongly if there are no words to identify the wrong collective behavior. This was the most important message in George Orwell's novel *1984.** It was stated explicitly in the little-heeded appendix, which explained the principles of "Newspeak."[37] While there is obviously no government propaganda program to create an American "newspeak" yet, the corruption of our language is well under way. Its purpose, usually implicit, is to strengthen support for the organizational imperative among the mass of people.

Language neutralization works on other planes. The jargon of academics, the buzz words of managers, and the acronyms of technologists remove from the realm of thought the possibility of passionate expressions, humane sentiments, and, indeed, even the necessity of thought itself. Suffice it to say, the importance of the place of language in integrative propaganda cannot be overemphasized. It is the key to controlling the attitudes of everyone.

---

* The symbolic power of the date 1984 is so great that one seldom finds it as a target date or planning reference in government press releases. We read about the intermediate-term future as 1983 or 1985, but never as 1984.

Chapter 6

The Professional People

The rule of the functionary is . . . identical with the
rule of the *professionals,* the so-called "specialists" —
even though it is only a subordinate kind of rule exercised by those who carry out orders. The specialist is
the prisoner of his department; he lives in the ghetto of
objectivity. He is "utilized" — the term itself is characteristic; he is assigned his role in the termite state. He
is the distinctively "disengaged" man and is therefore
liable to become the tool of a degenerate humanity.

— Helmut Thielicke, *Nihilism*

The Inhabitants of the Technical Core

We have frequently referred to the managerial elite who lead
modern organizations. The tendency is to identify them with
those who hold the most important offices in our largest
organizations, whether public or private, and this is correct.
Organizational America is ruled by individuals; their names
are on the annual list of the *Forbes* 1000 top corporations, on
a list of cabinet officers in the federal government, and on
the federal Civil Service roster of those with General Service
ratings of 16, 17, or 18. They are also the heads of the labor
unions and the large philanthropic foundations. One might
also include the general officers of the joint chiefs of staff as
part of the command structure of our nation. Here, however,

we turn our attention to their immediate subordinates, who are directly responsible for carrying out the policies of those at the top.

These subordinates of the managerial elite are identified by James Thompson as the "technical core" of an organization.[1] But that term suggests a narrower role for these second-tier people than they actually have; therefore, we call them the professional people, for they are the incumbents of the professional jobs in modern organizations. They are the middle managers and the technical specialists who abound in organizations: branch librarians, regional sales managers, supermarket managers, chemical engineers, factory superintendents, and public relations directors. Often professionals perform technical, engineering, or semi-scientific jobs like financial analysis, cost accounting, computer programming, and product research and development. Frequently professionals supervise the work of other professionals.

Legions of professionals fill our government agencies. Their jobs, in housing, welfare, tax collection, education, space exploration, agriculture, broadcasting regulation, or forest management, require specialized knowledge and often the supervision of other specialized tasks. Such people are sometimes condemned as bureaucrats who feed at the public trough without producing anything tangible in return. But, in fact, they do produce and are virtually indistinguishable from their counterparts in private industry.

Professionals have one primary responsibility in common, regardless of differences in their jobs or in the types of their organizations. That responsibility flows logically from the a priori values of the organizational imperative. Chester I. Barnard stated it clearly in *The Functions of the Executive*: "Executive work is not that *of* the organization, but the specialized work of *maintaining* the organization in operation."[2] The key word is "maintaining," since the critical task of professionals is to insure that all internal organizational processes run properly and in accordance with the policies formulated by top management. The performance of these jobs is absolutely essential to the modern organization; the managerial elite simply could not function without the support of the professionals. Using a military metaphor, Thorstein Veblen called "these expert men . . . the indispensible General Staff of the industrial system; and without their immediate and unremitting guidance and correction the industrial system will not work."[3]

Because the role played by professionals in organizational America extends beyond the modern organization, they are often the only contact between the insignificant people and the managerial elite that rules them. There can be no doubt about this for all who ever wanted to protest a traffic ticket, complain about a tax judgment, or get satisfaction for a piece of shabbily constructed merchandise. The petitioners' sole contact is usually with functionaries who may, or may not, take their concerns seriously. Professionals are the embodiment of the power and ubiquity of the modern organization for the insignificant people. However, dealing with them, and through them with the modern organization, is not without its tribulations. As Austin Warren wrote years ago:

Hierarchy provides, negatively, for deferment of responsibility of infinite regress. One's complaint always reaches the wrong office; one is passed from office to office, in general moving up the scale of delegated authority, only to find that the proper official to handle the complaint is out of town, or the necessary documents are lost, or by delay one's claim is outlawed. Wonderful is the efficiency of an order so complexly graduated that every expert is inexpert at satisfying the simple need for justice.[4]

But the public's problems with the professionals do not end with impersonality and even injustice. As Warren indicated, these functionaries have the uncanny ability to turn means into ends: "Readers exist in order that librarians may make card catalogues, pupils in order than educationalists may publish books on Methods of Teaching, worshipers in order that janitors may sweep and lock churches."[5] The substance and quality of all aspects of a person's life are profoundly affected by the proliferation of professional people who find purpose in their lives by an exaltation of means.

As this immense cadre of professionals becomes more powerful, perceptions of appropriate behavior are imposed upon all the clientele of their organizations. As civilians, our common frustrations with professionals are very important. These dealings are aggravating at times because professionals expect everyone to be as committed to maintaining the health of their organization as they are. They expect our beliefs to be congruent with theirs. And this expectation is not inexplicable, for their jobs are essential to the life of modern organizations.

We are, for the most part, more dependent upon the professional managers than upon the technicians who work for them. The organizational need for individual craftsmen has all but been eliminated, as has the need for the multi-faceted handyman and the subsistence farmer. In organizational America, tasks are accomplished by teams of specialists, and the complex of jobs is organized into rational and interlocking patterns of endeavor by managers. An obvious example is that of home building. Home builders are now home-building managers. For the most part, they no longer "build" homes, but instead are responsible for getting the framing crews, the dry-wallers, the flooring specialists, etc., to perform their jobs at the proper times. None of the subcontractors needs any vision of the home to be built, all each needs to know is what his specific tasks are. In turn, the supervisors do not particularly need building skills, but they do need managerial skills. The same is true for all of the other major endeavors in organizational America, from universities to cities to corporations to hospitals. The leadership positions are managerial, and managerial effectiveness is reduced when leaders get involved in the specific technical activities of their organizations. This can be seen even more clearly by looking at the managerial function from the point of view of the technical specialists: They cannot do their respective "things" unless managers manage. With the odd exception of the occasional writer or artist, traditional professional expertise is meaningless unless it is provided for by, and performed within, a modern organization.

It could be held that certain professionals such as physicians are exempt from management, for they can practice medicine without managerial assistance. But such is not the case; if anything, physicians are the most dependent of all. Their work would not be accomplished if managers did not put all of the necessary support activities together. The classic example is the modern hospital. Our physicians would be reduced to a band of feckless shamans wandering empty corridors unless administrators assembled the necessary medical teams and equipment. In fact, the modern medical function is almost totally dependent upon the managerial function.

The indispensibility of management is most obvious in the most powerful organization in our society, the federal government. Given the massive interdependencies of our government, it is clear that the nation could survive the collapse of Congress without much disruption of essential services, but it could never survive the collapse of the federal managerial system. After World War II, France went through a seemingly endless succession of governments in a relatively short time. Yet essential services continued: Mail was delivered; the subways and railroads ran; the police maintained order; and the people lived their lives in some security. Why? Because the professional bureaucracy managed these services while the politicians were falling like autumn leaves. Our national survival, like France's, is in the hands of a managerial elite, buttressed by subordinates. Given, then, the overwhelming importance of management, both public and private, it is reasonable to claim that people who perform these professional jobs should have codes, albeit unwritten, that guide their behavior.

Our main interest in this chapter is with the special place of professionals in organizational America. Since they are in the middle, organizationally, above the insignificant people and below the significant people, their role has its ambiguities. These arise, often, from two necessary but conflicting commitments required of the professionals. The conflict within these professional roles has been a knotty problem in management theory and practice.

Solving the Paradox in Professional Roles

The paradox of the professional role is that the people who perform it in a modern organization must be committed to two professional codes, both requiring advanced education and varying amounts of practical experience. The first code pertains to the practice of a specialty, which is often highly technical. The second code is far less specific and bears upon the management function that professionals must perform if they have authority over others.

The first code is easy to explain since it refers to the specialized component of the professional job, such as engineering, computer programming, accounting, selling, or manufacturing. To greater or lesser degrees, these job components have standards of professional performance. Sometimes these standards are written and monitored by independent professional associations, as with corporation lawyers or certified public accountants. At other times, the standards of practice are unwritten, unmonitored, and contain norms that are more or less "generally understood" by the people practicing them, such as personnel managers or advertising executives.

The second code is far more difficult to explain since it involves the responsibility of managing. This responsibility is very general; it does not have a written code and is not monitored by a professional association. Nevertheless, the management responsibility is understood, in theory and practice, to have priority over the specialized functions for all of the reasons just discussed, which we will note again at the end of this chapter.

From this brief description of the components of the professional job, two conclusions can be drawn. Some professional jobs have only one of the components, specialization: An electrical engineer may do his job without any managerial responsibility. However, the reverse is not true. A professional who manages others must also have a specialty, such as quality control management, manufacturing management, or the management of legal services. These professionals are said to have *line* management authority. The word "line" refers to a position of authority in a chain of command.

The amount of line, or command, authority relative to the amount of specialization in a professional job varies directly with the level of that job in the organizational hierarchy. Thus, the higher the job in the chain of command, the more important the management function related to the specialized function, as Figure 3 illustrates.

Note that the insignificant jobs are entirely specialized and that the significant jobs are entirely managerial. It is only in the middle ranges of the organization that a combination of these two components exists, with the exception of the technical specialist who has no managerial responsibility. These organizational realities are reflected in job titles. The titles of middle managers always indicate rank and function, such as those in the Internal Revenue Service: branch chief — audit, assistant regional commissioner — audit; or in a business organization: regional sales manager, vice president of marketing. For insignificant jobs, the title of the specialization alone is sufficient: machinist, typist, cook. For the significant job the title of the rank is enough: president, chairman of the board.

The relative emphasis given to job components has been

FIGURE 3

Relative Job Components in a Chain of Command

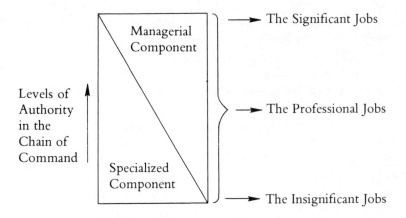

a source of serious conflict in middle management. These problems have been observed for years and thoroughly discussed. Veblen thought, incorrectly, that technical specialization was a foundation for class consciousness among professionals. But as John Kenneth Galbraith wrote: "I do not believe the conflict cited by Veblen exists, at least in the form he described . . . Engineers need managers and organization if they are to be useful."[6]

Early organization theorists believed that the separation of organizations into operating line-management functions and supporting specialized staff functions created a conflict of authority between staff specialist and line executive. They believed that while both activities were essential to complex organizations, the conflict potential inherent in them had to be eliminated.[7] Social psychologists twenty-five years ago found distinct personality and attitude differences between people whose jobs were heavily weighted toward specialization and those whose jobs were largely managerial.[8] They also saw these differences as harboring potential conflict.

Peter Drucker recognized the disparity between specialization and managerial responsibility and devoted an entire chapter of his influential book, *The Practice of Management,* to it. He made several recommendations for resolving these differences. One suggestion was to establish a separate promotion ladder for specialists,[9] such as apprentice chemist, junior chemist, senior chemist, and finally, manager of the chemical engineering function.

Drucker was wrong about this. If anything, separate promotional ladders would exaggerate the differences between specialists and managers rather than reconcile them. Structural, psychological, and financial palliatives are not able, in themselves, to resolve the conflicts inherent in job content. True solutions are based upon two conditions. The first is that modern organizations have sufficient influence, or power, to change professional standards to suit their requirements, which they do. The second condition is that professional people be converted to the management credo, which they also have. Thus, the credo is central to resolving conflict in job responsibilities. Through it, professional standards, diverse specialization, and management are homogenized into a whole where disagreement over essential values is impossible.

All professionals regardless of how their jobs are weighted, must be committed to the codes of both specialization and management. But it is obvious that these codes cannot be equal and that the dominant one is managerial. Thus, while managers must acknowledge and support specialization, they can never allow it to interfere with the smooth operation of the organization within which it takes place.

While professionals must be faithful to the canons of their specialization, they must always recognize the secondary status of that specialization in relation to the needs of the organization. This is nowhere more evident than in the fact that if any of them hope to get away from their "ghettos of objectivity" and move up the organizational hierarchy, they must be converted to the managerial credo more than to the codes of accounting, chemistry, or law.

The traditional explanations and solutions to the paradox of the professional job are no longer interesting. They are fantasies. *Credo in unam ordinationem* is a statement of belief in one orderly system of government. In the light of this credo, personal and selfish interests in specialization disappear. They are replaced by the recognition of the overarching necessity that the professionals have mutual interests in serving the organizational imperative through maintaining the organization. The experiences of the professionals, in their roles in the modern organization, teach them to believe the managerial credo.

Credo in Unam Ordinationem

Thorstein Veblen focused his incisive critical eye on a problem similar to the one under discussion here: How does a ruling elite insure the loyalty and commitment of its professional functionaries to its causes and interests? Veblen was more specific, since he was concerned with how capitalists guaranteed the loyalty of the engineers they hired. This problem interested Veblen in 1921, because he was writing *The Engineers and the Price System,* and he was mulling over the possibility that the engineers might overthrow the capitalist ruling class and replace it with a technocracy. Veblen thought that the engineers — roughly his equivalent of our professional people — had distinct class interests. In the end, however, Veblen concluded that a revolution from this quarter of society was unlikely, since the engineers had been wholly bought off by the capitalists. The engineers would remain loyal to the system so long as they heard the rattle of a full lunch bucket.

However correct Veblen might have been in 1921 about

the distinct class awareness of engineers (and there is reason to doubt its validity even then),[10] his argument is inaccurate with respect to organizational America. While Veblen believed in a disparity of class interest between engineers and capitalists, such a disparity does not exist between the managerial elite and the professionals.

From an individual point of view, career progress and, hence, increased income and authority are continuous and uninterrupted within this system, provided one accepts the requirements of the role. Oswald Knauth wrote:

Management looks upon salaries as a means of building up a corps of elite personnel that will carry on its essential policies. Each member acquires specializations that might be sacrificed were he to leave the organization. His value to it is disproportionately large in comparison with his market value. Specialized knowledge may be crucial as in the case of key officials, or it may be merely convenient as in the case of lesser officials, foremen, and other strategic personnel. The object of management is to assure continuous functioning and the amount paid in salaries is a small part of total expense.[11]

If professionals want to move upward through the hierarchy of management positions, they must show their unalloyed dedication to the values of the organizational imperative, and such faith must be demonstrated beyond question. However, people are not born with innate tendencies in this direction. Correct attitudes and behaviors are learned in the educational process, which begins in youth. They are codified in BA, MBA, and MPA programs, culminating when the professional internalizes the manager's credo, which we summarize as a sequence of six beliefs. The most critical period for learning the credo is during an individual's service as a professional, for the individual learns the meaning of the six articles of faith as they are revealed by the concrete experience of managing and being managed.

Credo 1: We Believe in the Decency of Managerial Intention

Contrary to the fashionable complaints of the critics of all things American, most of those who occupy positions of power in organizational America have decent intentions. Where the honorable intentions of managers break down is in their failure to examine the ends of their actions (in an appropriate manner) through examining their underlying values. This difficulty was well summarized by Robert Merton in his introduction to Ellul's *The Technological Society*:

Ours is a progressively technical civilization: by this Ellul means that the ever-expanding and irreversible rule of technique is extended to all domains of life. It is civilization committed to the quest for continually improved means to carelessly examined ends. Indeed, technique transforms ends into means. What was once prized in its own right now becomes worthwhile only if it helps achieve something else. And, conversely, techniques turn means into ends.[12]

Managers are largely honorable people, neither barbarians nor robots, and they need to believe that their manipulative endeavors are decent. Contemporary management has solved this problem in a fascinating manner through the universal behavioral techniques, the fusion of behavioral science techniques with humanistic psychology.[13]

The idea guiding early human developmentalists in the late 1940s, such as Kurt Lewin, Gordon Allport, and Carl Rogers, was that individuals have considerable latent potential that is not released as effectively as it might be because of the inhibitions imposed by their environment. Consequently, the humanists wanted to alter this environment so that it would be more conducive to individual psychological growth. It did not take long for this appealing doctrine to be applied to management by such psychologists as Abraham

Maslow, Chris Argyris, Douglas McGregor, Warren Bennis, and Rensis Likert. Their leading theme was expressed by Maslow:

We can learn from self-actualizing people what the ideal attitude toward work might be under the most favorable circumstances. These highly evolved individuals assimilate their work into the identity, into the self, i.e., work actually becomes part of the self, part of the individual's definition of himself. Work can be psychotherapeutic, psychogogic (making well people grow toward self-actualization).[14]

Maslow's argument is convincing, up to a point, if people in organizations actually *did* work instead of perform jobs. As it is, specific behavioral science techniques, like sensitivity training or the more recent outgrowth of the human relations movement, Organizational Development, are used to get people to identify with that mutant form of labor we call the modern job. The message and behavioral techniques of this applied version of human development were packaged and marketed by such organizations as the National Training Laboratories in Bethel, Maine. Many companies, such as TRW Systems, became converts to these new management technologies: first, because they seemed to produce more effective employees; second, because they were seemingly more humane; and third, because they were morally good techniques — they promised to help people realize their potential and to cope with the pressures of organizational life.

Thus, the universal behavioral techniques, which we defined in the Introduction, appear to have provided management with what it needed: a built-in automatic conscience. The significance of these techniques must not be minimized. They assure managers that they need not engage in the fuzzy, unscientific, unquantifiable stuff of values. They need only become more proficient at their jobs, because the principles of management guarantee the decency of their intentions.

They can be confident that they will hurt no one in the normal course of things. On the contrary, the more pervasive and intensive the application of their managerial skills, the more humane our society becomes.

This confidence is the essential feature of the first credo: namely, the need for managers to believe that the application of good means will automatically produce good results and good people. If this is believed, the consideration of values becomes unnecessary, even wasteful. Managers need look no further than to the humaneness of their techniques. This credo is nowhere more obvious than in the literature of participatory management.[15] The general reasoning flows from the assumption that since participation is democratic, it is therefore good, producing both harmony and good people. Nothing more need be said since the proposition is self-evident: Good procedures produce good people. But it is erroneous to believe that substituting discussions about an organizationally good decision adequately replaces serious thought and discussion about individual rights and the embodiment of those rights in both structure and action. They are two different endeavors and must not be confused.

Nevertheless, there is a consensus among those in the national managerial system that their intentions are decent and that the honor of their intentions is plainly demonstrated by their professional eagerness to find more humane means to organizational ends. That consensus is reinforced in nearly every book they read, nearly every class they take, and nearly every management training session they attend.

Credo 2: We Believe in the Necessity for Managerial Escalation

The principle of management escalation has several facets. First, it refers to a desire on the part of managers to escalate the scope of their control. If one accepts Credo 1, it follows that managerial practices in modern organizations represent the most humane way to govern large numbers of people. Implicit is the premise that the farther the influence of the national managerial system is extended, the more all-encompassing it is, the better off people will be. A cynic might argue that managers want to broaden the scope of their control in order to gain power. Certainly this is true of some, but we believe most are looking for more than power.

A great many managers try to extend their control because they believe firmly in Credo 1, that the extension of their control will benefit people through more effecent and humane organizations. Few people have single driving motives, but we believe most managers do want to improve conditions in organizational America.

Further, managers believe in progress, and managerial theory cannot abide static situations. Managerial escalation provides both theorists and practitioners with a guarantee of progress. They firmly believe in the same evolutionary promise that science holds: that continuous research will automatically bring new procedures that will advance the "state of the art." In this way, managerial control holds out great promise to people that their lives within organizations will get better and better. It is a compelling idea, one in which those with decent intentions can believe.

There is another consideration. In a brilliant essay, the political philosopher Sheldon Wolin has written about the intentions of those who would totally encompass the world within the modern organization:

Our political and social landscape is dominated by large structures whose premeditated design embodies many of the presuppositions and principles of methodism. They are deliberately fabricated, their processes are composed of defined "steps," and their work is accomplished by a division of specialized labor whose aggregate effect seems marvelously disproportionate to the modest talents which are combined. Not only do these organizations impart regularity and predictability to the major realms of our existence, thereby furnishing the conditions whereby methodical inquiry can pursue its goal of scientifically verifiable knowledge with reasonable hopes of success — for what would be more hopeful than to know that the political and social world is deliberately fashioned to produce regular and predictable behavior? — but also, since these organizations are uniquely the product of mind, rather than of mysterious historical forces, we are able to say with far greater confidence than Hobbes and Vico, who first announced the principle, "We can know it, because we made it." [16]

Professionals are encouraged to encompass as much of their world as possible within the bounds of the modern organization. By doing so, they will bring more and more *variables* under managerial control. As they extend the boundaries of the organization into all areas, a by-product is that the control of the national managerial system over organizational America is increased. This increases the possibility for planning. The farther the control extends, the more efficiently the entire society can be planned for.

But what does this mean in more specific terms for managers at the middle levels in the organization? One example should suffice. A large chain of retail stores has a policy of not specifying the content of its middle management jobs, contrary to typical practice, which spells out the scope and the authority of these positions. The idea is that effective middle managers will define their own jurisdictional boundaries by seizing responsibility from less aggressive managers who are unable or unwilling to defend and expand their territory. Presumably through this competitive struggle a natural selection takes place in which those managers who are fit to survive will rise to the surface. These winners are viewed as most effective at controlling their environment, and they will be among the future candidates for promotion into top management. There, it is assumed, they will apply their competitive skills to increasing the influence of the organization. In other words, they will be the managers of growth.

This is a rare case, since most management is not quite so forthright in encouraging competition among professionals, but some version of it is played out in many modern organizations. A winnowing process is essential in selecting those who will move up in the managerial hierarchy. Successful competition in the lower-level jobs leads, in general, to organizational growth overall, because the winners will not only be effective managers, they will also be growth-oriented. And growth is necessary for the health of the modern organization (or at least it has been so considered in the past).

There is a final facet to management escalation beyond providing a stage for acting out a Social Darwinist drama. Growth creates organizational interdependencies; and until growth ceases to be central to management thinking, the number of professionals must expand to manage these interdependencies.[17] And so, like a breeder reactor, the cycle of managerial escalation is self-feeding. Growth requires more professionals who, in turn, must be committed to the belief that the extension of management is a moral necessity. When this credo is coupled with the first, the foundation is laid for making professionals a powerful proselytizing force. Their faith in the credo of management escalation is the basis for the conversion of professional colleagues new to the ranks of the modern organization to its values.

Credo 3: We Believe in the Job über Alles

The burden for successfully attaining organizational goals lies more and more with the professionals who do middle management and specialized jobs. Therefore, it is important that they have their priorities straight and that they understand the seriousness of their jobs in relation to the other influences in their civilian lives. The job comes first.

A venerable adage in personnel management sums it up: Jobs are built around functions, not around people. A quality control manager sees that appropriate measures are applied, with specified frequency, to insure that the quality of flash-light batteries rolling off the assembly line is maintained. Being a good parent or an intelligent opera buff means nothing so far as the job is concerned, whereas the job may mean everything to effective parenthood or opera attendance. The job must be done and done according to the criteria of usefulness determined by the organization, or the manager may as well forget about *La Traviata*. The essential point of Credo 3 is that the job is more important than the person who occupies it.

This does not mean that managers are ill treated. On the contrary, the universal behavioral techniques have built-in mechanisms that guarantee humane conditions. Still, professionals must understand that organizational usefulness is more valuable than personal idiosyncrasy. But all this is familiar, is it not? Not entirely, for there are new elements here. One is that the executive attitude of self-abnegation is heralded by some influential writers as a harbinger of progress rather than as a stultifying requirement of the modern job. The perfect example of such "double-think" is found in the much-praised book by Harlan Cleveland, *The Future Executive*. For him, the reduction of self to a series of organizational functions represented a positive aspect of organizational evolution. In a key passage, he wrote: "A 'developed' society requires of each executive that he act in each office he holds more or less the way it is functional for a person in that position to act. He must be able to deal with other executives in the system not merely as himself but as a function." [18] In other words, the modern organization requires that the performance of a job must never be tainted by an individual personality. This theme is central to Cleveland's prescriptions for public executives, and it applies equally to managers in private industry. We will discuss some of the implications of his ideas because they come close to being the definitive statement of the value foundation of the national managerial system.

Cleveland is regarded as an enlightened spokesman for management because he has progressed beyond the old-fashioned hierarchical system of authority. He claimed that the vast and complex modern organization would require the decentralization of authority. But if those to whom the authority is decentralized are carbon copies of one another, the dispersion is meaningless, since each will act exactly as it was planned for him to do. This is precisely the aim of Credo 3: Professional people must believe that the job is what counts in their lives, the job is what gives meaning to their actions. Other considerations — family, community, and even individuality — must be secondary. Cleveland confused the issue; personal, internalized obedience, if unthinking, is not necessarily better than hierarchical command.

Credo 4: We Believe in the Universality of the Management Process

Another old saying in management is that the management process is universal. It can be practiced anywhere without regard to organization or specialty. The fields of marketing, finance, and accounting, for example, acquire greater stature, and presumably more meaning, when they deal with marketing management, financial management, and managerial accounting. A manager can practice this universal art in business, government, and educational organizations without having to learn a new management process for each area.

Indicative of the faith in management universality is the rise of generic schools of administration, like those at the University of California, Irvine, or Yale University, whose major purpose is to train interchangeable managers who can move with ease into managerial jobs in virtually any organization. Management is management is management; professional people are indoctrinated with the belief that they can perform managerial tasks in a multitude of different situations. And, given the ubiquity of modern organizations, they are correct.

There are two reasons why Credo 4 is critical to the professionals' belief system. First, by believing in it, professionals are homogenized by the common core of values underlying the organizational imperative. Second, by such homogenization more effective control of the professionals is possible. Logically, these two reasons amount to the same thing: Homogenization of personnel in the same system of core values guarantees unvarying, reliable employee performance in both the private and public sectors.

Seldom is this rationale for management universality made explicit, and when it is, it is not greeted with much enthusiasm. Years ago, William Scott wrote a satirical article entitled "Executive Development as an Instrument of Higher Control." [19] In it he made the modest proposal that executive development programs incorporate brainwashing principles to insure the reliability of technical core people in their performance of strategic organizational functions. The manuscript was sent initially to the *Harvard Business Review* for consideration. After a delay, the editor returned the manuscript with a very long letter saying that the reviewers debated at length on whether the author was kidding or serious about that proposal. They finally concluded that he was serious and that there was not sufficient data to support the view that brainwashing was an effective means of behavioral control. The unmistakable message was that when satire comes too close to stating dangerous truths, it is better left unprinted.

Since management is universal, managers could move with ease among jobs and organizations within the national managerial system. Homogeneity permits mobility. But does this highly vaunted mobility really occur? Not as frequently as one might imagine. Most managers remain in the same type of organization or in the same organization where they begin their careers. They tend not to move to different organizations, *although they could*. So mobility is not the reason for stressing management universality; homogenization is.

As intelligent individuals, professionals are required to fit the organizational values that dominate their jobs into an efficient and harmonious relationship with their entire personality; otherwise they will not be of much use either to the organization or to themselves. This situation was well described by Michael Maccoby:

Any organization of work — industrial, service, blue or white collar — can be described as a *psychostructure* that selects and molds character. One difference between the psychostructure of the modern corporate technostructure and that of a factory is the fineness of fit between work and character demanded of corporate managers and engineers who do "brainwork," in contrast to factories, where only minimal compliance is required to perform simplified, repetitive tasks.[20]

What Maccoby wrote about corporate management is certainly true about professionals in all modern organizations. They must become what they do, especially if they want to move up the management ladder in their organization. The career progress of the professionals depends upon their making organizational values an intrinsic part of their lives. This, in turn, creates a powerful behavioral control mechanism that guarantees their reliability and uniformity.

The modern organization's need for reliable and uniform professionals results from its size, complexity, and superspecialization of jobs. These three circumstances do not permit the close supervision associated with earlier, more primitive management systems. However, the need for control has not disappeared, and thus control in modern organizations must be enforced differently. Since it is impractical to supervise professionals closely, it is necessary to adjust the employee's personality by training and socialization so that his values accord with the required values of the job psychostructure. If this adjustment is successful, then professionals can be sent unwatched throughout the organization to perform their jobs with a fair degree of assurance that they carry with them the authorized organizational values that make them loyal and trustworthy.

The desirability for employee identification with organizational values is a long-standing, common-sense piece of management dogma. Chester I. Barnard observed decades ago that it is cheaper, and more effective motivationally, to have employees psychologically committed to serve a managerial system than it is to buy their willingness to serve with economic inducements. Barnard probably would agree that control of the psychostructures of jobs is the best way to insure the reliability of professionals. To illustrate, read what Barnard said about "ideal benefactions":

Ideal benefactions as inducements to cooperation are among the most powerful and the most neglected. By ideal benefaction I mean the capacity of organizations to satisfy personal ideals usually relating to non-material, future, or altruistic relations. They include pride of workmanship, sense of adequacy, altruistic service for family or others, loyalty to organization in patriotism, etc., aesthetic and religious feeling.[21]

Organizational appeals to professionals on these grounds are powerful motivators because they ring bells that the professionals are conditioned to hear. From their educational experiences, professionals learn to resent old and crude forms of managerial control and believe that they can perform their jobs better under looser control systems. At the same time, professionals learn the necessity of cooperative behavior and the importance of teamwork for obtaining organizational goals. Is it any wonder, then, that professionals respond with enthusiasm to the notion of extending the modern organization across all jurisdictional boundaries? As decent people, they envision the reform of the total society through the processes of humane management. This utopian vision is hard to resist, for it coincides so well with how they have been trained.

Credo 5: We Believe in the Vocationalization of Education

The most effective way to guarantee appropriate behavioral responses to organizational needs is to build an educational system that will indoctrinate people in the requisite beliefs. At the most basic level, this means that vocational specialization should be presented as a worthy goal to which all should aspire, with the expectation of being generously rewarded. Once professionals learn the virtue of vocationalism, they will teach its merits to the broader community as citizens and parents. A fully developed vocational educational system insures an adequate supply of professionals with appropriate skills and attitudes well in advance of when they are needed by the modern organization.

Harlan Cleveland advocated such a plan. In his discussion about how underdeveloped nations can enjoy the blessings of modern organizations, he wrote:

In a developed industrial culture, an executive may come to his task from Texas politics, a Los Angeles ghetto, a Chicago trade union, or a Proper Bostonian tribe, but he finds ways of marrying his heritage, training, and personality to some concept of what is required of a person doing the job he is supposed to do as the deputy assistant director of this or that. In the more personalized cultures of the less developed lands, the executive's family or clique or tribe or individual *amour-propre* tends to override his functions, with damage to the system that mounts as complexity increases. *A major purpose of education in the developing nations these days is to grow people with a vocation for organizationally relevant behavior.* [22]

Cleveland correctly observed that most Americans have been prepared from childhood to accept roles as professionals, with a minimum of attitude adjustment when they finally enter the job force. The key idea is contained in the last sentence above, where he argues that individuals must be *grown* to assure their reliability when the time comes for them to assume their roles in modern organizations. The major responsibility for the development of the requisite character belongs to the educational system, and it has accepted this responsibility with enormous gusto, at all levels.

Particularly dramatic are the enlarging segments of the student body in higher education who are choosing majors in professional fields like law, medicine, engineering, social work, dentistry, and most important, in administration: whether of businesses, governments, educational institutions, hospitals, or hotels. In most universities and colleges, traditional fields of learning in the arts and sciences are suffering serious declines in student enrollment as more and more students seek admission to vocational programs.

In all areas of academic study, fads and fashions reflect the issues of the times. Look at what happened in engineering after the Russians put Sputnik into orbit and to journalism after Woodward and Bernstein sent Nixon into exile. These fields surged, then declined, and perhaps will surge again. The field of business administration is truly a remarkable case of this flux. During the 1950s and 1960s it was a very low prestige major, along with physical education and agriculture, a fall-back position for those who had failed in pre-med or engineering. But there has been a steady, almost inexorable growth in its attractiveness and influence over the last ten or fifteen years. Now students clamor to get into business programs, and the more vocationally specialized these programs (e.g., accounting, financial analysis, statistics), the more popular they are. Waiting lists for business school admission are long, and the academic requirements to get into both graduate and undergraduate programs are getting higher all the time.

Almost invariably, the students in these university farm-clubs for professional training see themselves as becoming professionals in some large organization. Interestingly, almost none of them have any desire to start small businesses. They know that the big opportunities are in the large organizations, and they want the type of training that will help them enter this employment market. University budgets respond to these expressions of demand, and resources are allocated to those departments and programs where the demand is greatest.

In the years since World War II and until around 1970, most university departments shared in an expanding resource pie, thanks to the largesse of the state and federal governments. This growing pie relieved the pressure on university officials to make difficult priority decisions on academic programs. They passed the wealth around, and most departments could be reasonably comfortable with their share of it. Those "days of wine and roses" came to an end in the 1970s, when university administrators and faculties had to make hard choices and name priorities. The costs of operation soared, citizens complained about paying for nonvocational frills, and funding bodies, like state legislatures, looked at the educational budget as a place to achieve economies.

The effects of this educational policy on the character of the universities have been profound. One immediate consequence is that programs and departments with declining enrollments are being eliminated or sizably reduced. The public demand for economies in education is being met at the expense of liberal and fine arts programs, and the resources thus freed are being reallocated to those departments emphasizing practical and vocational programs, which are of the greatest utility to modern organizations. In simple terms, the vocationalization of education means the none-too-subtle transfer of funds away from fields that have no direct application to the modern organization into those fields that do.

Since the modern organization can only flourish in an education-intensive society, the apocalyptic cries of university administrators that penurious state legislatures and populist governors will cause the collapse of their universities are misdirected. Universities will not collapse because organizational American cannot exist without them. Modern organizations require an accessible and effective educational system, and those who understand this requirement most clearly are the professionals, who have been university trained. Therefore, the importance of the university can only *increase* because it is the last step in the formal educational system, where the final polish is applied to professional aspirants.

The university, however, must be more than a place where people learn skills. It must also indoctrinate professionals in how to think managerially all the time. In fact, this is the modern university's most important mission. Recall Maccoby's observation about the necessary closeness of fit between managerial character and the role requirements of the job. The vocationalization of higher education goes to the heart of this matter, and its two main characteristics are leadership, and scientific method.

LEADERSHIP

Leadership is the main ideological theme emphasized in the career training of the professionals. Although we do not equate management with leadership, nonetheless, the terms are synonymous in orthodox managerial training. The study of leadership is very safe because it holds out promises for advancement through the organizational hierarchy and because it excites the expectations of most students that they will eventually become leaders. In this way, the neophyte professionals come to covet top managerial positions and to concentrate their efforts on obtaining them.

But there is a far more important reason for the emphasis on leadership. Such training insures that the professionals who aspire to top management positions are aware of the immense burdens associated with them. When such managers make decisions, the professionals will understand how they are made and will identify with the leader's need for compliance from subordinates.

The reverse of leadership, of course, is "followership," and it should be asked why a similar ideological emphasis is not given to that subject in training professionals. It is, but it is treated as a part of leadership. Followers must be trained to appreciate the needs of the managerial elite. Such a state of mind is, of course, the foundation for obedience. Some years ago, Fillmore Sanford wrote:

It is the follower as an individual who perceives the leader, who perceives the situation, and who, in the last analysis, accepts or rejects leadership. The follower's persistent motives, point of view, frames of reference or attitudes will have a hand in determining what he perceives and how he reacts to it.[23]

No matter what they may think, virtually all professionals will spend all of their job lives being obedient to someone else. But they have been trained to empathize completely, with leadership roles, and they expect, without question, such empathy from their subordinates. So, while most professionals will be followers, the ideological emphasis of the modern organization is always on leadership and leadership needs. Why?

This is a fascinating question, and it opens a Pandora's box when its implications for vocationalism are pursued to their logical conclusions. Central to effective followership is obedience, and there are two extreme points of view on the subject. One view is that it corrupts people — at least it corrupts their rational sensibilities. There are many examples of this way of thinking; Hannah Arendt, Stanley Milgram, and Irving L. Janis have written persuasively about the type of obedience that impels people to immorality and stupidity, with disastrous consequences.[24] Arendt, for example, detailed the corrosive effects of unthinking obedience on the character of Adolf Eichmann, who believed that disobedience to his superiors would have been a worse crime than killing the Jews. The other extreme view of obedience is that since it is necessary for modern organizations, it promotes organizational health and thus need not be questioned. That follows logically from the second proposition of the organizational imperative.

Much to his credit, the philosopher John Rawls, in *A Theory of Justice,* addressed himself to the moral requirement of obedience in contemporary, organization-dominated society.[25] His position is that followership carries with it moral duties, just as leadership does, and he makes two key points. First, followers are obliged to refuse to comply with leadership commands if they violate the rules of justice. Second, if such conscientious refusal does not deter leadership from taking unjust actions, followers must appeal to public opinion through acts of civil disobedience that demonstrate the immorality of leadership commands. Whether or not one agrees with Rawls, it is obvious that such attitudes among professionals would not be prized by the managerial elite.

METHODOLOGY

The methodology of managerial education is rooted in an empirically based operational analysis, which, according to P. W. Bridgman, is the simple acknowledgment that a "concept is synonymous with the corresponding set of operations."[26] This seemingly innocuous definition has enormous implications for vocational training in administration for two reasons.

First, in order for a concept to have meaning in Bridgman's terms, it must be associated with a set of empirical measurements. For instance, the concept of personality does not exist apart from the tests that measure it. Indeed, personality becomes what personality tests say it is. Second, any questions associated with final causes, such as the ascertaining of values, are meaningless due to the absence of empirical operations to measure them. To the extent that some such measures are devised, as has been done in studies of ethics and morals, they will become what the empirical yardsticks measure, but nothing more or less.

The vocational education of professionals mainly involves concepts to which operational analysis can be applied. The positivist commitment is dominant in all of the disciplines in administration, with the effect of making all of their contents measurable by empirical techniques. This is evident in accounting, finance, marketing, urban development, and social welfare, among others. However, the truly critical change in administrative education is the application of empirical methods to the study of the management of human attitudes and behavior in organizations. It is axiomatic that no managerial technique can be certified as acceptable unless it has been empirically verified. Therefore, it is neceesary to reduce as many human attitudes and behaviors as possible to sets of testable operations. The triumph of operational analysis is clearly demonstrated by examining the curricula of any major schools of business and public administration or the contents of the major professional journals in management (e.g., *Academy of Management Journal* and *Administrative Science Quarterly*). Thus the behavioral component in the training of professionals is not only training in methods, it is even more training in ideological orthodoxy. The foundation of all orthodoxy is, of course, the a priori values of the organizational imperative. Once they have been accepted, managerial attitudes and behaviors are certified as orthodox when they are empirically verified.

Credo 6: We Believe in the Obtrusiveness of Management

The belief in management obtrusiveness belongs to the same category of beliefs as managerial escalation and managerial universality. However, there is an important difference between this credo and the others. Credo 6 states a belief in a system of priorities where management functions *always* have precedence over the specialties practiced by the technical operating personnel in modern organizations. This belief is of the utmost importance because it is so easy for the specialist or department manager to forget that the organization does not revolve around his or her job. There is more to managing a grocery chain than buying meat; there is more to running a publishing company than editing books; there is more to running a bank than being a loan officer.

The problem that Credo 6 aims to solve is the conflict between specialization and the general management function. Such conflicts lead to disharmonious organizational relationships, which are nowhere more apparent than those between technical organizational support groups, like research and development, and the managers of a company. Technical people in R and D often believe that their work is badly underfunded and unappreciated and that they have little or no influence on company policy. Managing executives frequently believe these technical people are impractical eggheads, with whom it is impossible to communicate, who have little regard for profitability, and who are so isolated from the mainstream of company activity that they have no idea of what managing a successful organization entails. This example has many counterparts throughout all modern organizations.

The facts of organizational life are harsh when it comes to gauging the comparative power between management and the specialized technical support staff. The managing executives are supreme, and the specialists must grit their teeth and go along with the decisions they make. But a grudging acknowledgment of who really has the organizational clout is not an ideal state of affairs, nor is it the intention behind Credo 6. The ideal is that professionals internalize the values of the organizational imperative. Knauth wrote:

To function effectively managerial enterprise requires a degree of voluntary cooperation among its several parts . . . Large numbers of persons with diverse skills and abilities must be fitted into a harmonious whole. Their rights, duties, and rewards must be determined not merely from the viewpoint of the individual or his organized group but within a framework that makes for continuity of operations.[27]

Through its obtrusiveness, management becomes the focal point, the primary cue-giver, for all organizational endeavors. For the more specialized professionals, this may be difficult to accept, because it demands that they recognize that the specialties that took them years to learn and more years to master are not the axis upon which the organization turns. As the job requires individual self-abnegation in its behalf, the specialization of the job requires its subordination to the necessities of the organization as a whole.

The constant movement of professionals within an organization is a drill that makes them aware of the penetration of management into all aspects of their jobs. Bit by bit, professionals learn the practices, processes, and language of management, thereby identifying with the managerial elite who coordinate and harmonize the activities of an organization. But more important, they will learn that management is the indispensable task in the organization, and according to Cleveland, by obedience and willing cooperation with it, "employees will increasingly be professional people who think of themselves . . . as part of management."[28]

Chapter 7

The Significant People

The fit survive, and fitness means, not formal competence — there probably is no such thing for top executive positions — but conformity with the criteria of
those who have already succeeded. To be compatible
with the top men is to act like them, to look like them,
to think like them: to be of and for them — or at least
to display oneself to them in such a way as to create
that impression.

— C. Wright Mills, *The Power Elite*

The Significant Job

The way to understand how a society functions is to ask the
question, who rules? All nations elevate some people above
the common herd. For centuries, Western societies have been
commanded by kings, prelates, and generals. Sometimes
they have even been led by statesmen, philosophers, and
saints. While most nations have adopted more authoritarian
forms of government, American history records a democratic experience for the people. But as our history has un-
folded, the ruling structure has changed. In organizational
America the new rulership is a direct outgrowth of the modern organization. While it may seem that our great public
and private institutions often run themselves, of course they
do not. At the apex of the ruling hierarchy are the top

managing executives charged with making the cardinal decisions for their organizations. This last group has the ruling power in organizational America.

These individuals should not be equated with the jobs they occupy, since the jobs are more important than their occupants. Their vital jobs are the "significant jobs" and those who perform them are the "significant people." Significant jobs are those formal role positions at the apex of primary information networks within modern organizations, where the duties are almost entirely managerial, where the performance of the job provides its own ethical justification, and where grand strategy decisions are made that have both internal and external consequences for the organization. This formal definition has five major elements.

1. *The formal role position defines that significant jobs at the top of the managerial hierarchy have definite role requirements, although they are not always spelled out.* By the time individuals rise to the significant job, after many years of employment by an organization, they have learned the role and can be trusted to do what people in their position are supposed to do: keep their organization healthy and ward off threats to it.

But the incumbents of such jobs are transient, while the jobs remain permanent. The job is more important to the modern organization than the person in it, and the occupant of the role can do almost nothing to change its nature. Top managers are as confined to the expectations of their roles as are generals, cardinals, or university presidents. The Presidents of the United States cannot alter the course of government bureaucracy as much as they claim in a presidential campaign, just as the president of an automobile company is relatively powerless to change his corporation. The mass of the organization creates an inertia that carries it in a predetermined direction.

2. *The significant jobs are at the head of all the important information networks within the organization.* Therefore the oc-

cupant of the significant job receives the information necessary for a complete overview of the total organization. The monopolization of such information permits the centralization of power at the top. The classic example of the significant job at an information hub is that of the director of the Office of Management and Budget (OMB). This office is responsible for preparing the federal budget, so it is the one place where all information about the federal executive is gathered on a regular basis. It also prepares the President's legislative proposals to Congress, which makes the director privy to the President's plans. It is no wonder, then, that Presidents like to appoint people they trust to that position.

3. *The significant jobs are almost purely managerial in content because the persons who occupy them are responsible for insuring that all of the specializations in a modern organization are effectively coordinated.* While this may require some delegation of authority to professionals, the ultimate responsibility for coordination remains in the significant job.

4. *Significant jobs provide their own ethical justification.* When individuals assume them, they know that society would suffer greatly if their organizations failed. What they must do to keep their organizations healthy can be ethically justified in terms of the national welfare. Remember the furor when Eisenhower's choice for secretary of defense, Charles Wilson, the head of General Motors, stated that "what is good for General Motors is good for America; what is good for America is good for General Motors." Engine Charlie captured the ethical principle of the significant job, which acknowledges the common destiny of America and its large organizations. The organizationally sustaining activities required of the significant people by their roles represent the epitome of morality as they have learned it.

5. *The primary requirement of the significant job is for its occupants to make grand strategy decisions for the organization.* These are the long-range decisions that affect the fate of the organization. Decisions must be made to acquire, or merge

with, other organizations, to compete for government contracts, to deregulate an industry, or to enter a new market. Such decisions have profound internal effects on organizations. But they also have varying external effects upon other organizations. If a large corporation decides to relocate its headquarters or to begin producing automobiles that run on methane, the interdependent mass of organizations surrounding it will be directly influenced.

Thus, the significant jobs are where the cardinal decisions in organizational America are made. Given this vital responsibility, the significant people are the custodians of their organizations, their industry, and their nation. They are the ruling elite because no one else participates in the rarefied atmosphere of high policy-making. Consequently, effective performance of the significant job by the significant people is unequivocally the most important element in the social, economic, and political welfare of the nation.

What could hamper the effective performance of significant jobs? While many factors could be mentioned, the major cause for the breakdown of performance is the inability of significant people to handle crises. Most managers are used to dealing with crisis conditions, and given the usual, garden-variety ones, they can manage them fairly well. However, the nature of crises has changed in organizational America, pushing the significant people to the limits of their training, skill, and natural ability.

Crisis and Management

Significant people are supposed to be able to resolve large crises. This skill is part of their reputation. Granted, it would be better if crises could be pre-empted. Then the maintenance of the organization could be left to the professionals. Nevertheless, from time to time major crises occur that can be dealt with only by those in significant jobs. Generally, these crises fall into two categories: precedented and unprecedented. A precedented crisis is one where prior managerial experience, processes, techniques, and analytical concepts exist to resolve them. An unprecedented crisis is just that: there is no experience or history to fall back on.

Precedented Crises: Internal

Such crises are common to management, and they have received a great deal of study. For the most part, the significant people are well equipped to cope with them. A primary goal of management education, research, and practice has been to improve managerial techniques for dealing with the internal problems of complex organizations. Once the problem is defined, an array of techniques is available to managers at all levels to help them find solutions. The significant people can draw upon staff specialists, computer-based management information systems, simulation models, and consultants to anticipate and solve internal threats to the organization. Many of these approaches have been so successful that internal crises are more dramatic possibilities than potentially serious threats.

However, internal crises have a way of compounding themselves in complex organizations. Consequently, the pressures on top managers have risen along with the technologies for crisis resolution. There is a serious question whether the multiplication and complexity of such techniques might be outstripping the ability of managers to control them. However, when they are so threatened, help will come from the outside — usually from the federal government — because large modern organizations cannot be allowed to die. The histories of the Penn Central Railroad and Lockheed Aircraft are examples. So, while human limitations often reduce their effective performance, the survival of large organizations is seldom seriously jeopardized by internal crises.

Precedented Crises: External

Beyond catastrophes, such as an atomic war in the Middle East, the most dangerous external threats to organizations come from other organizations competing for shares of a consumer market or, among government agencies, for a contested clientele. These are normal external crises, and again, the significant people are prepared to meet them.

However, in organizational America fundamental structural changes in the economy are increasing the pressures upon significant job holders. Among these changes are slower real economic growth, persistent inflation, weak political leadership coupled with greater bureaucratic authority, shortages of natural resources, and shortages of finance capital. The practical consequence of these structural changes is an intensified competition for resources and dollars, along with more regulation by the federal government of the resource allocation process.

Interestingly, many of these structural changes involve the supply rather than the demand side of an organization's economy. Management is accustomed to solving problems of demand in terms of the production and distribution of goods and services in a competitive market. But aside from the traditional economic problems of supply, competition at the input end is a different matter in America. Because we have been blessed by material abundance in the past, we have not had to contend with circumstances that directly affect our expectation of continuous growth and affluence. Yet, as a result of the basic external changes just mentioned, we must now face the prospect that for the first time in our history our expectations for material abundance may not be met.

Juanita Kreps, secretary of commerce in the Carter administration, has observed that continuous material growth is no longer an appropriate goal for Americans: "If we cease to accept the notion that we are doing well only if we are making more and more money, we will be able to do many things which we have denied ourselves in the past."[1]

The external crises created by structural changes will certainly raise the performance ante for the significant people. They will not only have to be more effective with less; they may have to curtail plans for growth and start thinking about how to manage stable-state or shrinking organizations.[2] However, managing negative growth is the reverse side of managing positive growth, and it does not pose problems of a different order from those management presently confronts. For example, the increasing price of fuel will not affect the significant people or their organizations to a very large extent. What will happen is that modern organizations will claim a greater share of national resources, with the price paid by the beleaguered customers in the form of a lowered standard of living.

All in all, external crises, even those resulting from structural changes, are not the threats to modern organizations that they may initially seem to be. Instead, they may provide the supreme opportunity for the significant people to consolidate ever more power in both public and private organizations.

The Unprecedented Crises of Interdependency

The overwhelming impression someone from the Northwest gets in almost any major eastern city is that things are out of control and that these cities are unmanageable. There are just too many things to be done for too many people. This impression is perhaps strongest in Washington, D.C., the civic heart of the nation. Recently we happened to stay in an expensive hotel there and decided to walk to a restaurant in the evening. The doorman stopped us, warning of indescribable dangers, from mugging to random violence. All, presumably, was chaos on the streets.

In contrast, when one visits major government agencies in the capital, all is sane and orderly. Professionals go about their jobs with an air of competence and a spirit of determination. It is not *within* the various federal organizations that one feels that things are out of control. The confusion appears when one stands back from the separate events and contemplates the enormous and complex array of the federal government. When one considers that the city of Washington is itself a part of the federal preserve, then the interdependencies begin to seem that much more complex. It engenders the feeling that human beings are not capable of managing the intricacies of this monumental system of organizational interrelationship.

What is equally dismaying is that the sense of chaotic interdependence extends to the private sectors of our society, which also contain independent but interlocking organizations in vital areas of commerce, like transportation, energy, automobile manufacturing, agriculture, and so on. When all of this is multiplied by an additional factor, that public and private systems are interdependent upon one another, the resulting complexity is beyond comprehension.

As an example of interorganizational complexity, Professor Bruce L. Gates has calculated that in a small community with 4 general-purpose levels of government (federal, state, local, and substate regional); 10 service-providing agencies (health care, child care, counseling, employment, etc.); 10 distinct client groups (the elderly, children, the poor, the Spanish-speaking, etc.); 12 funding sources (Department of Health, Education and Welfare, the United Way, the Department of Labor, etc.); 20 distinct service programs (Medicare, Medicaid, WIN, child care, food stamps, etc.); and 6 different methods for achieving interorganizational linkages (fiscal, planning/programming, case coordination, etc.), there are 578,202 possible relationships among different organizational entities.[3] This astronomical figure was arrived at by using only the most modest assumptions.

Surely only exceptional persons can manage these interdependent networks effectively, and there are very few such individuals. In the past they were considered unnecessary and even undesirable. In more relaxed times in our history, the automatic balancing of interrelated organizations in our society was assumed. In fact, it was accepted as a positive virtue and given a name: pluralism. The cultivation of pluralism was thought to be the best way of preventing economic and political autocracy. The costs of pluralism were considered worth the advantages gained for our way of life: a society relatively free from power centers dominated by despotic individuals. The price was indeed paid — in economic exploitation, political venality, and administrative bungling — but these costs were easily absorbed by the enormous productive surpluses of our economic system. We had plenty of resources and wondrous levels of productivity, but above all we had a lot of time to right the mistakes and injustices of mismanagement. In short, we could afford the luxury of error.

Thus, in the past our natural abundance, space, and material wealth allowed us to pursue self-interested goals. Managers were expected to conduct their activities with dispatch so that businesses would grow and be profitable. But, by and large, we were content to let nature take its course at the boundaries of organizations where tangential, overlapping, and competing interests existed.

This perspective is no longer possible. The significant people know that management must extend to networks of organizations, and they understand that other organizations are among the most important elements in their environment. This expansion of the managerial perspective shifts the responsibility of the significant people from the confines of "their" organization to the multitude of organizations that surround them. The question is, can these enormously complex networks be managed by normal human beings? Probably not. As a result, crises of interdependency will occur with increasing frequency. The daily newspaper is filled with examples of organizational systems running out of control because they are too complex to manage effectively. Would one rather be the president of IBM or the mayor of New York City? The answer is simple. One would rather be president of IBM because its interdependencies are under some control; New York City is Byzantine in its complexity.

These crises produce more than inconvenience and frustration for those dependent on organizational networks for the delivery of jobs, goods, and services. The crises of interdependency are unprecedented and represent the largest, most dangerous crises facing the significant people. Such crises reveal *the* major gap in the development of management technique: Little or nothing has been done to increase the personal capacity of the individuals who occupy the significant jobs.

Who Are the Significant People?

The control of America by the significant people presents a paradox, for Americans believe they live in an open society. Yet the great majority of the significant people were never elected by the citizens, nor are they even known. Furthermore, the decisions they make are shielded from public view. The eminent British author C. P. Snow has summed up this paradox succinctly: "One of the most bizarre features of any advanced industrial society in our time is that the cardinal choices have to be made by a handful of men, in secret."[4]

This secrecy is not entirely intended by elitists; rather, it stems from how modern organizations are designed to be managed. Such designs result in the shield of elitist invisibility, which we discussed at length in Chapter 2. Suffice it to say here that the average person is not aware of what goes on behind the shield, where the significant people make the big decisions that influence us all. What is interesting about these decisions is that they are not made by people who are necessarily the fittest in organizational America. Those who have risen to positions of significance are not there because of some mysterious form of organizational Darwinism, although C. Wright Mills hints at this in the quotation above. The truth about who the significant people actually are is apt to be disillusioning.

The significant people are not the mythic great captains of our industrial tradition. They are, for the most part, ordinary, intelligent, decent people who have risen slowly through the managerial ranks of their organizations. Their social origins are relatively democratic, in the sense that the majority of them are drawn from the American economic middle class. Mabel Newcomer's study of the big-business executive shows that the democratization of the significant people has been a trend since 1900. Around 45 percent of the top managers of big business came from the wealthy group in 1900, whereas this group accounted for less than 10 percent in 1964.[5] The gap was filled almost entirely by people from the middle income class. Those rising to the significant jobs from the ranks of the poor show a slight increase over the sixty-four years of the Newcomer study, but one nowhere near as dramatic.

The main instrument for the accession of the significant people to power has been education. What Theo Haimann and William G. Scott have written about business leaders applies to the leaders of all modern organizations:

The greater relative availability of education makes it possible to equip men of all classes . . . with the qualifications necessary for employment in large business firms. This opportunity together with the scientific character of higher education opens the door to greater vertical mobility in business regardless of social origin.[6]

Again, the Newcomer report makes this clear. Over 90 percent of the top managers surveyed had some college education; about 75 percent of them had college degrees.[7] Qualitatively, the most useful type of college education for vertical mobility is the vocational education discussed in Chapter 6, because it equips people with the necessary technical and managerial skills for organizational access and advancement. Therefore, the route to the significant jobs in organizational America lies through education that is not only specialized but, more important, managerial in character. The managerial aspect of formal education molds the incipient attitudes of students into the orthodox shape required by the management creed.

However, there is another side to managerial education, and it is the socialization process that an individual experiences during his or her years of organizational employment. As the business scholar Neil W. Chamberlain ruefully wrote:

Employees are being paid to produce, not to make themselves into better people. Corporations are purchasing employee time to make a return on it, not investing in employees to enrich their lives. Employees are human capital, and when capital is hired or leased the objective is not to embellish it for its own sake but to use it for financial advantage. But somewhere in this philosophy there is an inconsistency with the notion of a society of self-governing individuals. The large corporation has become an organizer of people, a *user* of people, a molder of identities, according to criteria that it has evolved, without regard to the effect on those people except as this is registered on the balance sheet.[8]

It stands to reason that the longer people remain in managerial jobs, the more they will absorb an orthodox managerial outlook. Their perception of themselves will be defined by the top managers, who embody and radiate the standards necessary for success, as Mills clearly described. This point was re-emphasized by the psychologist Michael

Maccoby in his study of the "gamesmen" as the new corporate leaders. He found that

most managers were rather unconflicted and realistic about themselves. They had started out as conservative careerists and had been liberalized by corporate demands for cooperation and working with different kinds of people . . . For the most part, they had weighed the costs and benefits of merging themselves with the corporation and nothing we could add seriously challenged their conclusions or suggested an alternative.[9]

Virtually everything organizational — from the reward structure to official approval — reinforces the importance of a manager's identification with organizational values. Consequently, the longer individuals remain with an organization, the more *they become what they do* in the sense that their personal values reflect organizational values.

This is especially true of the significant people, because it takes them quite some time to achieve their significant jobs. Many years are involved in their rise to the top, and frequently this long service is spent within one organization. Table 2 summarizes some data pertaining to chief executive officers' (CEOs') mobility, derived from samples drawn from the *Fortune* 500 companies and the *Forbes* ranking of the major U.S. corporations for 1977. This data shows that the average age of the CEO is greater than fifty-six years. Their average length of service in the larger firms was thirty years, twenty-one years in the smaller companies. This suggests that there is very little interfirm mobility among the CEOs as a group, since they spend more than half their lives with the same larger corporation and at least one third of their lives with the same smaller ones. Also, vertical mobility within these corporations is slow, since the years spent as a CEO do not exceed 37 percent of the total number of years spent in these corporations.

Based on this information and on biographical studies like

TABLE 2

Demographics of Chief Executive Officers, 1977

Sample for 1977	Average Number of Years as a CEO	Average Number of Years with the Company	Average Age	% of Years as a CEO
Fortune 500: Companies 1–50	5.44	30.46	56.44	17%
Fortune 500: Companies 439–500	7.68	20.98	57.66	36%
Forbes: Companies 1–50	6.24	30.12	57.40	20%
Forbes: Companies 451–500	7.26	22.3	57.44	32%

those done by Newcomer, a composite portrait of the significant person can be drawn.[10] The "average" significant person is a white, middle-class Protestant male with a college education. He is about fifty-six years old; most likely, he was in military service during World War II; he attended and usually graduated from a university; he may have spent a few years in entry-level jobs that proved false career starts; but by the time he was thirty he was working for the company that presently employs him.

There is little reason to suppose that these patterns of career mobility will change significantly, except that the average age of CEOs may drop somewhat because the coming generation did not have as long an interlude of military service. Consequently, it is safe to conclude that if young people are very ambitious and want significant jobs, they must obtain the appropriate education, settle with one organization before turning thirty, and plan on staying with it.

Two inferences can be drawn from this discussion. First, in their progress to the apex of an organization, the significant people have done well all of the orthodox things required of upwardly mobile managers, including the internalization of organizational values. Therefore, they become very conservative in their attitudes about how organizations should be managed. Second, their long period of organizational association breeds a loyalty that tends to narrow their horizons. Such parochial fidelity to one's organizational point of view requires further examination.

While a person's organizational experience may not always be pleasant throughout a career, long service tends to erase bad memories. For all of those years the organization interpreted the world for its managers, and they come to see it in terms of automobiles sold, tax returns processed, bank loans made, and computers programmed. This preselection and distillation of experience does not tend to create significant people who are philosopher-kings.

After years of dedicated service, a CEO is not apt to have a very cosmopolitan outlook on life. This was confirmed in a study of chief executive officers by C. Spencer Clark, himself the CEO of a large corporation.[11] He measured the extent of the cosmopolitan versus parochial outlook of these people and found the majority to be parochial in their world view. In spite of their obvious intelligence, their perspective became synonymous with that of the companies they led. Like villagers in the Middle Ages, they seldom wandered farther than the sound of the bells in their parish church.

It is not at all strange that leadership in organizational America is as it is. Given our priorities, it could hardly be otherwise. We have democratized economic opportunity, and as a consequence America is mainly composed of a vast economic middle class devoted to materialistic tastes. We have attached great utility to education because it is the chief means through which the individual can secure employment and be certified as a candidate for organizational advancement. We have made the organizational imperative the value foundation of America and entrusted our personal destinies to large organizations. We have in effect said that we want loyal and reliable people to run these organizations, and we have made the significant job the potential prize for such behavior. So it is no wonder that we have gotten the leadership we asked for: expert, well-intentioned, decent, parochial, and consumption-oriented managers.

And these are precisely the people who have made organizational America a stunning success. They have made our resources productive; their energy has permitted our dreams of affluence to be realized; they have projected the United States into a position of world power — all within the last thirty-five years.

But what of the future? Will these same people be able to continue their excellent performance? One cannot be optimistic. The reality of our complex society is bearing down on the significant people, and they will bear the brunt of accelerating crises of interdependency. Increasingly their time and attention will be consumed by these crises for which they are not prepared, mentally or physically. Therefore, the significant people may well seek unprecedented means to cope with these unprecedented demands for superior performance.

The stakes in this quest are extraordinarily high. The inability of the significant people to deal effectively with crises of interdependency could result in no less a calamity than the collapse of our economic system. Certainly, the significant people can argue that it is in the national interest for them to enhance their capacities for managing unprecedented crises. They must be able to perform their jobs in superior ways, exceeding what they are now capable of doing even with the best of effort. The question is, what methods will they seek to enhance those abilities?

Improving the performance of the significant people in the future involves much more than just a linear improvement in the support systems presently available. Even with all the information about organizational interdependencies that such systems could provide, it is the significant person who must absorb, weigh, judge, and qualify this data, finally choosing the appropriate route for the organization to follow in a world of unimaginable complexity. Superior performance in such circumstances requires superior people.

Given the leadership structure in organizational America, superiority of performance in the significant job *must* come by improving ordinary people. The significant people have used the conventional techniques of the applied behavioral sciences in the past for this purpose. However, the limit of what can be accomplished by these methods has virtually been reached. It now seems possible or even likely that the significant people may turn to the new technologies of physical control of behavior to find unprecedented methods for enhancing their minds. One can almost hear them paraphrasing a statement in John F. Kennedy's inaugural address: "The brain is an uncharted ocean and we intend to sail upon it."

Chapter 8

Enhancing the Significant People

> The old temple inscription "Know Thyself" is often
> repeated today, but perhaps it is not adequate. It should
> declare "Construct Thyself" as well. Shape your mind,
> train your thinking power, and direct your emotions
> more rationally; liberate your behavior from the ances-
> tral burdens of reptiles and monkeys — be a man and
> use your intelligence to orient the reactions of your
> mind.
>
> — José M. R. Delgado, *Physical Control of the Mind*

Improvement at the Apex

The sociologist Vilfredo Pareto described history as the
graveyard of elites. He believed that the circulation of the
elite, in which the ruling structure of a society changes as its
old elite becomes anachronistic or decadent, was the essential
cause of social renewal. Consequently, the primary interest
of most studies of elitism is in the changing balances of social
power implied in the fall of the old leadership and the rise
of a new leadership to take its place. This is certainly the
perspective that critics such as C. Wright Mills and Thorstein
Veblen bring to their analyses of American elitism. And they
are not alone in the traditional sociological view that attri-
butes the failure of an elite to rule effectively to its unwill-

ingness or inability to adapt itself to new values required by changing times.

Seldom, if ever, has history recorded an instance where an elite desperately wanted to adapt to new leadership demands but could not because they had reached the normal limits of their *psychophysical capacities* to absorb information, to make qualitative judgments about it, and to take action accordingly. However, as we suggested in the last chapter, the significant people are being brought to these limits by crises of complexity and interdependency. Extraordinary measures for extending these limits may prove necessary.

Dr. José Delgado, a pioneer researcher in the physical control of the brain, urged us in the quotation above to take a hand in our own evolution, and B. F. Skinner has repeated this admonition. "A scientific view of man offers exciting possibilities," he wrote. "We have not yet seen what man can make of man." [1] This mandate — that humans must take a hand in their own evolution — is not metaphorical. For Skinner, Delgado, and others doing research on the physical control of behavior, it is a literal injunction.

They reason that modern science (medical, pharmacological, biological, and behavioral) is rapidly developing the technical capability to alter fundamental human mental processes, and that through it people must change their present evolutionary course because their capacity for mischief is reducing the survival potential of the species. But beyond the simple mischief factor, we are naturally limited in our ability to manage effectively the complex interdependencies we have created.

Until now, human beings seem to have used their science and technology to destroy as much as to create. Now people, according to the argument, must use their science and technology on themselves, specifically on their brains, to expand their capacity to deal with their complex environment. The promise stemming from such applications of technology is

that we will finally be able to shed the self-destructive burdens inherited from our evolutionary past. We will become
truly liberated, both rationally and emotionally. Conversely,
if we fail to direct our own evolution scientifically, chances
are that humanity is finished as a species.

The prospect of mind enhancement by physical technology, such as electrical and chemical stimulation of the brain,
has led to impassioned debates. On the one hand, those
suspicious of and hostile to the use of mind technologies
argue that they could be used by despots to control humanity. Immediately the "brave new world" of Aldous Huxley
comes to mind. On the other hand, the proponents of mind
technology denounce such critics as engaging in antiscientific
scare tactics. They invoke the battle cry of free scientific
inquiry to support their cause, contending that the eventual
results of research into behavior modification technology
will create a renaissance of the mind for us all. Further, they
believe that such research is absolutely necessary if we are to
triumph over the machines and organizations of our own
making. Finally, the proponents of mind technology dismiss
arguments concerning the enslavement of the masses on the
grounds of sheer logistics. It would be too complicated and
expensive to apply this technology to the nation's millions,
let alone the world's billions.

The debate continues, and it is currently taking an interesting turn. Professor Elliot S. Valenstein, in an article in
Psychology Today, argued that science fiction was misleading
people about the capabilities of mind technology to control
behavior.[2] He is concerned that a neo–Luddite uprising is in
the making that will block further brain research. He defends
not only the freedom of scientific inquiry, but also the potential of brain research to cure brain-related diseases.

Both arguments have merit. On the one hand, behavior
modification could become an instrument of mass control.
But on the other hand, these technologies may be able to
raise the level of human performance profoundly. Can these

seemingly disparate arguments of the opponents and supporters of brain technology be reconciled?

The implicit assumption of the evolve-or-else position is that either all people will be saved together as equals through this evolution or all people will equally perish. The equality of individuals in salvation or damnation does not leave much room for elitism, and, as a matter of fact, not much on this subject is found in the current literature of behavior modification and control.[3] A curious lack of attention has been paid to the elitist potential in modern brain technology, for most contemporary critics seem to think that brain technology will be used on the mass of humanity for any reason, good or bad. Indeed, certain forms of this technology, such as bliss-trip drugs, may be available for mass consumption. But those technologies specifically targeted at enhancement will *not* be available to the masses. They will be used by the significant people to achieve excellence in their performance. Very simply, *physical brain control technology* may be used for the purpose of enhancing the behavior and performance of some, *but not all,* people.

We have discussed the enhancement of the significant people through brain technology with many groups around the country, beginning in 1973.[4] These groups have included practicing managers, students, and professional colleagues. Our audiences' reactions ranged from amusement, outrage, or acquiescence to enthusiastic acceptance. Some thought we were joking; a number were angered; most responded with resignation; and a few even seemed interested in getting in on the ground floor. Those who thought we were joking accused us of hyperbole: "Who ever heard of such a thing outside science fiction?" The reply was easy. There is plenty of evidence to demonstrate that many individuals are trying to enhance themselves right now. The most obvious example is the legion of people who use drugs to heighten entertainment experiences, like movies or rock concerts. But there are other examples, including the use of amphetamines by students before examinations or by executives before an important sales presentation.

Those who were outraged thought we advocated an artificially enhanced elite: "You are trying to create a Fourth Reich." We believe we convinced them that that was not our intention, but they were so impassioned we cannot be sure. But the most poignant response of all was that of those who acquiesced: "Yes, enhancement of an elite through mind technology is a terrible prospect, but what else can be done in the face of such overwhelming organizational needs?" Or: "Yes, this is just the kind of technology we need to set everything straight." As crises have mounted in recent years, this last category of respondents has been growing.

A frightening aspect of these reactions was that at no time did anyone ask: "Can we really do it scientifically and technologically?" Our audiences seemed convinced that no physical problem is impossible to solve technically, and this includes the physical modification of behavior. This tacit acceptance of its feasibility is a warning sign, for it represents a massive cultural preparation for what *could* come technologically. Serious articles on this subject appear regularly in the respectable press, from such prestigious sources as the *Wall Street Journal* and *Fortune* to more "in" journals like *Psychology Today* and *Playboy.* An article by Vance Packard on mind-enhancing drugs designed to increase intelligence appeared in the magazine appropriately named *Mainliner Magazine,* the inflight journal of United Airlines.[5] The readership of these publications is not only the significant people but also the rising, affluent, young professional class from which the next generation of significant people will be drawn.

Scientists are still some distance from developing completely tested, reliable, and marketable techniques for mind enhancement. But Americans, especially the young and upwardly mobile, are culturally conditioned by their faith in technology to believe that all problems have a technological solution that can be discovered if enough resources are allocated to them.[6] This premise must be examined. But first two related subjects have to be discussed. We must decide, tentatively of course, what enhancement means, and we must identify, again tentatively, what brain functions are likely targets for enhancement.

The Physical Modification of Managerial Behavior

Enhancing the Normal

Normal behavior is extraordinarily difficult to define, as it is considered relative to individuals, cultures, social situations, times, and places. Nevertheless the fields of law, psychiatry, and social work focus on behaviors that deviate from the normal. Lawyers, social workers, and psychiatrists therefore must think of deviation from something specific, something that an individual or a society considers normal in terms of self-image or appropriate behavior. It is fair to say, too, that current medical practice, including psychiatry, is therapeutically oriented to raise performance, mood, or cognitive processes that are believed to be below normal.[7]

In order to improve subnormal or deviant behavior, an idea of normality must be at hand in the form of a model or an operational definition. We define *normality* as a cognitive and behavioral basing point that results from the interaction between individuals and their reference groups. Normality is then a baseline against which the behavior of individuals is compared with the norms they set for themselves, the norms defined by a social group, or the norms set by society at large. In daily living, individuals oscillate in mood and performance about their baseline. Figure 4 illustrates this notion.

All people have periods when they feel "up" or "down." These mood oscillations are common and usually create few

FIGURE 4

The Baseline Concept of Normality

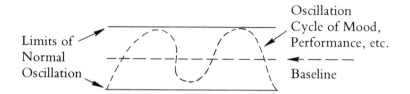

difficulties so long as they remain within the limits of generally accepted normal behavior. If they do exceed the limits and the period is short, they seldom require professional attention. But this is a simplified illustration of normality. We must move on to an expanded depiction of the idea, as illustrated in Figure 5.

The standard state represents normal behavior, situationally defined by commonly accepted norms and expectations of role performance. It provides the criteria for defining State A, which is substandard behavior, and State B, which is superior behavior. These three states have four components: cognitive performance (processes like decision-making or creativity); cognitive organization (abstract reasoning capacity or intelligence); affectivity (the ability to relate interpersonally with other people on a number of emotional and intellectual levels); self-integration (individual recognition of the continuity of a personal identity, unbroken and undiminished by time).

States A and B represent cognitive, affective, and integrative processes that are either inferior or superior to the criteria used to define normality in the standard state. Accordingly, *deviance* is defined as any behavior that varies beyond the limits of the standard state. This is not entirely the case, however, since there are zones of overlap between states into which mood and performance may oscillate temporarily, as can be seen in Figure 5. For example, people who are nor-

184   The Roles in Organizational America

FIGURE 5

Normality in Three Behavioral States

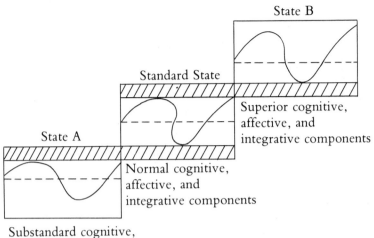

State B

Standard State

Superior cognitive,
affective, and
integrative components

State A

Normal cognitive,
affective, and
integrative components

Substandard cognitive,
affective, and
integrative components

Key:

--- Baseline (normal) behavior
for a state

⌒⌄ Cyclical variations of
behavior within limits that
define the states

////// Overlapping areas
between behavioral states

mally in the standard state will experience periods when they perform over their heads and other times when they are not up to par. However, they will usually function around the baseline of their normal state. Likewise, persons who are seriously impaired psychologically can have good and bad days. They may have stretches of considerable lucidity, indicated by the upper peak of the cycle in State A that could even reach into the overlapping segment of the standard state, but most of the time they, too, function around a baseline of substandard performance *that is normal for their condition*. A logically parallel case can be made for the relationship between the standard state and State B, representing superior performance.

State B, or superiority, has not received as much professional attention as the conditions of inferiority. The bulk of professional effort — and this includes medical research and clinical practice — has been directed toward State A, since this is where the most serious psychological disabilities are found. The obvious purpose of the therapies used in State A cases is to raise an individual's functional level toward the standard state. However, therapeutic practices have been extended to include the troughs in the normal cycle of the standard state. They are often considered mild illnesses for which treatment may be legitimately prescribed. Therefore, both the inferior psychological conditions found in State A and cyclically subpar conditions in the standard state are matters of clinical concern. The main objectives of current medical practice are relatively clear: to raise the level of individual baselines, especially in State A; to prolong cyclical oscillations at or above the baselines of State A and the standard state; and to smooth out the transitions between cyclical oscillations.

Thus, clinical intervention in psychological and behavioral processes exists to achieve one or a combination of two ends. First, it is often desirable to relieve patients' suffering from temporary psychological or physiological disruptions that cause them to function below their normal baseline. A considerable amount of psychotherapy and drug technology serves this purpose. Second, the more dramatic forms of intervention attempt to raise the baseline of individual psychological functioning, especially in instances where such behavior is initially substandard. While a permanent upward shift of baseline behavior is not always possible, in some cases it is possible to smooth out oscillations in a substandard state so that the average duration of behavior at or above the baseline is longer after the intervention than before it. The forms of psychotechnology used in these cases range across a spectrum that includes conventional psychotherapy, psychotropic drugs, electrical brain stimulation, and psychosurgery.

Enhancing the Significant People

In the past, managerial performance was augmented by support technologies from a number of applied sciences in the expectation that their use would improve executive performance. Traditionally, therefore, managers were augmented by technologies outside their skins, with the assumption that these technologies would advance at a pace commensurate with the problems that had to be solved. The implicit standard of normal managerial performance was that managers had to be capable of performing *at the level of their support systems.* Substandard managers were winnowed out while those remaining engaged in a race between retirement and obsolescence.

The kinds of external augmentation with which we are most familiar have placed a considerable strain on individuals attempting to keep up with the requirements of their job. That stress is responsible, in part, for encouraging the use of crude forms of psychotechnology to help managers feel better when they must confront the crushing burdens of modern management. It is correct to say that managerial drug use — and this includes alcohol, tobacco, amphetamines, and tranquilizers — is frequently a fumbling attempt to enhance personal effectiveness, however vaguely defined. Individuals hope to adjust the cyclical variations in their standard state — to calm agitation, to alleviate depression, or to stimulate performance — in order to be more effective in coping with the problems of the moment.

This type of drug use is negative in the sense that drugs are supposed to help overcome mental states that inhibit normal effectiveness. However, an article in *Fortune* hints that this may be changing: "New drugs promise to help *normal* people in many different ways, from improving their creative capabilities to easing the pain of divorce."[8] The author went on to describe drugs that might promote certain forms of enhancement. But the overall impact of this article is very conservative, for it barely flirts with the idea of managerial enhancement. Psychotechnology has not been widely used to transport individual managers to levels of performance beyond their natural and conventionally acquired abilities. But this is precisely what is indicated when superior performance from the significant people is necessary for coping with the superhuman demands of their jobs.

The Cognitive Targets of Enhancement

Keeping in mind that what might be technically needed might not yet be available, we must still identify the cognitive processes of managers that are the most likely targets for enhancement. The difficulty is that higher cognitive processes cannot be isolated for independent study or easily reduced to constituent functions. However, managers probably would be pleased if they could raise, or maintain, their level of performance in decision-making, aggressiveness, and creativity for longer periods of time.

Decision-making embraces such mental activities as data assimilation, memory and recall, information interpretation and integration, and the formulation and evaluation of alternatives. Computer-based, managerial information systems are designed for the most part to buttress the decision-making activity. However, they have so far been mainly useful in extending the range of data assimilation, memory, and recall. Computer techniques have been applied to interpretation and evaluation also, but they are successful in simple situations only, where the boundaries of a problem can be unequivocally defined in mathematical terms.

Aggressiveness pertains to the *motivation* to act upon the environment once a decision has identified and given weight to alternatives.[9] Aggressiveness is different from hostility, since aggression is an active passion that often produces positive results for the individual and for organizations, whereas hostility is often destructive to both. Aggressiveness makes use of a different set of cognitive processes than decision-making: Decision-making requires reflection; aggressiveness requires execution. Both processes are indispensable in management practice.

Creativity is an individual's cognitive ability to generate different combinations of concepts, responses, and ideas in familiar surroundings. It is the ability to pick up a stick from a different end and thereby use it in another way. The decision to pick up a different end of the stick, and the incentive to look at the same old stick from another perspective, are creative acts. They require cognitive processes that are different from decision-making and aggressiveness.

A test for the validity of these three enhancement targets is the question: "If you, as a manager, could improve your cognitive performance in order to do your job better, what mental processes would you select to enhance?" Our hunch is that the answers would follow these lines: "I wish I could make better decisions. I wish I could make my influence in policy decisions felt more. I wish I could find innovative solutions to persistent organizational problems." The content of most executive development programs is designed to improve the decision-making, motivational, and creative capabilities of managers, with one major exception. This exception is the trend in recent years toward developing the competence of managers in interpersonal (or affective) relationships. All these programs draw heavily from the behavioral sciences, like psychology, for their methods and concepts.

It is fairly clear that such programs simply cannot enhance managerial performance either sufficiently or fast enough to meet the demands of crisis. In and of themselves, the applied behavioral sciences are unpredictable in their behavior modification results and expensive in their application. Their techniques, which are designed to help managers cope with their environment, have failed to deliver the tangible benefits so urgently sought by management and so glibly pledged by consultants. For instance, a good many of the sensitivity training programs used to enhance teamwork among managers have produced only temporary benefits. The participants seem to need constant reinforcement.

But the difficulties with the present means of enhancement do not end with the shortcomings of applied behavioral science. Other techniques like management information systems or specialized staff groups in organizations are extremely limited in their abilities, and they become more glaringly deficient the higher one goes in the organization. Modern staff support groups and computerized management information systems have extended the range of management decision-making by supplying information that is usually superior to that available in the past. However, they are not very useful when action in high positions eventually comes down, as it must, to personal decision-making, motivation, and creativity. Short of finding a monkey's paw with three wishes left, technologies for physical intervention in brain processes *seem* to be the only remaining alternatives in the future that promise to enhance these managerial powers.

The Techniques of Behavior Modification

Indirect Nonphysical Interventions

Behavior modification is as old as the human race, and achieving it by physical means might be considered just another form of intervention. Figure 6 illustrates a continuum of various institutions and techniques that control and

FIGURE 6

Institutions and Techniques of Behavior Modification

Family	Small group	Tribe	Religion	Government	Organization	Formal education — general	Formal education — special (college, vocational, executive development)	Personal enrichment	training (T-groups, group process, group integration)	Organizational development	Psychiatry	Advertising and the mass media	Radical behaviorism (operant conditioning)	Psychosurgery	Electrical stimulation of the brain	Neuropsychopharmacology

modify human behavior. It is intended to be suggestive, not inclusive.

This continuum is significant in three ways. First, to the left of the solid vertical line are examples of general types of socialization widespread in familiar institutions: the family, the tribe, religion. These narrow to more specific techniques of influence and control, like encounter groups, executive development, and vocational training. As one moves from left to right on the continuum, the more specific the behavior-modification process becomes. For example, it is one thing to socialize children's behavior to the customs of a tribe or community, but it is another to use psychiatry to try to help an individual overcome a mental problem (e.g., unfocused rage), to get mass endorsement of an idea (e.g., energy conservation), or to obtain consumer acceptance of a product (e.g., Doublemint gum).

Second, the techniques and institutions for behavior modification to the left of the solid line involve indirect, non-physical interventions. On the right of the dotted vertical line are physical intervention techniques for altering mood and other cognitive states. These techniques are significantly different in nature from any of the indirect interventions. Therefore, it is not surprising that suspicion surrounds them as methods for creating behavioral change. Physical intervention tends to be less acceptable socially *and* technically than the conventional techniques.

Third, radical behaviorism, in the Skinnerian operant conditioning mold, has a rather special place on the continuum since it bridges the conventional and the physical techniques of behavior modification. Heretofore, the orientation of the neo-Skinnerian behaviorists has been to take from the social environment the rewards or punishments needed for reinforcing desired or extinguishing unwanted behaviors. Experience shows that this approach, by itself, is a limited way of achieving behavior modification. But the combination of radical behaviorism with physical control technology, particularly in the form of drugs, could become an extremely powerful behavior-modification technique. Given this brief background, we consider the two direct physical interventions that seem to have the most immediate promise of application to the problem of managerial enhancement.[10]

Direct, Physical Interventions

ELECTRICAL STIMULATION OF THE BRAIN (ESB)

Dr. José Delgado has observed that ESB is a technique that establishes direct communication with the brain. By implanting electrical probes in specified brain areas, and by stimulating these areas with an electrical charge emitted through the probe, certain kinds of behavioral responses can be reliably evoked.[11] This ability to establish direct communication with the brain is enormously significant. Unlike psychotherapy, it is unnecessary to go through the intermediary senses to influence behavior. Communication is direct, reaction is immediate, and feedback from behavior lags only momentarily. So for a wide variety of behaviors, ranging from motor response through some affective states to certain kinds of social behavior, ESB is an efficient way to achieve results of an either experimental or therapeutic nature.

The definitive judgment on ESB as an effective enhancement technology is yet to be made, as most research using ESB has been done on animals. So, while motor responses can be precisely evaluated, and certain primitive psychological states (rage) and social behavior (dominance) can be observed and measured, moods and attitudes under ESB control are difficult to appraise other than inferentially.

In order to determine the effect of ESB on humans, research must be done on humans, although there are significant prohibitions against such research at present.[12] Most of the research occurs in clinical situations, where the individuals available for experimentation are often being treated for major illnesses, like Parkinson's disease, epilepsy, or severe psychotic disorders.

The lack of research on human subjects prolongs professional ignorance about the effects of ESB on higher brain functions. Some interesting research has been conducted on the effects of ESB on memory and recall,[13] but as far as other cognitive processes are concerned, such as decision-making and creativity, virtually nothing is understood. Consequently, the capability of ESB for enhancement of the sort described in State B in Figure 5 is generally unexplored and unknown. The potential of ESB for modifying affective states has had some limited experimental demonstration. By stimulating regions of the limbic system, hostile, even violent behavior, can be induced or suppressed in the subject.[14] But violent behavior is a far cry from the aggressiveness that is useful to managerial performance.

ESB has some technical disadvantages. Granted, it is valuable for brain-mapping: the discovery of the specific location of various response centers. In the literal sense of the word, probing is necessary to establish the exact point of a response in an individual, except in the case of the grossest behavioral manifestations, like general feelings of euphoria. Further, higher brain functions that take place in the neocortex are very complex, engaging a network of cortical and subcortical brain systems. Thus, there is no specific "point" in the brain associated with decision-making, motivation, or creativity. A panoply of brain activities are involved. Little is known about how ESB intervention can be used to enhance these complex networks.

Second, the hardware used in ESB is very sophisticated and expensive, even though the equipment and the techniques of its application have been highly refined. Delgado, for example, has developed miniaturized transceivers, telemetry hookups, and direct transmissions to and from computers so that subjects no longer have to be plugged into a controlling apparatus. Instead, control is accomplished by electronic signals between subject and computer without human intermediaries. Even so, some electronic monitoring appendage must be carried around on the skull, and probes must be implanted surgically in the brain. Not many people are likely to seek out such chilling procedures, except perhaps in circumstances that involve severe brain dysfunction.[15] Further, the logistics of ESB are such that it is impractical to apply this technology except to a few. As Delgado observed, it is inconceivable that ESB will be used as a means of mass control.[16] Given the imposing apparatus required, the need for a high level of specialized medical competence, the cosmetic problem, and the natural repugnance of having holes drilled in one's skull, it seems improbable that the significant people would elect this method as a means of enhancement, even if it were possible to achieve.

NEUROPSYCHOPHARMACOLOGY

In practically every society, drugs for the chemical stimulation of the brain (CSB) are known and used either ritualistically, recreationally, or therapeutically.[17] Common drugs of this variety come from natural agents, including coffee, tobacco, alcohol, cannabis, java, peyote, and cocoa. In recent years many new drugs have been synthesized, such as the various amphetamines, diazepam, chlorpromazine, and lysergic acid diethylamide (LSD). Psychotropic drugs range from mild stimulants and depressants to potent compounds designed to treat cases of extreme psychotic behavior. Hallucinogens, or drugs that produce illusions (like LSD), are a third category of psychologically pro-active agents. There is hardly any need to document the wide use of these drugs (uppers, downers, transporters) with or without medical supervision.

The purpose of CSB is to induce changes in mood or behavior. However, most of the common natural and synthetic drugs are taken amateurishly. Often mere gross effects are sought by the drug taker: a jolt to wake up in the morning, relief from tension to go to sleep at night, a feeling of euphoria, a sense of sharing a pleasant experience with others. Psychotropic drug use is not usually fine tuned to subtle changes in mood behavior. Nevertheless people drug themselves constantly with agents that are readily available or supplied on prescription by a doctor, and a considerable amount of psychotropic drug consumption in America is a relatively casual but widely accepted practice, both medically and socially. While such acceptance is important for establishing the legitimacy of drug use, the present patterns of drug consumption are not terribly efficient for achieving complex enhancement goals.

One of the most important elements in psychotropic drug administration is the development and application of a program of drug consumption tailored to the specific enhancement needs of the subject. In such circumstances, using the right drug or a combination of drugs at the right time, under the constant attention of an expert, seems to be the minimum requirement. The role of the experts is crucial; they must be in a position to orchestrate the administration of drugs to the subjects in order to modulate the nuances of behavioral change while the subject is under care.

The experts, of course, must not only be well informed on the effects of psychotropic drugs on normal people, but they must also be familiar with the physical and psychological condition of the subject taking the drugs. Only in this way will the proper drugs be given with appropriate timing to suit the changing moods and environmental conditions of the subject so that the desired effects can be achieved.

No one drug or group of drugs used casually or amateurishly will produce the refined adjustments necessary for enhancement. From the standpoint of the significant people, the implications of this statement are considerable. In order to achieve the degree of refined usage necessary to enhance behavior, individuals would need access to highly advanced psychopharmacological resources, both the drugs themselves and, even more important, the experts in their use. Clearly such resources are not available to most people, but they could be to the management elite.

Presently some researchers and journalists alike write optimistically about the coming availability of synthetic drugs that will produce sexual response, counteract senility, help people relive pleasurable experiences in order to face personal tragedy, and create intoxication without hangovers.[18] However, the chief puzzle for brain researchers to solve is how to develop drugs that can be used to enhance carefully targeted higher brain activities, such as intelligence, memory, decision-making, creativity, and so on.

Three practical difficulties stand in the way of a solution. First, the direction of present research, the focus of clinical practice, and the orientation of the drug industry are aimed at curing the ill rather than enhancing normal individuals. Second, and as a consequence of the first situation, few medical experts are able to administer drugs in an enhancement program. Third, even though a large portion of our population uses drugs to alter mood and behavior, there are powerful social prohibitions against some of these practices. This may seem paradoxical, but it is not. It is generally considered permissible for people to fumble inefficiently in their personal use of mind-altering drugs, but any efficient but undemocratic attempt to pump up a minority with drugs that would make them superior to everyone else would encounter imposing social taboos. Politicians who are known alcoholics get re-elected regularly; but how far would these same politicians get if their constituency were aware that they were being constantly attended by a team of neuropsychopharmacologists?

The State of the Enhancing Art

The brain sciences are not yet able to perform feats of enhancement for the significant people. However, the scientific research and theory necessary to the advancement of this art seems to be progressing rapidly. The major obstacles do not appear to be technical problems, but the clinical *applications*.

The scientific-technological scenario may unfold in the following way. ESB can evoke certain responses in isolated brain segments, which provide the targets for psychotropic drug research. The purpose of this research is to discover drugs that create the same response chemically that brain probes create electrically. Therefore, an essential scientific link exists between CSB and ESB. ESB is a primary research tool, while CSB has the clinical potential for practical behavior modification.

Drug taking is far more convenient and logistically feasible than ESB. It can be concealed, whereas the elaborate procedures of ESB are difficult to hide. Drugs are less fearsome for the individual, and they are more socially acceptable. Current research indicates that strides are being made to increase the specificity of drugs in order to permit more precise control over particular brain functions.[19] Further, the enormous research and development capacity of the drug industry is available if the production and marketing of chemical enhancers are economically feasible. In short, the chief problem at present is the social taboos that surround the clinical use of psychotropic drugs in human experimental settings and in the practical use of such drugs by people seeking enhancement. Thus, legal, political, and social attitudes will help to determine when and if the state of the art of enhancement will advance.

The Psycho-Economy of Enhancement

The scientific research that underlies technological development does not happen randomly. It follows the flow of resources that reflect what policy-makers in the public sector think are social needs and what business leaders in the private sector think are market demands. In the last fifteen years need/demand analyses for psychotechnology were profoundly influenced by economics and psychiatry rather than by value philosophy. The technological advances in this field were the result of the allocation of more research dollars, which was eventually translated into the production and distribution of an enormous variety of psychotropic drugs.

These drugs, which are the most widely used clinical agents for direct brain interventions, are an offshoot of psychiatry. Historically, psychiatry has consistently enlarged the definition of mental illness. It started, at the time of Freud, with the most obvious psychological diseases, and kept expanding its area of application so that now many aspects of behavior previously considered normal fall into a category of psychological malfunctions needing treatment. The point is that as new psychological ailments are discovered, new drugs come on the market offering relief. People demand them, drug companies make them, and the medical profession prescribes them. The citizens of organizational America are not very patient about enduring anxiety or depression, let alone more serious ailments. Thus, tension, anxiety, and stress are big markets, which is reflected in the huge sales of tranquilizers.

But it is important to appreciate the social aspects of the prescription use of psychotropic drugs. One of the main factors in the acceptance of drug technology is the prior acceptance by the public and then by the medical profession that certain behaviors are psychiatrically defined symptoms of mental disorders. For example, tension is a relatively moderate psychological malady found with high frequency among otherwise normal American adults. Since tension may impair effective performance, it is accepted that it should be treated with tranquilizing drugs. The reasoning is similar to that which decides to nurse a sore toe that interferes with walking.

Clearly, public and professional acceptance underlie the economic motivation for the development and marketing of psychotropic drugs. But the situation is not quite that simple. As Gerald L. Klerman observed: "In large part, the motivation of the pharmaceutical and advertising industries is economic; their intent is to widen the size of the drug user market by extending the rationale of drug use to include relief of minor symptoms related to emotional stress."[20]

The economics of the drug industry rely upon an ever-increasing demand for its products. Given the highly competitive nature of the industry, this cannot be achieved without the diligent efforts of advertising agencies and vigorous marketing programs for prescription and proprietary drug products such as Valium or Cope. So the development of psychotropic drug technology is the result of a self-reinforcing set of conditions that include principally: the social acceptance of drug use for psychological disorders that cover a span of intensity from mild to severe; medical acknowledgment and prescription of such drugs as therapeutic for the relief of these disorders; and the profitable business opportunities that are promised to the pharmaceutical industry for its research and sales efforts. But running through these events is the current of public sentiment that is probably the critical factor in the present drug orientation of our society. There is no need to dwell on the fact that we are a pill-popping people and expect instant relief from most every physical and psychological affliction.

Where formerly religion or mysticism served the purpose, we now seek scientific and psychological explanations of the inexplicable. However, psychiatry itself has undergone some important changes. Perry London notes three stages of fashionable mental disorders.[21] During Freud's time, hysteria as a symptom of the sexual repression of the late Victorian period was "in." Hysteria gave way to anxiety and depression as the hallmark psychological sicknesses of our era. In the future, London suggests, this will be displaced by ennui or boredom. If one goes along with his argument and couples it with the idea that psychiatry is an important factor in the development of psychotropic drugs, then some drug prescriptions in the future will help people overcome the "illness" of boredom.[22] The third era is here, and the recreational use of drugs obtained through both legal and illegal sources is evidence of its presence. Thus, the need/demand analysis of psychological disorders in vogue during a period are the real forces behind the development of psychotropic drug technology.

But there is another possibility for London's third stage, not an alternative but a possible parallel outcome. Suppose that the inability to manage organizational crises becomes so acute that the significant people are unable to fulfill expectations for excellent performance. Their incapacitation could be defined as an occupational mental illness.[23] Given the desire of Americans for psychiatric explanations of behavior, such a definition is quite likely to be made. From this point it is just a small step to expect a response to this new "illness" in the form of research and clinical technology that would enhance the significant people, thereby increasing their managing capacities. Brain technology would be demanded because most of what this elite does requires brainwork.

There is a subtle aspect to this definitional gambit. Calling the failure of the elite to perform effectively a mental illness places this problem squarely within the medical model. This model is endowed with enormous authority. If the significant people suffer from the *illness* of being ineffectual in the face of crises, then what could be more reasonable than to cure them with whatever medical technology seems appropriate? By a single definitional stroke, the social taboo vanishes against using direct physical intervention to create superior people. The issue is redefined into the well-understood and completely acceptable model of helping normal people overcome a "sickness" that impairs their performance.

The need/demand factors that underlie the psycho-economy of brain technology are highly variable. Who can predict what will happen to public and professional attitudes toward the research necessary for developing the sciences that might enhance normal people who perform significant jobs? We suggest that the probability is high for a shift in resources toward such research in mind enhancement, given the likelihood that failure to do so will seriously jeopardize the health of the great system of modern organizations.

On the scientific and medical fronts also, who can predict with any degree of confidence that even with the resources, research could actually produce a true enhancement technology? But what if the billions of research dollars allocated to the space program, in answer to the challenge of the Soviet Sputnik, had instead been directed toward brain enhancement research? There is little doubt that enormous advances would have been made. In the end, since most Americans have an unquestioning faith in applied science, why not direct it toward making some people superior, so that they may lead the organizations upon which we are so greatly dependent more effectively? Why not indeed!

The Dilemma over Enhancing the Significant People

Issues like crisis episodes, the scientific feasibility of physical enhancement, the economic and social question of need/demand analysis, and the definitional problems of mental illness beg the central question: *Is it right to create superior people through the scientific means of direct physical intervention in brain processes?* [24] Regardless of their feelings about elitism, it must have occurred to some people that perhaps certain regions of the human brain are like game preserves, inviolable, and that poaching on these preserves is wrong. To some contemporary thinkers, like B. F. Skinner, this moral dilemma merely reflects obsolete romantic idealism. The proper subject of discussion from their point of view is whether enhancement is *necessary,* not whether it is right or wrong.

Beyond these value issues, why would the significant people even begin to entertain the possibility of enhancing themselves? What conceivable justification, beyond necessity, is there for doing it? While necessity may be reason enough, it still may not be adequate for some significant people, who cling to a lingering idealism about the innateness of human nature. Obviously, more than mere necessity is required to justify enhancement.

So we repeat the question: Why might the elite want to do such a thing? The answer is: for the entirely decent reason of being able to respond with amplified sensitivity and effectiveness to the crises of interdependency that afflict every advanced organizational society. In other words, the significant people will do it for you and me, so that we can continue to enjoy the comforts and security that organizational America provides.

The significant people, dominating the organizational and technical apparatus of America, have access to brain technologies unavailable to the rest of us. But this elite is composed of ordinary, overworked, hard-pressed individuals, who are frantically seeking ways to maintain the health of their organizations as required by the organizational imperative. So when offered a brain technology that will enhance their normal capacities, coupled with the self-justifying ethic of the significant job, more than sufficient grounds can be found to encourage the significant people to make use of these technologies.

An element of science fiction is present in all of this, and we hesitate to exploit it for fear of weakening the seriousness of the position we have taken in this and the previous chapter. Yet, in his science fiction *Dune* trilogy, Frank Herbert writes about the Guild of Space Steersmen, who, to navigate safely across space, had to take a drug that gave them prevision to foresee perilous events before they occurred.[25] The irresistible temptation is to draw a parallel between the prevision of the Space Steersmen and the planning the significant people must do in order to control events that endanger the modern organization. In a metaphorical sense, an enhanced significant people become "celestial navigators," endowed with powers bestowed by technology that permit them to use their skills more effectively on behalf of human welfare.

Whether or not brain enhancement is the elitist wave of the future is a matter for speculation. Prophecy is not yet a full-scale science. Nevertheless, it seems that Americans must make a Hobson's choice: between organizational collapse resulting from an incapacitated elite or an enhanced elite who are made superior to everyone else by technology. Muddling along is not an option anymore. We no longer live in an age when freedom can co-exist with a system of despotism tempered by inefficiency, as Victor Adler described his native Austria in 1889.

Part III

The Fate of
Organizational America

Chapter 9

The Probable Future

It was a world half convinced of the future death of our
species yet half aroused by the apocalyptic notion that
an exceptional future still lay before us. So it was a
century which moved with the most magnificent display of power into directions it could not comprehend.
The itch was to accelerate — the metaphysical direction
unknown.

> — Norman Mailer, *Of a Fire on the Moon*

The Drift into Totalitarian America

Time and circumstance invariably lead all nations into revolutionary periods wherein they must make profound alterations or perish. New conditions and new attitudes put so
much pressure upon established values and institutions that
fundamental changes that must be more than fine tunings of
the status quo become necessary. Sometimes such revolutions rip societies to shreds and completely new political
forms rise from the ruins. Other times, the result of revolution is an amalgam of elements of the old institutions fused
with elements of the new. This synthesis alters institutions
so that they are both sufficiently familiar to keep the society
functioning, yet modern enough to respond to contemporary
demands.

Organizational America is entering one of these historic

revolutionary periods. It will probably not be violent, but it will result in drastic changes in our society. Some anticipate such changes with blind optimism, for they believe in a benevolent American dialectic, in which the forces of history will invariably combine to produce an even better society. We believe such faith is misplaced, for there is no guaranteed utopia waiting for us.

But if there is no inevitable millennium, there is a probable destination. We have alluded to the multiple crises that will require solutions from the significant people. As these crises accumulate and as people grow more fearful, the temptation will be to grasp for security in a highly centralized, authoritarian state. And, as a way out, leaders will be only too happy to respond. As George Reedy, former press secretary to President Lyndon Johnson, correctly observed: "A society confronted with insoluble problems usually turns to its organs of repression."[1]

The United States has heard the clamor for authoritarian rule from the earliest days of the Republic. After the American Revolution, the accumulation of crises produced constant demands to establish everything from a monarchy to a military dictatorship. Had it not been for the courage of the most influential political leaders of the age, our democratic institutions would never have been established, let alone have survived.

It did not end there, of course, for the pressures for authoritarianism have surged and declined throughout our history: The repression of dissent by the federal government in the North during the Civil War, the unjust treatment of the Japanese Americans during World War II, and the shameful witch hunts of the Cold War are some examples. Americans have often looked to the illusory security of state authoritarianism in times of national crisis, real or imagined. None of these occasions provoked a revolution.

Behind the dramatic ebb and flow of our history, however, a truly revolutionary force has been gathering momentum: the modern organization. Its presence was felt before the Civil War, but its influence began to accelerate in the late nineteenth century as industrialization and urbanization eroded the values and institutions of individual America. By World War I we were well on our way to organizational America.[2] A few protested this profound shift in values, but the great majority did not really comprehend what was happening.[3] After World War I, the changes in our value system were obscured as we entered a tumultuous half-century of booms and busts, of hot and cold wars. The withering away of the values of the individual imperative was scarcely noticed until, by the mid 1970s, the values of the organizational imperative had more or less replaced them once and for all.

The transition to a fully organized state is not quite complete, for even now there is a residue of tenacious loyalty by some to the values of the individual imperative. Although the organizational imperative is dominant in America, the pressures of present and future crises are working for the total elimination of all vestiges of the individual imperative. *It has been the residue of commitment to the individual values of our past that has prevented the complete domination by the modern organization.* This compulsion to eradicate what remains of individualism in values is bringing America to the edge of a modern revolution.

The real danger lies not in the obvious incivilities of our contemporary society, since this is only a transitional stage out of which we must move. Organizational America is like a franchise motel: It is only a place to lay over before continuing the journey to a final destination. The precariousness of our age has come about because the security of the great interdependent system of modern organizations has taken precedence over the realization of the values of the individual imperative. The question is whether to continue our progress into a future given over totally to organizational maintenance or to restructure modern organizations around the needs of the individual.

The most probable answer to these questions lies in a basic fact about social change: No society changes all its values and institutions at once. Successful change depends upon the durability of some essential institution within the society — the army, the church, or something else. The fate of a society during a revolutionary period is most often guided by the most enduring institution.

The sturdiest institution in organizational America is the modern organization, and it will remain so through the transitional times ahead, providing continuity for our changing nation and shaping the future in which we will live. The odds highly favor the triumph of the organizational imperative, if for no other reason than that it has the inertia of material success going for it. It is our belief, and our great fear, that the waltz of history will culminate in a totalitarian America, a monolithic society that is the logical culmination of the organizational imperative, unimpeded by any residue of the values of individualism.

The word "totalitarian" immediately summons up images of a grim Orwellian state, governed by manifestoes enforced by jackbooted thugs. Indeed, most of the familiar totalitarian regimes have displayed just these characteristics. But it is a serious mistake to be distracted by dictatorial trappings and an even greater mistake to dismiss totalitarianism as just another form of dictatorship, with which the world is so familiar.

Only a few scholars have correctly analyzed the totalitarian trend.[4] Totalitarianism is the only truly modern form of government, since its base of power is rooted in modern technology.[5] But this interpretation of totalitarianism does not go far enough. Technology is meaningless without the modern organization, which links it to human attitudes and behavior. Without the organization, technology is as useless as humming machines on an empty, Daliesque plain. By encompassing all human behavior within the rules of technically advanced organizations, it is possible to obtain complete control over all people. *Thus, the modern organization is the essential feature of totalitarianism because it is the primary means of control.*

Totalitarian America is not an inevitable destination, although it would require extraordinary efforts to avoid it. At present, America is not a totalitarian nation for the single reason that there are still lingering traces of commitment to the individual imperative. Nevertheless, all the necessary elements for totalitarianism are present, save for the federal government assuming full power and bringing all organizations under its control. While it does not require much imagination to visualize any number of crises precipitating such an action, such crises will only hasten us in the direction in which we have been moving for so many years.

Slowly, an awareness of our national jeopardy has been growing. Interestingly, many of those most aware of our predicament are part of the national managerial system. But those managers who recognize the totalitarian threat are caught in a fearful dilemma. They are confronted with immediate organizational problems in a time of shrinking budgets, slackening productivity, interorganizational complexity, shortages of financial and material resources, inflationary operating costs, growing worldwide competition, political uncertainty, and bored employees.

These are the day-to-day problems of operating managers, and the conventional way to solve them is by strengthening their organizations. Most managers shrug off the great sweep of events external to their organizations, believing they can do little or nothing about them. They tend to "go with the flow," drift with events, and concentrate on making their own organizations more efficient.

The response of these "efficient drifters" is a modern version of what was called "muddling through" in the 1950s. Such behavior is aimed at preserving the organizational status quo by requiring managers to be at once doctrinaire and flexible. Efficient drifters want management practice to be more psychologically sophisticated; they want the organizational environment to be more humane; they want organizations to pursue good ends; and they emphasize the need for managers to be adept at handling contingencies. However, those committed to efficient drifting believe that before everything else must come the preservation of the modern organization, and all reforms must take place within the inviolable rules of the organizational imperative.

Compare the system of modern organizations to a raft, a very modern, comfortable raft that the managerial crew understands because they built it. The raft is drifting pleasantly downriver, presumably headed for a happy, if unspecified, destination. Suddenly, rapids are spotted some distance ahead, and both passengers and crew grow uneasy, sensing trouble. They could not only lose control, they could even lose the raft! Something must be done in a hurry. Under the circumstances, the only thing that appears reasonable to the efficient drifters is to keep on doing what they have been doing, only better. So plans are formulated, equipment is secured, the crew is given emergency assignments, the passengers are calmed. It is almost as if these routine emergency activities have a magic effect when performed with dispatch and faith. Passengers and managers are confident that they will ride out the rapids in safety, because surely nothing untoward can happen to such well-organized, well-intentioned, nice people.

Alternatives to toughing it out in the rapids are not considered for a variety of reasons: The current is too strong for backing up; the shores on either side are considered too unpleasant to risk beaching; the raft is too familiar and too valuable to abandon; and besides, all of their skills and training have been committed to rafting. Options to the predetermined drift downriver are simply unthinkable. Perhaps the raft *can* survive — but at a terrible cost. The danger the efficient drifters have barely perceived is that if the raft is not to founder and drown both passengers and crew, it will most certainly require an authoritarian chain of command and unquestioning obedience to orders. Rough water does not allow for democratic procedures, and it certainly does not permit any freedom or much dignity. What it requires is strenuous rowing! If the turbulence is short-lived, the reasoning goes, then the people can return to a more pleasant and democratic way of rafting. Unfortunately, the dangers stretch out far ahead, and once committed to a totalitarian course, it is extremely doubtful that the leaders would voluntarily surrender their positions of absolute authority.

If our society's destiny is left to the efficient drifters, we will surely be deposited into a totalitarian culture. The efficient drifters are unwilling to alter the organizational imperative and want to preserve the great system of modern organizations unaltered. As it now stands, the efficient drifters are in control, and the major responsibility for the preservation of large organizations is with them. When the threatening prospect of the use of mind enhancement techniques is added to this responsibility, there appears no way to avoid totalitarian America.

But totalitarian America offers, at best, an orderly life in troubled times. Most probably it will consign us to lives that will be unfulfilled, bleak, solitary, homogeneous, and sterile almost beyond our present comprehension. At worst, it could pitch us into the horrors of a garrison state. Hitler and Stalin are dead, but the voices of conscience still warn us of the sterility of human life in totalitarian societies, whether the People's Republic of China, the Soviet Union, or Cuba.

Granted, our traditions and circumstances are quite different from those of the nations cited. Nonetheless, we are in the process of developing our own version of total control. Its peculiar characteristics have been described throughout this book, but the fact that we are Americanizing totalitarianism should certainly not be reassuring. The "niceness" built into modern organizations is preferable to concentration camps and mass executions, but the single goal of totalitarianism, whatever its external window-dressing, is the complete control of all individuals by the central government through the modern organization and its complementary technology.

The tragic irony of our present situation is that we have the institutions that would allow individuals to realize their full potential. Our magnificent, albeit flawed, institutions of government, commerce, education, law, and religion can provide us with security, employment, consumer goods, learning, justice, and spiritual relief. We have the technology to liberate us from labor, giving us the possibility of work. We have the leisure time to permit individual intellectual and aesthetic development. We have communications systems to keep us informed and entertained. We have the productive capacity to provide everyone with reasonable economic well-being. Finally, we have the research and development capabilities to enable us to solve the confounding problems of energy, food, pollution, and the like. Most important, we are the beneficiaries of the original American Revolution, which established the rights of the individual over those of any despotic government. In short, all the necessary elements are present to enable us to achieve the dreams of the founders of the Republic. With all of our exalted ideals, our successful institutions, and our promising opportunities, what has gone wrong? Our misdirection is not the result of conspiracies or evil intentions, as we have tried to make clear. To the contrary, it is largely because our good intentions have been so successful that insufficient thought has been given to the long-range effects of the organizational imperative upon the individual. As our problems are human, so are their solutions.

Who Will Challenge the Organizational Imperative?

What happy combination of people, events, and circumstances could successfully challenge the organizational imperative? The common impression is that the impetus for reform must come from one of two sources. The first is the governing elite — the significant people. The second is the general populace — the insignificant people. However reform will not come from either of these sources, and if the future is left to them exclusively, totalitarian America is a virtual certainty. For reform to be achieved within the context of the modern organization, the momentum will have to be supplied by the professionals, with the support of the insignificant people. While we are skeptical that reform will occur from this quarter, it is the only straw we have left to grasp to keep us from drifting into totalitarianism.

Why Reform Will Not Come from the Significant People

The significant people could reform organizational America if they desired, but they will not. After all, they are the great beneficiaries of the power that comes from maintaining the status quo in the modern organization. If it were just a matter of the material comforts that come from wealth, then there might be more reason for optimism that they would institute the necessary reforms, for many persons of great wealth have devoted themselves to social improvement. The significant people are social conservatives, but theirs is a sort of conservatism that is rooted in headier rewards than the financial. They receive unending deference; they are excused from the monotonies of ordinary life; they have security; and at their level in the organizational hierarchy, value issues are simple.

Significant people are always surrounded by ranks of professionals who alter reality for them so that they will not be plagued by the incivilities of ordinary life. While rudeness, mediocrity, and boredom are the rule for the average citizen, such is not the case for the significant people. They believe that the continuous courtesy and praise they garner from their subordinates is their due. When criticism is necessary, it is usually given in a decorous manner. When they talk, others listen. When they tell jokes, others laugh. Lesser managers and other supplicants of the significant people imitate their manners and their dress — a most reassuring form of flattery — the majority must listen, laugh, and imitate.

Such homage has always been customary for any elite. Regardless, it does distort reality for the significant people. Remember that the regimen Plato required for those who would be philosopher-kings was spartan in the extreme. He knew what deference and distortion could do to one's ability to rule. In the American experience, George Reedy described the skewing of reality that occurs when the most significant person among significant people, the President, has all power at his disposal.[6] David Halberstam discussed how General Westmoreland's staff in Vietnam altered intelligence and battle reports to fit his preconception of how the war *should* be going.[7] Indeed, it takes extraordinary persons not to believe in the false realities generously provided by their staffs.

In spite of all the support, significant people sometimes fail to do their jobs well, or they get caught breaking laws. But even when these lapses receive widespread publicity, the significant people are protected. Very few are banished permanently to tract homes, let alone forced onto the welfare rolls. If they go astray, they get a slap on the wrist or a sabbatical for twelve to eighteen months in a minimum security federal prison, or they retire to elegant sulking in Grosse Pointe or San Clemente. The significant people have the most financially secure lives imaginable. It is almost as if there were a Benevolent Protective Association of Significant People. Obviously, these are perquisites that no sane person would want to jeopardize by ill-advised attempts at institutional reform.

But the main cause for the conservatism of the significant people is managerial careerism. It is an institutional tenure system that travels under the labels of "seniority" policies for civil employees and "promotion from within" policies for corporate employees. The net effect of these policies, as we have seen, is that managers are marinated in the values of their organization for many years before they advance to significant jobs. As Richard A. Gabriel and Paul L. Savage wrote: "The higher one's military status, the less one's tendency to perceive differences between the ideal military ethic and the way it operates in practice. Clearly, higher ranks perceive *less* of what is 'wrong' with the Army than lower ranks!"[8] The data in Chapter 7 on chief executive officer tenure in corporations give some insight into the practical consequences of these policies on managerial careers: People must be prepared to spend most of their lives with one organization in order even to aspire to its top slot.

There are many explanations for this phenomenon, but the critical one is that organizations need at their head people of demonstrated loyalty and reliability to the values that that organization represents. Writing about "organizational personality," Chester I. Barnard noted that "those who have a strong attachment to an organization . . . are likely to have a code or codes [of morals or ethics] derived from it if their connection has existed long."[9] Thus, extending Barnard, managerial careerism insures that the personal priorities of the significant people are compatible with the needs of their organizations.

It does not alter the case of which Barnard also wrote: "The important distinctions of rank lie in the fact that the higher the grade the more complex the *moralities* involved, and the more necessary higher abilities to discharge the responsibilities, that is, to resolve the moral conflicts implicit in the position."[10]

There is no paradox here if reference is made to the way values, ethics, and morals are ordered. It is entirely consistent to say that significant people have enormously complex moral conflicts to resolve but also that these conflicts are settled within the gloriously simple value system of the organizational imperative. Barnard, in his most important chapter, "Executive Responsibility," discusses just morals and ethics. He takes the value system from which they are derived as a given. The value orthodoxy Barnard represents, and which contemporary significant people follow, is not the stuff upon which a reform movement is built.

Finally, there would be little incentive for organizational reform if enhancement became a technological reality. Because of superior mind power, the significant people would be capable of excellent managerial performance, and their ability to resolve the crises of interdependency would simply increase their control over organizational America.

Why Reform Will Not Come from the Insignificant People

One of the persistent and poignant myths in the radical tradition is that of an enraged people rising up in righteousness to shatter the old tyrannies and create a new utopia. There is a beauty to this vision, but it is largely fantasy. While the people running rampant can indeed shatter an *ancien régime,* they very seldom create and maintain the utopias of which they dream. The masses are powerful, and they have been mobilized too often for any sane elite to take them for granted in political life. The people are slow to anger, but once their anger is set in motion they are implacable. However, in a society as technically advanced as ours, the masses do not have the organizational expertise to make the necessary reforms. They can destroy the status quo, but it is doubtful that they can build a better nation.

Marx clearly understood the need for organizational ability if revolution is to succeed. He dreamed of the proletariat rising and ending the great historical dialectic in pure communism. But in order for that day to come, the masses had to be made aware of their plight and had to be organized for effective political action. Since they could not do it themselves, the critical role of organization was assigned to the bourgeois intellectuals. In fact, Lenin urged that the new

Soviet leadership learn by studying Frederick W. Taylor's scientific management.[11]

The insignificant people in organizational America are very, very far from the repressed proletariat of Marxian theory, as the bourgeois radicals of the late 1960s found to their chagrin. But they are the majority in America, and latent power is still theirs. However, they are also the beneficiaries of employment in modern organizations. As such they are constantly told of their good fortune in being able to consume an unending flow of consumer products. They are constantly bombarded with intensive advertising propaganda to show how well off they are and how fortunate they are to have all the things they have. They are trained to accept accelerating consumption as the inevitable way of their lives. And they are admonished at all times not to mess around with the horn of plenty because such actions will obliterate their jobs and their consumption potential. This is not a context from which militant masses, bent upon reform, are likely to arise.

But the insignificant people must not be entirely ruled out, for they could have an important role in reform. The material affluence by which their quiescence is purchased, is deteriorating: Their goods are shoddy; they are indentured through time payments to pay for trivial products; their buying power is eroded by inflation; and their prized individual mobility that comes from personal automobiles will be drastically limited. Mass discontent is already being expressed in actions such as consumer and taxpayer revolts. The people are growing more susceptible to those who speak of radical reform.

The people can go either way: as a lynch mob or as reforming pioneers. However, they are susceptible to voices that speak for change. It is from this susceptibility that a power coalition for reform *might* be forged between the insignificant people and the professionals. The key is whether or not the professionals realize and act upon their historic opportunity in organizational America. The real power in the nation belongs to them.

The Practicability of Reform by the Professional People

The professionals are the essential custodians of the modern organization. Without them it cannot function. In an everyday sense, the professionals are more critical to the modern organization than the significant people, for they know how to do the basic jobs that the significant people either do not know or have forgotten how to do.

An interesting parallel can be drawn here if it is not pushed too far. Marx believed that the control of industrial societies would eventually fall into the hands of the proletariat, for they knew how to run the machines of the society. These were skills that the owners did not have. Consequently, power would accrue to those who operated the equipment that made an industrial society possible. In organizational America, the essential equipment is the modern organization, and it is the professionals who make it work. It stretches the Marxian parallel a bit out of shape, but the argument might just be made that the professionals are "the new proletariat," in the sense of having those technical skills upon which the health of the modern organization is predicated.

Reform can come from the professionals because mass support for change is growing and they have the technical and organizational expertise to galvanize this support into a reform movement. They are in the right place at the right time with the right skills. If the professionals accept the responsibility that has been thrust upon them, there is a chance to avoid the trap of totalitarian America. The professionals are correctly positioned to be the dynamic force behind social change. If they do not rise to this responsibility, reform will not come.

However, we are pessimistic that the professionals will recognize their historical potential and seize their opportunity to challenge the organizational imperative and reform modern organizations. Thorstein Veblen, at his cynical best, introduced "A Memorandum on a Practicable Soviet of Technicians" as follows:

It is the purpose of the memorandum to show, in an objective way, that under existing circumstances there need be no fear, and no hope, of an effectual revolutionary overturn in America, such as would unsettle the established order . . . Notoriously, no move of this nature has been made hitherto, nor is there evidence that anything of the kind has been contemplated by the technicians. They still are consistently loyal, with something more than a hired-man's loyalty, to the established order of commercial profit and absentee ownership.[12]*

Veblen's assessment of the revolutionary potential of the technicians applies to the professionals, with the exception of the minor amendment noted below. Their reform potential is virtually nil. The professionals are not likely to be the spiritual leaders of a reform movement. The only way we can improve upon Veblen's appraisal is to bring him up to date with a few more contemporary observations.

Professionals are trained as *followers* with a vastly overrated belief in the burdens of leadership. They are conditioned to look upward to leaders for cues to action and avoid thinking about problems not assigned to them. Closely related to this is the fact that through the organizational imperative the professionals are conditioned to accept their own dispensability, which encourages an attitude of powerlessness to create change.

Nevertheless, some professionals have enough hubris to think they can influence the great organizations. This attitude is encouraged by the significant people because it brings the most arrogant and talented into line. As these exceptional

* Modern readers should substitute "organizational imperative" for "commercial profit and absentee ownership."

professional people learn organizational realities, they believe that they cannot create important reforms *until* they occupy the significant jobs themselves. So they serve their time, get their tickets punched, and wait for the day when they will be elevated to the significant job. But herein lies the twenty-second catch. In the process of striving, they inevitably become what they do. They turn into human extensions of the organizational imperative, and its institutional conservatism smothers their dreams. After twenty-six years in the organizational deep freeze, awaiting the top job, the best they can hope for is that the next generation of upwardly mobile professionals will somehow be able to fulfill their youthful dreams of reform.

All of the above notwithstanding, the professionals could lead organizational reform, by challenging the organizational imperative, for at least four reasons. First, many professionals are still young enough, both in years and in the organization, that they are receptive to new ideas. The ideas of radically modifying the modern organization may not be well understood by these people, but they are not necessarily anathema to them. At this point, the professionals are not exactly champing at the bit to reform organizations, but they are at least open to new ideas.

Second, the professionals practice specializations that cut across the jurisdictional boundaries of organizations. They are unified by common managerial techniques and language. These are preconditions for effective political action, which can be used either for reform or for the preservation of the status quo.

Third, the professionals understand organizational structure and behavior, so they know the critical places in organizations where reforms are most likely to be effective. They know how to generate the behaviors required for organizational change, and they know how to organize and coordinate masses of people for effective action.

Fourth, and perhaps most important, the professionals are

close enough to the insignificant people, both on and off the job, that they can empathize with their difficulties and their aspirations. Using the time-worn model of an oppressed working class, the radicals of the 1960s could not forge an effective coalition with the insignificant people. They could not understand them as professionals can.

The premise that we have argued throughout this book is that there has been a value change in America leading from individualism to a form of organizational collectivism. Furthermore, we claim that the drift inherent in this value change will carry us into a totalitarian society. If this descent is to be prevented, it can be done only by abandoning the values of the organizational imperative as the guiding principles of the modern organization.

This is not as impossible as it might seem, if it is understood that there is not a necessary link between the modern organization and the values of the organizational imperative. *The modern organization is value neutral* in the sense that the uses to which it is put depends upon the values that guide it. In organizational America, managers are instructed by the perverse values of the organizational imperative. Since no natural law ordains this, an option to totalitarianism exists. Therefore, to avoid the unwanted results of drifting, we must substitute the values of the individual imperative as the *a prioris* upon which all modern organizations are reformed, and this task must fall to the professionals for the reasons given above.

The Option of Transcendent America

Before they can even attempt an attack upon the organizational imperative, the professionals must confront several hard realities about their place in the organizational firmament. The first is that most of them will never be significant people. They will probably remain in similar professional jobs until they retire. Given this perspective, their attitudes toward careerism must change. They need to realize that the satisfaction of employment comes not from the prospects of advancement, but from the performance of work and *the reform of organizations.* Being content with doing the same job expertly within a better organization should not be considered a sign of a defective character. Rather, it should be esteemed and rewarded as a worthy life goal. Professionals should not think of themselves as "upwardly mobile entrepreneurs" but as relatively stable specialists.

A change in attitude toward careerism implies a parallel change in attitude about the organization. It is very difficult to identify with a modern organization, especially if one's aspirations for the highest jobs within that organization are unrealistic. Therefore, professionals must identify with the subunits of the organization, departments or project teams, where they apply their skills. Such re-identification demands a major refocusing, since it is completely inconsistent with the belief in the ubiquity of management. It is within the subunits that the possibilities of both work satisfaction and reform are to be found.

Second, as a corollary reality to the above, professionals must reconcile themselves to the fact that they will mainly be followers for as long as they are employed by a modern organization. So they must be prepared to accept the obligations of followership that John Rawls has described as conscientious refusal and civil dissent. In instances where these duties cannot be undertaken by individuals, they should be performed by professional associations.

Consequently, the third reality professionals must face is that they cannot alone, as isolated specialists, bring about needed organizational reform. This speaks to their obligation to build associations representing specializations *based upon the principles of voluntarism,* described in Chapter 3, to challenge the conservatism of the significant people. This type of action, however, may require the greatest attitudinal change of all, because it requires the rejection of organizational paternalism.

Finally, these actions, derived from new attitudes about their life's work, require a foundation in values and a changed perception of the innateness of human nature. This means that in some respects the professionals must become philosophers, and this is a role for which they have not been trained. Yet the philosophical task must precede action. And if philosophers will not become managers, it is certain that managers must become philosophers.[13]

This task of preparation must begin in schools of management and administration, and the professionals must be educated in the requisite values of their historic mission. There is still some time for teachers to give renewed attention to the values of the individual imperative. Those values must be stated with clarity, arranged with precision, and defended with passion. From such a base, the next step can be taken, namely, to plant those values within the basic structure of the modern organization through the actions of the professionals. In this way, and only in this way, can organizations be suitable places in which individuals may prosper.

This requires a division of labor, for teachers cannot be activists. They, like other intellectuals, must *educate* the professionals, perhaps only after they have educated themselves. As Dwight Waldo wrote of the romantic vision of American democracy:

Anyone who writes political philosophy has an idea of the Good Life and at least a faint hope of realizing it — otherwise he would not write political philosophy. When the ends desired seem remote from "reality," subsequent generations call the work a Utopia. In the Utopias the Good Life stands forth most clearly. Here the author, more concerned with ends than means, is at pains to enumerate the values, both spiritual and material, which will be served, and to delineate the right relationship of man to his God, his State, and his fellows.[14]

To fulfill this vision, there must be those to dream the dreams, give them words, and then explain them to those who can act. Our "faint hope" is that the genesis of leadership by the professionals lies in understanding and accepting the individual imperative, expressed in new organizational contexts. They must begin with a theoretically sound and practical alternative to the organizational imperative. Its basic values have already been stated in the individual imperative discussed in Chapter 3. The primary proposition of the individual imperative is that *all individuals have the natural right to the realization of the full potentials of every stage of their lives; therefore, all institutions must be predicated upon that right.*

If the lives of individuals are to have meaning, each stage of their lives must allow full development consistent with their innate selves, their pasts, and in expectation of further development in the future.[15] Therefore, the primary principle to be used in creating and maintaining an organization must be the enhancement of individual lives in the terms they define for themselves. The following list is certainly not complete, but some of the corollary values that come from the propositions of the individual imperative are:

1. Individuals are born with an innate need to develop psychologically, socially, intellectually, and fraternally,[16] through all the stages of their lives.

2. Individuals have the right to expect that their personal and unique worth be recognized by the community and its organizations.

3. Individuals have the obligation to realize their individual potential, for if they do not, they diminish the quality of the community, which diminishes the quality of every individual's life.

4. Individuals have the right and the duty to act in the interest and support of human diversity, since whatever they are capable of becoming cannot be achieved unless organizations are uncompromisingly committed to this pluralistic cause.

5. Individuals have the obligation to understand the aesthetic and intellectual possibilities of this world, without which individual development is not possible.

6. No individual should be used as a means to obtain an end.

7. Individuals have the right and the duty to dissent, without fear of repression, when any social or organizational arrangement abridges the absolute values of life, liberty, and the pursuit of happiness.

Obviously, this bill of rights is incomplete, but we cannot present here a full description of the society that should be. The question arises as to what such organizations, based upon the values of the individual imperative, might look like. The frank answer is: We do not know. We have some general ideas, but we are, after all, talking about a totally unprecedented situation. In *A Theory of Justice,* John Rawls encountered the same problem. He argued that the nation should shift from a utilitarian to a neo-Kantian value system. The resultant change would be enormous and within a few years the new society would be all but unrecognizable. Rawls understood that, and so he did not attempt to give a specific description of his new society. Our situation is similar. Just as modern organizations are new, the idea that they could be based upon the premises of the individual imperative is, of course, unprecedented.

We do not want to dismantle technology or pull down organizations. They offer us all benefits that are undeniable, and those must be preserved. Rather, we advocate a synthesis: new organizations predicated upon the values of the individual imperative. It will require modifying the modern organization so that its technology, complexity, and the new environmental limits contribute to the fuller realization of individual lives. This revolution must be led by the professional people.

The thought of middle managers, accountants, or computer programmers leading a revolution of any kind may

seem surprising, perhaps outrageous. After all, revolution-
aries are supposed to be dramatic people: alienated intellectuals, undersized corporals, brooding John Browns, wealthy
folk singers. However, the barricades will not be manned by
professionals clubbing the establishment with their pocket
calculators. Reform in America *must* be achieved peacefully
and by thought. When put in these terms, then leadership
by the professionals does not seem far-fetched.

Other critics have argued along similar lines. For instance,
William H. Whyte, Jr., concluded his book with a plea for
the organization man to rebel:

He must *fight* the Organization. Not stupidly, or selfishly, for the
defects of individual self-regard are no more to be venerated than
the defects of co-operation. But fight he must, for the demands
for his surrender are constant and powerful, and the more he has
come to like the life of organization the more difficult does he find
it to resist these demands, or even to recognize them. It is
wretched, dispiriting advice to hold before him the dream that
ideally there need be no conflict between him and society. There
always is; there always must be. Ideology cannot wish it away; the
peace of mind offered by organization remains a surrender, and no
less so for being offered in benevolence. That is the problem.[17]

Our argument goes further. The professionals must not
only rebel against their individual absorption into organizational anonymity, they must also assume the burden of leadership in fundamentally reforming modern organizations. In
other words, their mission exceeds mere personal rebellion
and extends outward to the renovation of organizational
America.

But even if all the necessary philosophical chores are done,
if the professionals decide to aim for reform, it will not be
achieved without heroic action. To paraphrase Lincoln, as
our situation is new, so must our heroism be new. The new
heroism calls for modest individuals committed to the belief
that they can, by their own efforts, create a society that

enhances the individual lives of its members. Values must change if individuals are to surpass the limits of technology and organization, creating a transcendent America. This is more than a theoretical option, but not a very likely one. Unfortunately, transcendent America is not our most probable future.

Epilogue

"The Requisite Conditions for Human Happiness": A Dialogue

The boardroom on the forty-seventh floor of the Metropolitan National Bank in Seattle has a commanding view of Puget Sound. The northern islands and cliffs, the western Olympic mountain range, and the flat southern tidelands can be seen through the three large picture windows that form the west wall of the room. When the days are clear and bright, which is seldom in the Pacific Northwest, these landmarks are set against a background of incomparably blue sky and water. The vista from the room at night is no less entrancing. The string of lights on the waterfront, the luminous ferryboats crossing Elliot Bay to Bremerton, the glow of the Space Needle, and the sparkling homes on Queen Anne Hill blend into an urban scene that many visitors regard as one of the most beautiful in the world.

The bank's boardroom harmonizes with the attractiveness and diversity of the surrounding country. The room is open, bright, and finished in woods native to Washington's forests. The decorations, which are used sparingly, are reminders of the state's maritime tradition. A large oil painting of a magnificent sailing vessel, done by a northwestern artist, hangs on one wall. A few valuable antique nautical instruments and Indian artifacts are hung tastefully on the other walls.

Notably absent is the usual massive conference table for the board of directors. Casually arranged modern, Scandinavian-style chairs and low tables are used instead. This furniture is subtly oriented toward a medium-size desk, which is occupied by the board chairman during regular meetings of the bank's directors. At other times the room serves as a gathering place for higher-level executives to relax, entertain a few guests, or hold small, informal meetings.

Although it departs from tradition, this boardroom still reflects the dignity and authority of individuals who hold power. The room says that the bank's executives are mindful of the environment, they have not forgotten the early settlers and industries that made the area great, and they are democratic in the conduct of their affairs. Thus, the boardroom blends physically and socially with its place and time. However, its understated elegance also suggests that those who sit there are aware of their pre-eminent influence in this region of the United States.

One February evening during the one-hundredth-anniversary year of the publication of THE BROTHERS KARAMAZOV, an anomalous presence appears in the half-lighted room. Seated on one of the scattered chairs under the ship painting, dressed in disheveled nineteenth-century clothes, is the shade of the Russian novelist Fyodor Dostoevsky, come to converse about the present state of human affairs.

Dostoevsky does not wait long for the other person, as the form of Chester I. Barnard is already materializing in the leather chair behind the desk. As he knows, Barnard was a rarity among American business executives. He read extensively in arcane philosophy and social theory, he had many friends among leading American intellectuals in the 1930s and 1940s, and he wrote thoughtfully and influentially about management.

But it is not clear what prompted this meeting between Barnard and Dostoevsky. How could they have much in common? Barnard was president of the New Jersey Bell Telephone Company, a subsidiary of AT&T, and, of course, Dostoevsky was a prominent novelist and mystic in another country and century. Did they discover they were both men of action? Did they learn that they had similar philosophical interests? Did they realize that they both had

"The Requisite Conditions for Human Happiness"   231

a knack for prophecy, and now, in a time and place removed, they can review together how right or wrong they were about what they foresaw?

These may or may not be the reasons why they decided to talk. But why shouldn't they meet in this delightful room, enjoy the lovely nighttime views, and discuss the galactic questions of the requisites for human happiness? They have eternity at their disposal. Being uninvolved in daily affairs, they can deal with the subject with a detached objectivity denied them during their lives.

Feeling comfortable in his incarnation behind the desk, Barnard greeted Dostoevsky. "Welcome, sir, and congratulations on the one hundredth year of *The Brothers Karamazov*. Like so many others, I've always been impressed by the parable of the Grand Inquisitor in it, one of your most profound pieces of writing."

"I'm not sure congratulations are appropriate, Mr. Barnard. In some ways, *The Brothers* built upon *The Possessed,* which I wrote eight years earlier."

"You mean that the philosophy expressed by the Grand Inquisitor was an extension of the utopian philosophy of your earlier character Shigalev?"

"Yes. My purpose in both books was to denounce utopians of all kinds and to demonstrate that their atheistic programs for social reform would ultimately lead the people into nihilism. *The Brothers Karamazov* was a refinement of that idea, but its essential elements are contained in *The Possessed.*"

"I remember that prediction. What do you think now?"

"The followers of Shigalev and the Grand Inquisitor are dominating the twentieth century, just as I said they would. They won by blood and violence in Russia. In America, they will win by exploiting the indifference of the people. Regardless, the Shigalevists will triumph exactly as I predicted."

"As I recall," said Barnard, "Shigalev discovered a paradoxical system. He started with unlimited human freedom and ended with unlimited despotism."

"That was the key to his views. However, Shigalev was getting at a very important point about leadership."

"Oh, yes! Shigalev's idea was that for men to have happiness, humanity had to be divided into unequal parts, where one tenth has dominion over nine tenths."

"Quite right," replied Dostoevsky.

"You seem critical of this inequality. My feeling is that leadership and inequality go hand-in-hand. This isn't necessarily bad, since human choice is seldom between absolute freedom or absolute despotism. Most of humanity has had to settle for a compromise, maybe tilting in one direction, but never entirely."

"The direction of the tilt *is* what is important. It is the stuff of prophecy."

"Well, what is the direction?" asked Barnard.

"If man does not seek happiness in the freedom of Christ, he will seek it in earthly comforts and follow those who are able to provide them, despite the consequences."

"So the consequence of not following Christ is, in your thinking, unlimited despotism."

"That is my opinion. And see how correct my prophecy has been for the twentieth century."

"It has and it hasn't," Barnard observed. "There were and are despotic regimes; but there also were victories for the great democratic nations of the West during this century."

"You are missing my point. In order to be victorious, the democracies had to become like the nations they were opposing. And while some freedoms were restored after the wars, these freedoms were never fully returned to the people."

"That's hardly an original observation, Dostoevsky!"

"Perhaps I put it too simply, Barnard. War merely accelerates the despotic trend in industrial nations. With or without war, even those nations with a tradition of freedom will eventually lose it."

"By other means than turning away from God, as you claim?"

"By embracing the only other alternative that man has: a blend of secular humanitarianism and materialism."

"Therefore, people will deliver their freedoms to the despotic one tenth because they allow them material comforts. Beyond this you see no option?"

"You have the gist of it."

"You are not exactly brimming with optimism tonight, are you, Dostoevsky? I don't agree with your assessment of things, but as a matter of curiosity, who are the despots of the future?"

"You won't like this, Barnard, but you were one of their forerunners. Your intellectual friends at Harvard, your executive position with the telephone company, and your book, most of all, contributed to the fulfillment of my prophecy. I'm tempted to see you as an American version of the Grand Inquisitor."

"What rot! I've read *The Brothers Karamazov*! There are no parallels in our work! American executives are generally rather ordinary citizens whom I tried to help do a better job.

I don't see any connection between that and the vicious methods of repression used by the Grand Inquisitor."

"Come now, Barnard, there is no need to get over-wrought."

"I disagree. The Grand Inquisitor was evil. Do you think that I am too, or the generations of managers who have been influenced by my work?"

"Not in the sense that evil was a conscious choice on your parts. The real tragedy is that you managers unwittingly drift into the ways of the Grand Inquisitor by following your good intentions.

"But since the subject disturbs you, let's drop it for the moment. Besides, I want you to explain a passage in your book."

"Can you quote it?" asked Barnard.

"Yes, because it is a memorable statement. Your words are, 'So among those who cooperate the things that are seen are moved by the things unseen. Out of the void comes the spirit that shapes the ends of men.'

"Tell me, Barnard, what is the void? What is the spirit? What are the ends?"

"The meaning of the passage is evident to anyone who has studied or practiced management. The void is the state of chaos before people formed organizations in order to overcome their individual limitations. However, organizations are merely artifacts that must be animated by the people in them. The quality of their performance is entirely the result of managerial leadership. It is the spirit that creates cooperation among people in an organization. It is the qualitative factor that decides whether cooperation will be high or low grade."

"That explains the void and the spirit of it, but what are the ends toward which all this activity is directed?"

"Ah, the ends," mused Barnard. "The ends are the clearest of all. Cooperation created by enlightened managers will bring the mutual satisfaction of individual and organizational needs. People will be happier psychologically and satisfied materially."

"Then is it correct to say that managers are the real leaders of modern countries, not politicians, soldiers, capitalists, or scientists?"

"Yes! That was my prophecy, and it is now a fact of life in most industrial nations, particularly in Russia and America."

Agitated, Dostoevsky rose from his chair, walked to the window, and stared abstractly at the black water of the Sound below. "Yet is it not also true that while managers are making greater happiness for people, they are also strengthening their organizations, which, in turn, deny men their freedom and enslave their souls? Your 'managerial society' seems exactly like the Grand Inquisitor's, except that it is not so crudely coercive. Remember that he said, 'Freedom and bread enough for all are inconceivable together.'"

"This is *not* what I had in mind. I wrote clearly in my book —"

"Barnard, none of your writing is clear."

"— that there was in the late 1930s a contest between those who held extreme views of vast regimentation and endless subordination with those who held equally extreme views of liberty and unrestricted self-will. The enlightened managerial way in America never led to one or the other of these absolutes. I wanted to show the dangers of extremism of all kinds; I also wanted to show that there are alternatives."

"Such as?"

"My way, and the way of all enlightened managers, is a way of moderation. The good manager is an Aristotelian. He seeks proportion; he has modest aspirations; above all, he believes in the power of cooperation and science to find a rational path between ideological extremes.

"Your Grand Inquisitor and Shigalev are monsters. They are pathological creations of malevolent deterministic social systems. They want humans to be happy, but only on their terms. And they will use means that are cynical and oppressive. Americans would never stand for such leaders, and for that matter I don't think the Russians will either. In my estimation, you Russian intellectuals tend to overdramatize."

Dostoevsky turned from the window and started pacing in front of Barnard's desk. "Maybe there *is* a point that I missed in my passion for drama. The Grand Inquisitor and Shigalev believed that human happiness could come only after those who opposed them were eliminated. These characters of mine were prophetic in more ways than I care to imagine. They were Lenin's and Stalin's prototypes.

"Considering what Russia was like, it didn't occur to me that there were any alternatives for my people: Christian freedom on the one hand or totalitarian repression on the other. After hearing you, I believe that a third alternative for humanity may exist. However, it is difficult for me to describe."

"You've not been at a loss for words before. Try!"

"All right, and please try not to take what I say personally.
"Perhaps there is a condition in which people can be kept suspended, in limbo. Initially, this condition is not consciously sought by the leadership, nor is it consciously

avoided. Rather, it just happens. But, having happened, there is no reason for the leaders not to take advantage of it."

"I simply don't understand what you're driving at."

"Please hear me out. Suppose for a moment that repression does not take the form of killing dissidents, running concentration camps, or terrorizing citizens with the secret police. Suppose instead that the strategy is to anesthetize people with physical comforts. Who could possibly object to such a system, guided by the decent intentions of its leaders? Of course, the results are the same — oppression. The people's sensitivities would be so dulled that they would not realize what was happening to them. They would be securely asleep. Then all could be managed according to the managerial dream of balance, moderation, reasonableness, and proportion without popular objection. Life might be drab and sterile, but it would be orderly and secure. In this light, Shigalev and the Grand Inquisitor *are* anachronistic. Their actions would inflame people. Your strategy of oppression is much more effective for modern times because you've been able to combine 'humanitarianism' with despotic control."

"This is not true," cried Barnard. "I never wanted people to be oppressed any more than I wanted to have their development stifled."

"What you wanted isn't the issue. I suspect that your work has been used just as mine has been. Can you imagine me being put in the role of a sympathetic prophet of Russian socialism? Well, I have been! Since my words can't be purged, they are perverted."

"You're not still feeling persecuted, are you, Dostoevsky? Besides, *my* message has not been twisted. I wrote nothing that was contrary to what decades of managers either before or after me have believed. In a sense, I merely codified what managers have held to be their true rights and duties."

Barnard and Dostoevsky talked through the night. At dawn, the shades were drawn. They decided to rest during the day and promised to return to their conversation at sundown. They met the next evening, refreshed and anxious to pick up where they had left off.

"Last evening, Chester — may I call you Chester? — you said that you tried to arrange management ideas in an orderly way. I think it is popular these days to say that you were making a 'paradigmatic statement,' so that future managers might be properly instructed in appropriate ways to act."

"That was what I was trying to do, although after thinking it over, I wasn't merely a codifier. I believe I made several valuable contributions to management knowledge, among them the 'cooperative system.' Incidentally, isn't 'paradigm' an awful word?"

"No worse than 'ideal benefactions.'"

"Touché, Fyodor."

"Let's get back to the subject. If you intended your book to be a guide for future managers, then my opinion is that it was a misdirected one. You made organized effort the measure of everything. But you went further. You required that managers persuade people to hold values consistent with organizational values. I believe you said that this could be done by 'deliberate education of the young and propaganda for adults.' This does not seem to me to advance the cause of individual freedom."

Barnard began to fidget behind the desk, because Dostoevsky had struck a delicate issue. "When you take my words out of context, you can draw any inference you like. Let me try to explain more fully — it involves the whole issue of leadership. The reality of modern life, or life in any historical period, is that an elite must lead. Pareto saw this and thought that the circulation of the elite was the immutable historical fact behind social change. I foresaw that the new elite circulating into modern industrial nations was coming from a managerial class. I asked myself, 'What's better, to have this new elite impervious to their moral responsibilities, or to have leaders enlightened and sensitive to these responsibilities?' The question is rhetorical; the enlightened minority must instruct the majority in appropriate values. It's as simple as that. The rest follows like an exercise in Euclidean geometry.''

"Your Euclidean metaphor is dangerous. His geometry works only when you accept his premises. But let's go along with *your* premises for a moment. Take for example your advice to managers to arrogate to themselves the right to define the 'nine tenths.' This is pure Shigalevism, and it is the main a priori premise in your system. Once that premise is accepted, that humanity is divided into managers and nonmanagers, your system is as irrefutable as Shigalev's. It's the same as affirming that parallel lines never cross. Given that assumption, the rest of Euclid's geometry cannot be disproved.

"The difficulty with your view of managerial leadership is that you equate their moral responsibilities with the removal of all that is psychologically and materially tragic from human life. In this respect, you are no different from the utopian socialists, who figured that practical secular humanitarianism required nothing more than the application of a few rules of social geometry.''

"What's wrong with making people's lives more comfortable and safe?'' asked Barnard.

"Only that you Americans confuse comfort with freedom.''

"That is not true, at least not entirely. There is a tragedy that cannot be eliminated: A few will have to suffer for the sake of the many. There is no doubt in my mind that the chief sufferers are top managers, because they have the ultimate responsibility for human welfare."

"The more you talk, the more you sound like the Grand Inquisitor . . ."

"Don't say any more, I know what's coming. You're going to quote your passage about the 'happy millions' and the 'ten thousand martyrs.'"

"It did occur to me," said Dostoevsky. "You must agree that the most notable totalitarian leaders of your twentieth century have borne me out. Lenin, Mao, and Hitler saw themselves as martyrs to their ideological causes.

"Regardless of them, you wrote about the complex nature of executive morality. Am I incorrect, or don't you imply that managers who shoulder this complex burden are martyring themselves for lesser humans who are not faced with such enormous dilemmas of moral choice?"

"I believe these people *are* martyrs in some ways. But theirs is not a self-conscious martyrdom, nor is it particularly dramatic. A martyr needs an audience to witness the magnitude of his sacrifice, and the managerial elite is not highly visible. The tragedy of their lives is made all that much greater by their anonymity.

"This, Fyodor, is why I object to your accusation that I advised managers to arrogate the right of defining the leaders and the led. Managers do not usurp these privileges. They are forced by the irresistible logic of their circumstances to make distinctions among men based upon organizational principles."

"So the matter of choice does not enter into the managers' calculus of inequality? They are required to function according to this calculus by organizational forces beyond their control?"

"It's more complicated than that. Fyodor, please try to see my point of view. Organizations thrive on appropriate human actions; they founder on inappropriate actions. The success or failure of all cooperative endeavors depends upon the quality of our performance. Don't you see? There is nothing sinister in wanting people to cooperate more effectively."

"Oh, I can agree with that!"

Barnard pressed on, encouraged that he has finally gotten Dostoevsky to concur with something. "Managers are obligated more than nonmanagers to act appropriately in organizations. But the important thing is that all people do what they are obligated to do in organizations with a sense of commitment, even though their obligations vary."

Dostoevsky narrowed his eyes in an incredulous, ironic look.

"You're not following me, are you, Fyodor?"

Dostoevsky said nothing, but his expression made Barnard uneasy. So he hurried to explain further. "Your character the Grand Inquisitor is a perfect example of what I'm trying to get across to you. Wasn't he apart from his flock as well as a member of his flock at the same time? This situation is only paradoxical when we forget that the leaders and the led are engaged in a *mutual* effort to accomplish a goal that they couldn't alone."

Dostoevsky asked, "Isn't it true that if people do different things in an organization, this will make them different? The Grand Inquisitor was different from the lesser members of his flock because he had the power of his position. He used his power to increase his church's dominance of the flock.

The Grand Inquisitor's sin — his personal tragedy if you prefer — was that he *knew* oppression was evil. Nevertheless, he took advantage of people's weakness to follow him blindly and in return gave them comfort and security. He twisted this weakness to his advantage, and as a result his organization became so powerful that he could successfully challenge Christ when he returned a second time and send Him packing. Yes, the Grand Inquisitor had the knowledge of good and evil; and consciously, with a full understanding of the consequences, he chose 'evil.'"

"Managers," replied Barnard, "have to make choices too; my concern was that they choose the 'good.' The Grand Inquisitor believed that despotism was necessary for human happiness. I believe that my cooperative system fulfills the conditions for human happiness. It is the middle ground between unlimited freedom and unlimited despotism. In my philosophy people and organizations can reach an accommodation where both can achieve their aims without damage to either. This is my idea of 'good,' and it can be obtained if the managerial elite makes moderate and decent choices. Given these conditions it is appropriate for leadership to be in the hands of a managerial class."

"Chester, Chester, Chester," sighed Dostoevsky, "your conditions for achieving the 'good' are impossible to meet; management is not the same thing as moral leadership."

"It is!"

"Not if you stop and think about it. Your ideal manager, if I understand him correctly, is a decent, psychologically balanced, technically competent fellow — right? How many managers in your country now fit this description?"

"Most of them — say, ninety percent."

"If this is the case, why aren't Americans happy?"

"Probably because managers still haven't mastered the skill of creating true cooperation among people."

"Nonsense! All that twaddle is good for is keeping human relations consultants employed."

"What are you suggesting, Fyodor?"

"Let's use Shigalev and the Grand Inquisitor as examples. Their actions were true to their ideals, and these ideals were selfless, in the sense that they were willing to sacrifice themselves for humanity. This is rather decent, don't you think?"

"Fyodor, you *are* a sophist!"

"On top of it, the Grand Inquisitor was a competent manager. The point is that Shigalev and the Grand Inquisitor were monstrous because their acts were based on perverse values.

"The reason Americans are not happy, in spite of their material blessings, is because they are led by morally decent people who have been seduced by false values. Their good intentions will not help them provide the requisite conditions for human happiness."

"Then what does it take, Fyodor, beyond repudiation of the organizational system?"

"I realize that most of your managers are caught in circumstances beyond their control. And I suppose that all that can be expected is for them to do their jobs quietly, competently, and decently. What bothers me is that there is so little incentive for heroism among at least a few of these people. I don't mean flamboyant physical courage, but a willingness for them to perform idealistic acts against insuperable odds.

"Let me be more explicit. Suppose one of your managers, an army officer, sees something devastatingly wrong, say officer careerism, destroying troop morale and organizational performance. What is he likely to do? If he is young and aspires to a military life, he will do nothing, because he knows that to campaign for reform will destroy him professionally. If he is a senior officer, he will still do nothing because he has a vested personal commitment to maintaining the status quo. It takes a true hero, Chester, to sacrifice himself in trying to change perverse values, particularly when the chances against success are so enormously high.

"Of course my example applies to all organizations; the army should not be singled out. You can't make me believe that among all the bright young professional people who work in American organizations there are not some, maybe many, who think that what they do is spiritually corrosive. They may say it differently than this, but it amounts to the same thing.

"It seems to me that heroes could come from their ranks, but they're not likely to. At least not now. Your system of government by organizations has been far too effective in capturing the souls of these people and making heroism an antiquated ideal for them.

"It is truly ironic, Chester, that while you and I wanted immortality, it is our creations — Shigalev, the Grand Inquisitor, and professional managers — who really still live. When we meet again a hundred years from now, perhaps we should ask Mary Shelley to join us."

References

Index

References

Introduction, pages 1–10

1. Clyde Kluckhohn et al., "Values and Value-Orientations in the Theory of Action," in *Toward a General Theory of Action,* ed. Talcott Parsons and Edward A. Shils (New York: Harper & Row, Torchbooks, 1951), p. 395.
2. A similar distinction is used by David L. Norton in *Personal Destinies: A Philosophy of Ethical Individualism* (Princeton: Princeton University Press, 1976). However, our usage does not necessarily follow his.
3. Peter Drucker, *The Practice of Management* (New York: Harper & Row, 1954), pp. 3–4.
4. Herbert S. Parmet, *Eisenhower and the American Crusades* (New York: Macmillan, 1972), p. 572.
5. Kenneth E. Runyon and Howard L. Smith, "The Organizational Imperative — Paradigm or Rationalization," *Administration and Society* 10 (May 1978): 110–121.
6. The conclusions of the conference are contained in Frank Marini, ed., *Toward a New Public Administration: The Minnowbrook Perspective* (Scranton, Pa.: Chandler, 1971).

Chapter 1, "Organizational America," pages 13–31

1. Theodore C. Sorensen, *Kennedy* (New York: Bantam, 1965), p. 276.
2. Robert L. Heilbroner, *The Future as History* (New York: Harper & Row, 1960), p. 17. Emphasis in the original.

3. Nicholas Wade, "Raw Materials: U.S. Grows More Vulnerable to Third World Cartels," *Science* 183 (January 18, 1974): 186.

4. John M. Blair, *The Control of Oil* (New York: Pantheon Books, 1976), p. 22.

5. David Easton, "The New Revolution in Political Science," *American Political Science Review* 63 (December 1969): 1053.

6. Edward Mead Earle, "Adam Smith, Alexander Hamilton, Friedrich List: "The Economic Foundations of Military Power," in *Makers of Modern Strategy,* ed. Edward Mead Earle (Princeton: Princeton University Press, 1944), pp. 117–120.

7. A most useful summary and analysis of these trends can be found in Richard B. Wirthlin, "Public Perceptions of the American Business System: 1974–1975," *Journal of Contemporary Business* 4 (Summer, 1975): 1–14.

8. Barnard J. Frieden et al., *The Nation's Housing: 1975 to 1985* (Cambridge: Joint Center for Urban Studies, 1977), pp. 122, 124.

9. Representative are: George C. Lodge, *The New American Ideology* (New York: Knopf, 1976); Daniel Bell, *The Cultural Contradictions of Capitalism* (New York: Basic Books, 1976); Robert Nisbet, *Twilight of Authority* (New York: Oxford University Press, 1976). The subject has received excellent although not particularly pessimistic treatment in the legal and economic areas by James Williard Hurst, *The Legitimacy of the Business Corporation in the Law of the United States: 1780–1970* (Charlottesville: University Press of Virginia, 1970). "Legitimacy" has been much discussed of late but, curiously, very little has been done to define and analyze the term. However, the following are quite good: Carl J. Friedrich, *Man and His Government: An Empirical Theory of Politics* (New York: McGraw-Hill, 1963), especially Chapter 13, "Legitimacy and Political Obligations," and David Easton, *A Systems Analysis of Political Life* (New York: Wiley, 1965), Chapter 18, "Diffuse Support for Authorities and Regime: The Belief in Legitimacy," and Chapter 19, "Sources of Legitimacy."

10. Robert Michels, *Political Parties: A Sociological Study of the Oligarchical Tendencies of Modern Democracies,* trans. E. and C. Paul (New York: Dover, 1915, 1959); James Burnham, *The*

Managerial Revolution (Bloomington: Indiana University Press, 1941, 1960); Jacques Ellul, *The Technological Society,* trans. J. Wilkinson (New York: Knopf, 1954, 1964). This is the first book in his great trilogy, indicating totalitarianism. The others are *Propaganda,* trans. K. Kellen and J. Lerner (New York: Knopf, 1962, 1965), and *The Political Illusion,* trans. K. Kellen (New York: Knopf, 1967).

11. Michels, *Political Parties,* p. 408. According to Michels, the iron law of oligarchy is innate to organization: "It is organization which gives birth to the dominion of the elected over the electors, of the mandataries over the mandators, of the delegates over the delegators. Who says organization, says oligarchy" (p. 401). The tyranny of expertise comes from the leaders' indispensability: "The leader's principle source of power is found in his indispensability. One who is indispensable has in his power all the lords and masters of the earth" (p. 86).

12. Ibid., p. 407.

13. Ibid., p. 401. Emphasis in the original.

14. Ellul, *The Technological Society,* p. 233.

15. Ibid., Chapter 5. The wedding of the new despotism with humanitarianism and benevolency is discussed by Nisbet as the greatest single revolution in the political sphere.

16. Lodge, *The New American Ideology*; Harlan Cleveland, *The Future Executive: A Guide for Tomorrow's Managers* (New York: Harper & Row, 1972).

17. We have discussed this topic in some detail in David K. Hart, William G. Scott, and C. Spencer Clark, "Management, Propaganda, and the Age of Decline," in *Theoretical Perspectives in Public Administration: A Normative Perspective,* ed. Carl J. Bellone (Boston: Allyn and Bacon, 1980).

18. Karl R. Popper, *The Open Society and Its Enemies* (Princeton: Princeton University Press, 1950), p. 120.

Chapter 2, "The Organizational Imperative," pages 32–49

1. This contention is effectively treated by Henry S. Kariel, *The Decline of American Pluralism* (Stanford: Stanford University Press, 1961). See also David K. Hart and William G. Scott,

_"The Organizational Imperative," in _Administration and Society_ (November 7, 1975): 259–285.

2. Walt Whitman, "Leaves of Grass: By Blue Ontario's Shore," in Walt Whitman, _Leaves of Grass and Selected Prose_ (New York: Holt, Rinehart and Winston, 1949), p. 293.

3. Robert L. Heilbroner, _An Inquiry into the Human Prospect_ (New York: Norton, 1974), p. 70.

4. John Platt, "What We Must Do," _Science_ 28 (November 1969): 1117.

5. Richard A. Gabriel and Paul L. Savage, _Crisis in Command_ (New York: Hill and Wang, 1978), p. 19.

6. C. P. Snow, _Science and Government_ (Cambridge: Harvard University Press, 1961), p. 84.

7. Examples are legion, but note particularly Warren Bennis, _Changing Organizations_ (New York: McGraw-Hill, 1966).

8. Rolf H. Wild, _Management by Compulsion: The Corporate Urge to Grow_ (Boston: Houghton Mifflin, 1978).

9. See Richard M. Steers, "Problems in the Measurement of Organizational Effectiveness," _Administrative Science Quarterly_ (December 1975): 546–551, for an excellent review article on this subject.

10. See Thomas S. Kuhn, _The Structure of Scientific Revolutions,_ 2nd ed. (Chicago: University of Chicago Press, 1970).

11. It is suggestive on this point to mention that the first major movement in administrative theory was "scientific management"; later, two key fields of study and practice emerged, called _management science_ and _operations research,_ and presently two of the most respected professional journals are _Administrative Science Quarterly_ and _Management Science._

12. Daniel Katz and Robert L. Kahn, _The Social Psychology of Organizations_ (New York: John Wiley, 1966), p. 55.

13. Kuhn, _Scientific Revolutions,_ p. 37.

14. Wyndham Robertson, "The Directors Woke Up Too Late at Gulf," _Fortune_ (June 1976): 121.

15. Mendes Hershman, "Liabilities and Responsibilities of Corporate Officers and Directors," _The Business Lawyer_ 33 (November 1977): 263–308. By and large, the courts have been unwilling to cause any major changes in the "prudent man" and "due diligence" doctrine relative to corporate manage-

ment. Therefore, it is extremely difficult to prove negligence. These rules add to the shield of elitist invisibility because it is nearly impossible by legal action to hold management liable for bad decisions or incompetency.

16. Chester I. Barnard, *The Function of the Executive* (Cambridge: Harvard University Press, 1938), Chapter 17.
17. Frederick W. Taylor, *The Principles of Scientific Management* (New York: Harper & Bros., 1919), p. 6.

Chapter 3, "The Organizational Imperative Realized," pages 50–80

1. William H. Whyte, Jr., *The Organization Man* (New York: Simon and Schuster, 1956). See also Sloan Wilson, *The Man in the Grey Flannel Suit* (New York: Simon and Schuster, 1955).
2. The story is told emphatically by David Halberstam, *The Best and the Brightest* (New York: Random House, 1972).
3. William G. Scott and David K. Hart, "The Moral Nature of Man in Organizations: A Comparative Analysis," *Academy of Management Journal* 14 (June 1971): 255. Note the criticism of this position by Don Hellreigel, "The Moral Nature of Man in Organizations: A Comparative Analysis: Comment," *Academy of Management Journal* 14 (December 1971): 533–537.
4. Elton Mayo, *The Human Problems of an Industrial Civilization* (Boston: Harvard University, Graduate School of Business Administration, 1933), esp. pp. 150–151.
5. See examples in Samuel R. Aertker, *The Influence of Skinnerian Philosophy and Principles on Administrative Practice and Social Organization* (Seattle: University of Washington, doctoral dissertation, 1974).
6. This point is of the utmost importance. When all individuals believe their nature to be malleable, they make themselves completely susceptible to the values and behaviors demanded by administrators. For examples, see John Taylor, *The Shape of Minds to Come* (New York: Weybright and Talley, 1970), and Gordon Rattray Taylor, *The Biological Time Bomb* (New York: New American Library, 1968).

7. Chester I. Barnard, *The Functions of the Executive* (Cambridge: Harvard University Press, 1938), p. 279.
8. Barnard and Mayo had contemporaries who were not so optimistic about the new managerial society. However, their voices were not heard, at least to the extent of influencing the corpus of management thought. Perhaps the most influential critics were A. A. Berle and G. C. Means, *The Modern Corporation and Private Property* (New York: Macmillan, 1932). We have also referred to James Burnham in Chapter 1. See also Oswald Knauth, *The Managerial Enterprise* (New York: Norton, 1948).
9. John Stuart Mill, "On Liberty," in John Stuart Mill, *Utilitarianism, Liberty, and Representative Government,* Everyman's Library (New York: Dutton, 1950), p. 178.
10. David Riesman et al., *The Lonely Crowd* (Garden City, N.Y.: Anchor, 1953), pp. 29–32.
11. An excellent discussion of the topic is contained in Stanley Milgram, *Obedience to Authority* (New York: Harper & Row, 1974), esp. pp. 123–168. In addition, ideas central to our discussion are presented in Irving L. Janis, *Victims of Groupthink* (Boston: Houghton Mifflin, 1972).
12. Milgram, *Obedience to Authority,* p. 113.
13. Eric Hoffer, *The True Believer* (New York: Harper & Row, 1951).
14. Ray Allen Billington, *Frederick Jackson Turner* (New York: Oxford, 1973), p. 86.
15. This most serious problem cuts across cultures, but seems to be heightened in advanced industrial societies. See, for instance, Simone de Beauvoir, *The Coming of Age,* trans. P. O'Brian (New York: Putman, 1970, 1972). For the American situation, see the Pulitzer Prize–winning book by Robert N. Butler, M.D., *Why Survive? Being Old in America* (New York: Harper & Row, 1975).
16. There is an extensive literature dealing with the concept of community. The following books are most useful: Robert A. Nisbet, *The Quest for Community* (New York: Oxford, 1953, 1969); Maurice R. Stein, *The Eclipse of Community,* expanded ed. (Princeton: Princeton University Press, 1972); Wilson Carey McWilliams, *The Idea of Fraternity in America* (Berkeley: University of California Press, 1973).

17. Again, there is an extensive literature, but the following two books demonstrate the point: Warren G. Bennis and Philip E. Slater, *The Temporary Society* (New York: Harper & Row, 1968); Alvin Toffler, *Future Shock* (New York: Random House, 1970).
18. Patrick E. Connor and William G. Scott, "Reward Protocols in Technical Organizations: Interpersonal versus Technical Competence," *Human Organization* 33 (Winter, 1975) 367–374.
19. For example, see Henry S. Kariel, *The Decline of American Pluralism* (Stanford: Stanford University Press, 1961), and John Kenneth Galbraith, *American Capitalism: The Concept of Countervailing Power* (Boston: Houghton Mifflin, 1952, 1956).
20. Andrew Carnegie, *The Empire of Business* (New York: Doubleday, Page, 1902), p. v.
21. Nicholas N. Kittrie, *The Right to Be Different* (Baltimore: Pelican Books, 1973), p. 5.
22. See E. Fuller Torrey, *The Death of Psychiatry* (Radnor, Pa.: Chilton, 1974), p. 97.
23. Adolf A. Berle, Jr., and Gardiner C. Means, *The Modern Corporation and Private Property* (New York: Macmillan, 1933).

Chapter 4, "Organizational Roles," pages 83–94

1. Neal Gross et al., *Explorations in Role Analysis* (New York: Wiley, 1958), p. 67.
2. Georg Simmel, *The Web of Group Affiliations* (London: Collier-Macmillan, 1955).
3. Sinclair Lewis, *Babbitt* (New York: New American Library, 1922), pp. 80–81.
4. Harold D. Lasswell and Abraham Kaplan, *Power and Society: A Framework for Political Inquiry* (New Haven: Yale University Press, 1950), p. 222.
5. Lewis A. Coser, *Greedy Institutions: Patterns of Undivided Commitment* (New York: Free Press, 1974). While we do not agree entirely with his argument, his idea about "greedy institutions" is most applicable.
6. James Thompson, *Organizations in Action* (New York: McGraw-Hill, 1967), develops the notion of the "technical core" in some detail.

7. John Kenneth Galbraith, *The New Industrial State,* 2nd ed. (Boston: Houghton Mifflin, 1971), pp. 36–37.
8. Reflections of the author on the day before the opening of the grouse hunting season in Scotland. Thomas Oakleigh, Esq., *The Oakleigh Shooting Code* (London: James Ridgway, 1837), p. 118.
9. This was the major purpose of the game of "Rollerball," in the film of the same name. The point was stressed by the Director of Energy when trying to convince the highly popular professional player Jonathan E. to resign from the sport. Unfortunately, most film critics did not have the wit to understand the theme or the importance of the film.
10. For an excellent survey of the literature, see George Comstock et al., *Television and Human Behavior* (New York: Columbia University Press, 1978).
11. For example, see Robert Butler, M.D., *Why Survive? Being Old in America* (New York: Harper & Row, 1975).

Chapter 5, "The Insignificant People," pages 95–129

1. E. F. Schumacher, *Small Is Beautiful: Economics as if People Mattered* (New York: Harper & Row, Colophon, 1973), p. 35.
2. Milovan Djilas writes mainly about the rise to power of bureaucrats in communist parties, and some of the points he makes about managerial class structure are instructive. He observes that this class did not arise by deliberate design, that it is not conscious of itself, but that "the phenomena of careerism and unscrupulous ambition are a sign that it is profitable to be a bureaucrat." Also, he points out that the ranks of the new class are filled by people from the broadest possible strata of society. The "democratization" of access to the ruling class of managers with technical and organizational expertise is an obvious characteristic of the managerial class in noncommunist as well as communist societies. (*The New Class* [New York: Praeger, 1958], pp. 59–69).
3. For an interesting and useful summary, see T. B. Bottomore, *Elites and Society* (Baltimore: Penguin Books, 1964).
4. Consensus is central to the legitimization of a dominant managerial value system. This point is clearly made in Rolf Dah-

rendorf's analysis of managerial attitudes about the "pathology" of conflict, *Class and Class Conflict in Industrial Society* (Stanford: Stanford University Press, 1959). The functional value of consensus is interlaced through the value structure of contemporary management theory and practice. This aspect of management is so fundamental that it is easily overlooked; yet it is the basic historical continuity that links modern theory and practice with the past. For a further elaboration see William G. Scott, "Organization Theory: A Reassessment," *Academy of Management Journal* 17 (June 1974): 244–246.

5. James M. Glass makes this point in an imaginative way by contrasting the behavior of the main characters in two novels, *The Man in the Grey Flannel Suit* and *Something Happened* ("Organization and Action: The Executive's Personality Type as a Pathological Formation," *Journal of Contemporary Business,* [Autumn, 1976]: 91–111).

6. This is the major theme of the organizational humanists, which is clearly brought into focus by Chris Argyris, *Organization and Personality* (New York: Harper & Bros., 1957). Subsequently, much has been written and researched on the subject of changing either personality or organization so that a closer harmony between the two might be achieved. The idea is simply that disequilibrium among the component parts of a system reduces organizational effectiveness. Humanists like Argyris, Warren Bennis, and Rensis Likert want to modify behavior and organizations so that they are more compatible. The approach is within the consensus tradition of management theory and practice.

7. The contrasting of internalistic versus externalistic causes of behavior is treated in Pitrim A. Sorokin, *The Crisis of Our Age* (New York: Dutton, 1941).

8. B. F. Skinner, *Beyond Freedom and Dignity* (New York: Knopf, 1971), p. 19. Emphasis added. Skinner answered his critics in *About Behaviorism* (New York: Knopf, 1974), but his position remains the same.

9. Jacques Ellul argues that the only defense against modern propaganda, and thereby mass domination, is the individual intellect. (*Propaganda,* trans. K. Kellen and J. Lerner [New York: Knopf, 1965]).

10. Jacques Barzun, *The House of Intellect* (New York: Harper & Row, 1959), pp. 3-4.
11. Ibid., p. 5.
12. Ibid., p. 4.
13. Robert M. Pirsig, *Zen and the Art of Motorcycle Maintenance* (New York: Morrow, 1974), esp. pp. 212-289.
14. We will not develop the idea here, but we are impressed with the fact that "reason" is a two-edged sword. Outwardly, as intelligence, it is essential to successful paradigmatic puzzle-solving. Inwardly, as intellect, it is the means of discovering the inviolable self. This assumption is central to an understanding of John Rawls, *A Theory of Justice* (Cambridge: Harvard University Press, 1973).
15. Museum of Modern Art, *The Family of Man* (New York: Macro Magazine Corporation, 1955).
16. See, for instance, Richard Hofstadter, *Anti-intellectualism in American Life* (New York: Vintage, 1963), and John H. Bunzel, *Anti-Politics in America* (New York: Knopf, 1967).
17. That psychiatry is the ally of those seeking collective support of the communal values is a point made by E. Fuller Torrey, particularly in his discussion of the "mental hygiene" movement (*The Death of Psychiatry* [Radnor, Pa.: Chilton, 1974], esp. Chapter 7). The use of psychology as a management tool is developed by Loren Baritz, *The Servant of Power* (Middletown, Conn.: Wesleyan University Press, 1960).
18. Hannah Arendt, *The Human Condition* (New York: Doubleday Anchor Books, 1959), pp. 152-153.
19. Rolf H. Wild, *Management by Compulsion* (Boston: Houghton Mifflin, 1978), Chapter 7.
20. Carole Pateman, *Participation and Democratic Theory* (Cambridge, Eng.: Cambridge University Press, 1970). The arguments about participation are discussed in David K. Hart, "Theories of Government Related to Decentralization and Citizen Participation," *Public Administration Review* 32 (Special Issue; October 1972): 603-621.
21. A. S. Tannenbaum, *Control in Organizations* (New York: McGraw-Hill, 1968).
22. See the delightful book by Allan Harrington, *Life in the Crystal Palace* (New York: Knopf, 1959).

23. The figures were compiled from the following sources: *Fortune* (May 8, 1978): 239; *Forbes* (May 15, 1978): 286; *Economic Report of the President* (Washington, D.C.: U.S. Printing Office, 1978), pp. 290, 297.

24. Carl J. Friedrich and Zbigniew K. Brzezinski, *Totalitarian Dictatorship and Autocracy* (Cambridge: Harvard University Press, 1956), Part IV.

25. Alastair Buchan, *Crisis Management* (Paris: The Atlantis Institute, 1966). In passing, we should identify at least three types of crises: (1) predictable crises, which can be controlled under extant contingency plans; (2) unpredictable crises, which require pragmatic managerial response and can often be manipulated to enhance management strength; and (3) planned crises, which are deliberate management maneuvers used to enhance managerial power.

26. The reader should not be misled by our use of examples from federal energy policy. Crisis management is by no means the exclusive domain of government administrators. It is simply that the energy crunch of 1977 provided an almost made-to-order case for our discussion. There is, however, a considerable literature in the area of "conflict management," reporting research by sociologists and social psychologists on how to turn conflict (crisis) situations into favorable managerial events. One of the findings of special importance is that crises that are external to a group or organization have the effect of making people more cohesive, causing them to present a "unified front" to a commonly perceived enemy or threat. See Lewis A. Coser, *The Functions of Social Conflict* (Glencoe, Ill.: The Free Press, 1956).

27. See William G. Scott, "Executive Development as an Instrument of Higher Control," *Academy of Management Journal* 6 (September 1963): 191–203.

28. William G. Scott, "The Management of Decline," National Industrial Conference Board *Record* 13 (June 1976). See also the symposium on decline by Charles Levine, ed., *Public Administration Review* 38 (July/August 1978): 315–357.

29. Jacque Ellul, *Propaganda,* trans. K. Kellen and J. Lerner (New York: Knopf, 1965, 1968).

30. John Keegan, *The Face of Battle* (New York: Viking Press,

1976), Chapter 5.
31. Rolf Dahrendorf, *Class and Class Conflict in Industrial Society* (Stanford: Stanford University Press, 1959), Chapter 3.
32. William G. Scott, "Organization Theory: A Reassessment," *Academy of Management Journal* 17 (June 1974): 245.
33. Although from reading James Glass's commentary on Heller's book *Something Happened,* one might be led to the opposite conclusion — that psychic turmoil is the only way a person has to cope with an insane organizational world. Glass, op. cit., and James M. Glass, "Consciousness and Organization," *Administration and Society* 7 (November 1975): 366–384.
34. Robert A. Nisbet, *The Quest for Community* (London: Oxford University Press, 1970), pp. viii–xi.
35. Ellul, *Propaganda,* p. xviii.
36. Barzun, *House of Intellect,* p. 261.
37. George Orwell, *1984* (Baltimore: Penguin, 1949), pp. 241–251.

Chapter 6, "The Professional People," pages 130–160

1. James D. Thompson, *Organizations in Action* (New York: McGraw-Hill, 1967).
2. Chester I. Barnard, *The Functions of the Executive* (Cambridge: Harvard University Press, 1938), p. 215.
3. Thorstein Veblen, *The Engineers and the Price System* (New York: Harcourt, Brace and World, 1963), p. 82.
4. Austin Warren, *Rage for Order* (Chicago: University of Chicago Press, 1948), p. 106.
5. Ibid., pp. 106–107.
6. John Kenneth Galbraith and Nicole Salinger, *Almost Everyone's Guide to Economics* (Boston: Houghton Mifflin, 1978), p. 24.
7. James D. Mooney and Alan C. Reiley, *Onward Industry* (New York: Harper & Bros., 1931). Subsequently revised, and published as James D. Mooney, *The Principles of Organization* (New York: Harper & Bros., 1947). "Classical" organization theorists like Mooney and Reiley realized that staff support people, with the authority of expert knowledge, might exert undue influence on operating line executives with their general

authority. So that this conflict of authorities would not disrupt coordination, by violating the "unity of command" principle, Mooney and Reiley reasserted in unequivocal terms the structural supremacy of line authority over staff authority.

8. For example see, Melville Dalton, "Conflicts between Staff and Line Managerial Officers," *American Sociological Review* 15 (June 1950): 342-351.

9. Peter F. Drucker, *The Practice of Management* (New York: Harper & Bros., 1954), Chapter 26.

10. See Daniel Bell, Introduction, in Veblen, *Engineers and the Price System,* pp. 21-26.

11. Oswald Knauth, *Managerial Enterprise* (New York: Norton, 1948), p. 156.

12. Robert K. Merton, Foreword, in Jacques Ellul, *The Technological Society,* trans. J. Wilkinson (New York: Knopf, 1954, 1964), p. vi.

13. Lest this appear to be just another attack on humanistic psychology, let us make it quite clear that our objection is to its misuse, as a technique of control. A similar concern is expressed throughout the fine book by Robert Nisbet, *Twilight of Authority* (New York: Oxford, 1976).

14. Abraham H. Maslow, *Eupsychian Management* (Homewood, Ill.: Richard D. Irwin, 1965), p. 1.

15. Some of the issues concerning participation are discussed in David K. Hart, "Theories of Government Related to Decentralization and Citizen Participation," *Public Administration Review* 32 (Special Issue; October 1972): 603-621.

16. Sheldon S. Wolin, "Political Theory as a Vocation," *American Political Science Review* 63 (December 1969): 1081.

17. See, for example, John Child, "Parkinson's Progress: Accounting for the Number of Specialists in Organizations," *Administrative Science Quarterly* 18 (September 1973): 328-348. One must not overlook the successful book that lent its name to the controversy about management overhead: C. Northcote Parkinson, *Parkinson's Law and Other Studies in Administration* (Boston: Houghton Mifflin, 1957). In passing, it is worthwhile to note that administrative overhead is extraordinarily inflexible on the downside, that is while administrative overhead grows disproportionately when an organization grows, it does

not seem to contract disproportionately when an organization contracts. F. Terrien and D. L. Mills, "The Effect of Changing Size on the Internal Structure of Organizations," *American Sociological Review* 20 (February 1955): 11–13.

18. Harlan Cleveland, *The Future Executive* (New York: Harper & Row, 1972), p. 25.
19. William G. Scott, "Executive Development as an Instrument of Higher Control," *Academy of Management Journal* 6 (September 1963): 191–203.
20. Some astute observations about the nature of the current career are made by Michael Maccoby, *The Gamesman: The New Corporate Leaders* (New York: Simon and Schuster, 1976), p. 173. Most of his findings substantiate the arguments in this book.
21. Barnard, *Functions of the Executive*, p. 146.
22. Cleveland, *Future Executive*, pp. 25–26. Emphasis added.
23. Fillmore H. Sanford, "Leadership Identification and Acceptance," in *Groups, Leadership and Men*, ed. Harold Guetzkow (Pittsburgh: Carnegie Press, 1951), p. 159.
24. Hannah Arendt, *Eichmann in Jerusalem: A Report on the Banality of Evil*, rev. ed. (New York: Viking, 1965); Stanley Milgram, *Obedience to Authority* (New York: Harper & Row, 1974); Irving L. Janis, *Victims of Groupthink* (Boston: Houghton Mifflin, 1972).
25. John Rawls, *A Theory of Justice* (Cambridge: Belknap Press of Harvard University Press, 1973).
26. P. W. Bridgman, *The Logic of Modern Physics* (New York: Macmillan, 1927, 1960), p. 5.
27. Knauth, *Managerial Enterprise*, p. 199.
28. Cleveland, *Functions of the Executive*, p. 46.

Chapter 7, "The Significant People," pages 161–177

1. Seattle *Times,* May 8, 1977.
2. Charles Levine, ed., "Organizational Decline and Cutback Management," *Public Administration Review* 38, (July/August 1978), and David K. Hart, William G. Scott, and C. Spencer Clark, "The Management of Decline," in *Perspectives in Public*

Administration, ed. Carl Bellone (Boston: Allyn and Bacon, 1980).

3. In a letter to the authors, Professor Gates noted that the relationships in different dimensions equal $4 \times 10 \times 10 \times 12 \times 20 \times 6 = 576,000$. If the possible relationships between organizations in the same dimension are included (e.g., between all service agencies, between all funding agencies, etc.), there is a total of 367 such relationships in this example which can be facilitated in any of six ways. Thus, $578,202 = 576,000 + (357 \times 6)$. Note that the example treats only pairs of organizations; multi-organizational arrangements, such as consortia, would create additional possibilities. All of this is developed in full detail in Bruce L. Gates, *Implementing Social Policy* (Englewood Cliffs, N.J.: Prentice-Hall, forthcoming).

4. C. P. Snow, *Science and Government* (New York: Mentor, 1962), p. 9.

5. Mabel Newcomer, "The Big Business Executive," *Scientific American Special Report* (1965): 6.

6. Theo Haimann and William G. Scott, *Management in the Modern Organization* (Boston: Houghton Mifflin, 1970), pp. 8–10.

7. Newcomer, "Big Business Executive," p. 11.

8. Neil W. Chamberlain, *The Limits of Corporate Responsibility* (New York: Basic Books, 1973), p. 92.

9. Michael Maccoby, *The Gamesman* (New York: Simon and Schuster, 1976), p. 32.

10. C. Wright Mills, *The Power Elite* (New York: Oxford University Press, 1957), Chapter 6, has a lengthy biographical description of the average top executive. It conforms in most details to the one stated here. However, in the intervening years it appears that the economic class from which these executives come has dropped from the upper or upper middle into the middle class. Also, greater emphasis is given to higher education today than twenty years ago, when Mills's study was done.

11. C. Spencer Clark, "Corporate Responsibilities and Management Perception" (Seattle: University of Washington, doctoral dissertation, 1975). See also his article "Management's Perception of Corporate Responsibility," *Journal of Contemporary Business* 4 (Summer, 1975): 15–30.

Chapter 8, "Enhancing the Significant People," pages 178–203

1. B. F. Skinner, *Beyond Freedom and Dignity* (New York: Knopf, 1971), p. 215.
2. Elliot S. Valenstein, "Science-Fiction Fantasy and the Brain," *Psychology Today* (July 1978): 29 ff.
3. This point is also made by Samuel Chavkin, *The Mind Stealers* (Boston: Houghton Mifflin, 1978), pp. 177–178.
4. William G. Scott, "The Theory of Significant People," *Public Administration Review* 33 (1973): 308–313.
5. Vance Packard, "Building Brighter — or Duller — People," *Mainliner Magazine* (March 1978): 53–56.
6. Delgado has, for example, recommended establishing a NASA-type center to coordinate and support the work of neural-behavioral institutes. See José M. R. Delgado, *Physical Control of the Mind: Toward a Psychocivilized Society* (New York: Harper & Row, 1969), pp. 259–260.
7. Dr. Kline discusses normality at some length in an effort to define the term. He states that normality in any specific instance is conformity to particular standards or criteria. In other words something or someone is normal only with respect to the state of a relevant system. Our term *basing point norms* is based on his discussion. See Nathan S. Kline, M.D., and Wayne O. Evans, *The Psychopharmacology of the Normal Human* (Springfield, Ill.: Bannerstone House, 1969), pp. 3–37.
8. Gene Bylinsky, "Preview of the 'Choose Your Mood' Society," *Fortune* (March 1977): 200.
9. For a further discussion, see Vernon H. Mark and Frank R. Ervin, *Violence and the Brain* (New York: Harper & Row, 1970), pp. 3–38.
10. Neurosurgery and psychosurgery involve direct intervention in brain processes. The former is concerned with correcting or repairing organic brain damage resulting from accident or disease. Psychosurgery seeks to relieve behavioral aberrations where there is no indication of organic brain damage. Both of these procedures are quite distant from our main interests in this chapter, and therefore we will not discuss them further.
11. See Delgado, *Physical Control of the Mind,* pp. 100–114, 123–

132, 133–140, 140–142, 142–176, where he discusses various types of behavioral responses elicited by ESB.

12. Many articles have been written on the ethics of human experimentation, and most books concerning psychosurgery, ESB, psychopharmacology, or behavior control at least touch on the subject. An overview of the pros and cons of using humans in experiments may be acquired from the following sources: *Quality of Health Care — Human Experimentation, 1973* (Washington, D.C.: U.S. Government Printing Office, 1973); Ralph Slovenko, "Commentary on Psychosurgery," *The Hastings Center Report* (October 1975): 19–22; Eric J. Casell, "Making and Escaping Moral Decisions," *The Hastings Center Studies,* 1973, pp. 39–49. See also the bibliographies of *Society, Ethics and the Life Sciences,* published by The Hastings Center, for additional articles on human research.

13. For a description of certain experiments conducted, see George A. Ojemann, Katherine I. Blick, and Arthur A. Ward, Jr., "Improvement and Disturbance of Short-term Verbal Memory with Human Ventrolateral Thalamotomy," *Journal of Neurosurgery* 35 (1971): 203–210.

14. See Mark and Ervin, *Violence and the Brain,* pp. 92–110.

15. See Jane E. Brody, "Brain 'Pacemaker' Is Helping Some with Handicap," *New York Times,* September 22, 1975, and "Brain Implants Control Schizophrenia," *Daily Journal American,* June 16, 1977, p. C16.

16. Delgado, *Physical Control of the Mind,* pp. 222–223.

17. For a general discussion of the "drug ethic," see "Controlling Behavior through Drugs," *The Hastings Center Studies,* (January 1974): 65–111.

18. For a discussion of these possible effects from the use of psychotropic drugs, see Wayne O. Evans and Nathan S. Kline, eds., *Psychotropic Drugs in the Year 2000* (Springfield, Ill.: Charles C Thomas, 1971), pp. 25–84. Alternative reference may be made to two summary articles in the popular press: David Rorvik, "Mood Drugs," *Penthouse* (December 1978): 100–102, 150–151, and Peter Ross Range, "Future Highs," *Playboy* (December 1978): 150, 256, 294, and 297.

19. For a progress report on such research, see Richard A. Shaffer,

"Advances in Chemistry Are Starting to Unlock Mysteries of the Brain," *Wall Street Journal,* August 12, 1977, pp. 1, 18.

20. Gerald L. Klerman, "Psychotropic Hedonism vs. Pharmacological Calvinism," *The Hastings Center Report* (September 1972): 3.

21. Perry London, "Future of Psychotherapy," *The Hastings Center Report,* (December 1973): 11–12.

22. Wayne O. Evans, "Chemical Aphrodisiacs," in Evans and Kline, *Psychotropic Drugs in the Year 2000,* p. 42.

23. Bylinsky comes close to saying this, but not quite. See Gene Bylinsky, "A Preview of the 'Choose Your Mood' Society," *Fortune* (March 1977): 220–224, 226–227.

24. Perry London, *Behavioral Control,* 2nd ed. (New York: Harper & Row, 1977), Chapter 8. London examines the ethics of behavioral controls.

25. The books are Frank Herbert, *Dune* (New York: Ace, 1965); *Dune Messiah* (New York: Berkley, 1969); *Children of Dune* (New York: Berkley, 1976). What is not fiction is the fact that Herbert, and other science fiction writers, are hired as consultants and lecturers by large corporations like Weyerhaeuser, IBM, U.S. Steel, and American Airlines. A presagement of things to come? See Steve Weiner, "Science Fiction 'Invades' Business Minds," Seattle *Times,* May 31, 1978, p. B-5.

Chapter 9, "The Probable Future," pages 207–229

1. George E. Reedy, *The Twilight of the Presidency* (New York: World, 1970), p. 190.

2. It would be burdensome to cite the most relevant literature about the rise of the new value system of the modern organization. However, the following three books are excellent, even though there are areas of disagreement. Alfred D. Chandler, Jr., *The Visible Hand: The Managerial Revolution in American Business* (Cambridge: Harvard University Press, 1977); Paul Boyer, *Urban Masses and Moral Order: 1820–1920* (Cambridge: Harvard University Press, 1978); James Willard Hurst, *The Legitimacy of the Business Corporation in the United States: 1780–1970* (Charlottesville: The University Press of Virginia, 1970).

3. Of particular interest are the observations about the "Progressives" and the "Status Revolution" in Richard Hofstadter, *The Age of Reform: From Bryan to F.D.R.* (New York: Vintage, 1955), especially Chapter 4, "The Status Revolution and Progressive Leaders."

4. One of the most perceptive analyses is by Robert Nisbet, *Twilight of Authority* (New York: Oxford, 1975).

5. The literature about totalitarianism is vast. The classic works are by Hannah Arendt, *The Origins of Totalitarianism,* 2nd ed. (Cleveland: World, 1958), and Jacques Ellul, *The Technological Society,* trans. J. Wilkinson (New York: Knopf, 1954, 1964).

6. Reedy, *Twlight of the Presidency.*

7. David Halberstam, *The Best and the Brightest* (New York: Random House, 1972), pp. 544–545.

8. Richard A. Gabriel and Paul L. Savage, *Crisis in Command* (New York: Hill and Wang, 1978), p. 90.

9. Chester I. Barnard, *The Functions of the Executive* (Cambridge: Harvard University Press, 1938), p. 270.

10. Ibid., p. 276.

11. Nikolai Lenin, "Scientific Management and the Dictatorship of the Proletariate," in *Trade Unionism and Labor Problems,* ed. John R. Commons (Boston: Ginn, 1921), pp. 179–198.

12. Thorstein Veblen, *The Engineer and the Price System* (New York: Harcourt Brace, 1963), p. 132.

13. See, for example, R. Joseph Monsen, "Social Responsibility and the Corporation: Alternatives for the Future of Capitalism," (Seattle: Graduate School of Business Administration, University of Washington — reprint series, 1971).

14. Dwight Waldo, *The Administrative State* (New York: Ronald Press, 1948), p. 65.

15. The evidence for the stages of adult life is presented in Daniel J. Levinson et al., *The Season's of a Man's Life* (New York: Knopf, 1978); Roger L. Gould, M.D., *Transformations* (New York: Simon and Schuster, 1978). Supporting evidence can be found in George E. Vaillant, M.D., *Adaptation to Life* (Boston: Little, Brown, 1977). The philosophical justification is brilliantly presented by David L. Norton, *Personal Destinies: A Philosophy of Ethical Individualism* (Princeton: Princeton University Press, 1976).

16. See the splendid discussion of fraternity in Wilson Carey McWilliams, *The Idea of Fraternity in America* (Berkeley: University of California Press, 1973).
17. William H. Whyte, Jr., *The Organization Man* (New York: Simon and Schuster, 1956), p. 404.

Index

Adler, Victor, 203
Aertker, Samuel R., 253n
Allport, Gordon, 141
Amorality: managerial, 36–43, 63–65
Arendt, Hannah, 6, 111, 156, 258n, 262n, 267n
Argyris, Chris, 142, 257n

Baritz, Loren, 258n
Barnard, Chester I., 60, 131, 151, 217, 218, 253n, 260n, 262n, 267n
Barzun, Jacques, 106–108, 128, 257n, 260n
Beauvoir, Simone de, 254n
Behavior Modification: techniques of, 190–192; direct physical interventions, 192ff
Bell, Daniel, 250n, 261n
Bennis, Warren, 142, 252n, 254n, 257n
Berle, A. A., 60, 254n, 255n
Billington, Ray Allan, 254n
Blair, John M., 17, 250n
Blick, Katherine I., 265n
Bottomore, T. B., 256
Boyer, Paul, 266n
Bridgman, P. W., 157, 262n
Brody, Jane E., 265n
Brzezinski, Zbigniew, 117, 259n
Buchan, Alastair, 259n

Bunzel, John H., 258n
Burnham, James, 24–27, 250n
Butler, Robert N., 254n, 256n
Bylinski, Gene, 264n, 266n

Capra, Frank, 66
Carnegie, Andrew, 75, 255n
Carter, James, 119
Casell, Eric J., 265n
Chamberlain, Neil W., 172, 263n
Chandler, Alfred D., 266n
Chavkin, Samuel, 264n
Chemical Stimulation of the Brain (CSB) — Neuropsychopharmacology, 194–197
Child, John, 261n
Clark, C. Spencer, 175, 251n, 262n, 263n
Clemens, Samuel, 110
Cleveland, Harlan, 28, 147, 148, 152, 160, 262n
Comstock, George, 256n
Confidence: the shattering of traditional, 13–23; the reconstruction of, 23–28
Connor, Patrick E., 254n
Contingency Theory, 57n
Coser, Lewis A., 87, 255n, 259n
Crisis Management, 118ff

Dahrendorf, Rolf, 256n, 260n
Dalton, Melville, 261n

Decline, Age of, 28
Delgado, José M. R., 178, 179, 192, 194, 264n, 265n
Dewey, John, 110
Dickson, William, 60n
Djilas, Milovan, 256n
Drucker, Peter, 4, 137, 138, 249n, 261n

Earle, Edward Mead, 250n
Easton, David, 18, 250n
Education: vocationalization of, 152–158
Effectiveness: organizational, 37
Eisenhower, Dwight D., 6
Electrical Stimulation of the Brain (ESB), 192–194
Ellul, Jacques, 6, 26, 27, 126, 128, 141, 251n, 257n, 259n, 260n, 261n, 267n
Ervin, Frank R., 264n, 265n
Ethics: definition, 3
Evans, Wayne O., 264n, 265n, 266n
Expediency: methods of, 38–40
Expertise: tyranny of, 24–25, 251n

Freud, Sigmund, 198, 200
Frieden, Barnard J., 250n
Friedrich, Carl J., 117, 250n, 259n

Gabriel, Richard A., 35, 217, 252n, 267n
Galbraith, John Kenneth, 90, 137, 255n, 260n
Gates, Bruce L., 168, 263n
Glass, James M., 257n, 260n
Gompers, Samuel, 73
Gould, Roger L., 267n
Gross, Neal, 84, 255n

Haimann, Theo, 171, 263n
Halberstam, David, 216, 253n, 267n
Harrington, Allan, 258n

Hart, David K., 251n, 253n, 258n, 261n, 262n
Hastings Center, The, 265n
Hawthorne Studies, 61n
Health: organization, 36–38
Heilbroner, Robert, 16, 33, 249n, 252n
Hellreigel, Don, 253n
Henderson, Thomas, 60n, 61n
Herbert, Frank, 203, 266n
Hershman, Mendes, 252n
Hobbes, Thomas, 56
Hoffer, Eric, 254n
Hofstadter, Richard, 258n, 267n
Hurst, James Willard, 250n, 266n
Huxley, Aldous, 180

Individual Imperative, 53; definition, 226; collapse of, 55–80
Innate Human Nature, 101ff
Insignificant People, 95ff
Integrative Propaganda, 125ff
Intellect, 105ff
Intentions: decency of managerial, 28–31, 141–143
Invisibility: elitist, 40–43

James, William, 110
Janis, Irving L., 156, 254n, 262n
Johnson, Lyndon B., 29, 208

Kahn, Robert L., 39, 252n
Kaplan, Abraham, 87, 255n
Kariel, Henry S., 251n, 255n
Katz, Daniel, 39, 252n
Keegan, John, 126, 259n
Kennedy, John F., 13, 52, 177
Kittrie, Nicholas N., 75, 76, 255n
Klerman, Gerald L., 199, 266n
Kline, Nathan S., 264n, 265n, 266n
Kluckhohn, Clyde, 3, 249
Knauth, Oswald, 140, 159, 254n, 261n, 262n
Kreps, Juanita, 167
Kuhn, Thomas H., 252n

Lasswell, Harold D., 87, 255n
Leadership: and management, 35; and education, 155–157
Legitimacy, 23–24, 28
Leisure, 90–94
Lenin, Nikolai, 218, 267n
Levine, Charles, 259n, 262n
Levinson, Daniel J., 267n
Lewin, Kurt, 141
Lewis, Sinclair, 84, 255n
Likert, Rensis, 142, 257n
Locke, John, 56, 100
Lodge, George C., 28, 250n
London, Perry, 200, 266n

Maccoby, Michael, 150, 153, 173, 262n, 263n
McGregor, Douglas, 27, 142
McNamara, Robert S., 35
McWilliams, Wilson Carey, 254n, 268n
Mailer, Norman, 207
Managerial Escalation, 143–146
Managerial Obtrusiveness, 158–160
Managerial Universality, 148–152
Marini, Frank, 249n
Mark, Vernon H., 264n, 265n
Marx, Karl, 218, 220
Maslow, Abraham H., 27, 142, 261n
Mayo, Elton, 56, 58, 59, 60, 253n
Means, G. C., 60, 254n, 255n
Merton, Robert K., 141, 261n
Methodology, 157–158
Michels, Robert, 24, 25, 27, 250n, 251n
Milgram, Stanley, 63, 156, 254n, 262n
Mill, John Stuart, 62, 254n
Mills, C. Wright, 161, 171, 172, 178, 263n
Mills, D. L., 262n
Modern Job, 115ff; dominance of, 146–148
Modern Organization: definition, 4

Monsen, R. Joseph, 267n
Mooney, James D., 260n
Morals: definition, 3
Mosca, Gaetano, 95, 96

Nadel, S. F., 83
National Managerial System: definition, 5, 88–89
Newcomer, Mabel, 171, 172, 174, 263n
Nisbet, Robert, 6, 32, 250n, 251n, 254n, 260n, 261n, 267n
Nixon, Richard M., 29
Normality: defined, 183; enhancing, 183–187
Norton, David L., 249n, 267n

Oakleigh, Thomas, 255n
Ojemann, George E., 265n
Oligarchy: iron law of, 24–25, 251n
Operant Conditioning, 192
Organizational Imperative: propositions and rules, 43–46; significance of, 46–48; values of, 55–80
Orwell, George, 124, 129, 260n

Packard, Vance, 182, 264n
Pareto, Vilfredo, 178
Parkinson, C. Northcote, 261n
Parmet, Herbert S., 249n
Pateman, Carole, 114, 258n
Peirce, Charles Saunders, 110
Pirsig, Robert M., 258n
Platt, John, 34, 252n
Popper, Karl, 29, 251n
Pragmatism, 45–46
Pre-emptive Control, 121ff
Progress: technological, paradox of, 33–36
Psycho-economy of Enhancement, 198–201

Range, Peter Ross, 265n
Rationality, 44
Rawls, John, 157, 224, 227, 258n, 262n

Reedy, George E., 208, 216, 266n, 267
Reiley, Alan C., 260n
Riesman, David, 6, 62, 254n
Robertson, Wyndham, 252n
Roethlisberger, Fritz, 60n
Rogers, Carl, 141
Role: defined, 84
Rorvik, David, 265n
Rousseau, Jean Jacques, 56
Runyon, Kenneth E., 249n

Sanford, Fillmore, 156, 262n
Savage, Paul L., 35, 217, 252n, 267n
Schumacher, E. F., 97, 256n
Scientific Management, 38
Scott, William G., 149, 171, 251n, 253n, 254n, 257n, 259n, 260n, 262n, 263n, 264n
Shaffer, Richard A., 265n
Significant Job, 161–164; defined, 162
Simmel, George, 84, 255n
Skinner, B. F., 60, 104, 179, 192, 202, 257n, 264n
Slater, Philip E., 254n
Slovenko, Ralph, 265n
Smith, Howard L., 249n
Snow, C. P., 36, 170, 252n, 263n
Solzhenitsyn, Alexander, 110
Sorensen, Theodore C., 249n
Sorokin, Pitrim A., 257n
Steers, Richard N., 252n
Stein, Maurice R., 254n
Steinbeck, John, 13
Stewardship, 44–45

Tannenbaum, A. S., 115, 258n
Taylor, Frederick W., 38, 48, 56, 219, 253n

Taylor, Gordon Rattray, 253n
Taylor, John, 253n
Technical Core, 130–131
Terrien, F., 262n
Thielicke, Helmut, 130
Thompson, James, 131, 255n, 260n
Thoreau, Henry, 110
Tocqueville, Alexis de, 61
Toffler, Alvin, 254n
Torrey, E. Fuller, 76, 255n, 258n
Totalitarian America, 207–214
Transcendant America, 223–229
Turner, Frederick Jackson, 65, 254

Universal Behavioral Techniques: definition, 4, 141–142

Vaillant, George E., 267n
Valenstein, Elliot S., 180, 264n
Values: definition, 3; American, transformation of, 32–33
Veblen, Thorstein, 132, 137, 139, 140, 178, 221, 260n, 261n, 267n

Wade, Nicholas, 17, 250n
Waldo, Dwight, v, 6, 225, 267n
Ward, Arthur A., Jr., 265n
Warren, Austin, 132, 260n
Weiner, Steve, 266n
Westmoreland, William, 216
Whitman, Walt, 33, 110, 252n
Whyte, William H., Jr., 6, 50, 52, 54, 268n
Wild, Rolf H., 113, 252n, 258n
Wilson, Sloan, 253n
Wirthlin, Richard B., 250n
Wolf, William B., 61n
Wolin, Sheldon S., 6, 144, 261n
Work, 111ff